Women in Terrorism

Women in Terrorism

Case of the LTTE

Tamara Herath

SAGE www.sagepublications.com
Los Angeles • London • New Delhi • Singapore • Washington DC

First published in 2012 by

SAGE Publications India Pvt Ltd
B1/I-1 Mohan Cooperative Industrial Area
Mathura Road, New Delhi 110 044, India
www.sagepub.in

SAGE Publications Inc
2455 Teller Road
Thousand Oaks, California 91320, USA

SAGE Publications Ltd
1 Oliver's Yard, 55 City Road
London EC1Y 1SP, United Kingdom

SAGE Publications Asia-Pacific Pte Ltd
33 Pekin Street
#02-01 Far East Square
Singapore 048763

Published by Vivek Mehra for SAGE Publications India Pvt Ltd, typeset in 10/13 Berkeley by Diligent Typesetter, Delhi and printed at Chaman Enterprises, New Delhi.

Library of Congress Cataloging-in-Publication Data Available

ISBN: 978-81-321-0695-1 (HB)

The SAGE Team: Gayeti Singh, Swati Sengupta, Anju Saxena and Rajender Kaur

This book is dedicated to the brave, sensitive and caring women who chose to take some control of their space, their environment and of their lives.

Thank you for choosing a SAGE product! If you have any comment, observation or feedback, I would like to personally hear from you. Please write to me at contactceo@sagepub.in

—Vivek Mehra, Managing Director and CEO,
SAGE Publications India Pvt Ltd, New Delhi

Bulk Sales

SAGE India offers special discounts for purchase of books in bulk. We also make available special imprints and excerpts from our books on demand.

For orders and enquiries, write to us at

Marketing Department
SAGE Publications India Pvt Ltd
B1/I-1, Mohan Cooperative Industrial Area
Mathura Road, Post Bag 7
New Delhi 110044, India
E-mail us at marketing@sagepub.in

Get to know more about SAGE, be invited to SAGE events, get on our mailing list. Write today to marketing@sagepub.in

This book is also available as an e-book.

Contents

Notes on the Language Conventions

Note on Citations

I have used the commonly accepted English language spellings for Tamil words, such as, *Thambi* (younger brother) or the name, Prabhakaran, for ease of accessibility.

Note on Transliteration

The usage of Tamil words in the text are based on phonetics as reflected in the writings of Tamil-speaking authors.

Note on Research Informants

Most participants were monolingual (speaking only in Tamil), while a few were bilingual (speaking both Tamil and English).

Acknowledgements

I would like to thank the women combatants of the Liberation Tigers of Tamil *Eelam* (LTTE) and the Tamil civic women of Jaffna who were willing participants of this research. I am grateful to them for giving their time freely and feel highly privileged for being allowed access into their lives.

I am deeply indebted to the family of S (Jaffna), who took me in as their own and taught me to appreciate the people and the culture, and to focus on the positive and the good in all situations. I am beholden to Anil and Deanne M., the late Mrs Mae Paternott and Malkanthi (Colombo) for taking very good care of me during my field research period in Sri Lanka. I am extremely grateful to Chitra S. (London) who became invaluable for developing my understanding of the Tamil language and its culture, specifically on the topic of Tamil women of Jaffna. My thanks also to Social Scientists' Association (Colombo), Women's Education and Research Centre (Colombo) and International Centre for Ethnic Studies (Colombo) for granting me access to their libraries.

I would like to thank Professor Mary Kaldor (Global Governance), Dr Clare Hemmings, Professor Diane Perrons, Ms Hazel Johnstone (Gender Institute), and Professor Anne Phillips (Government Department) of the London School of Economics and Political Science, London, UK, for their guidance and wisdom in this research and writing process. I am also indebted to Professor Baroness Haleh Afshar (Department of Politics) of York University, UK, for her suggestion that I should turn my research into a book.

I am grateful to BTP and Centrex (Bramshill, UK) for awarding me a Fellowship that facilitated my research and personal development. A special thanks to John Hennigan MBE, BTP (London), who believed in my ability and gave me all the assistance I needed throughout the life cycle of this project. I would also like to thank Adrian Dwyer OBE, BTP (London), Peter Villiers and Peter Abbott, Centrex (Bramshill), for their support at the initial stages of this project.

I would also like to thank my feminist friends Drs Maki Kimura, Roona Simpson and Sabine Grenz for their debates and discussions when analysing complexities in gender-related cultural issues. I am particularly grateful to my friend Dr Roisin Ryan–Flood for insisting that I publish my research findings and give a voice to the combatant women and civic women of the LTTE conflict.

I wish to include a very special note of gratitude to Stephen B. for his support in reading every single word I have written in this book and offering suggestions and corrections throughout. I would like to acknowledge Gloria Tanner, Aiden, Ciaran and Markrid Dermody for their total faith in me. I am also indebted to Alex C. for his valiant effort in checking the final draft thoroughly and diligently.

Thanks also to Sugata Ghosh and Gayeti Singh at SAGE Publications for all their help and support in the publishing process.

I wish to thank my family for their faith in me, especially my father, H.M.G., for his unwavering encouragement; my very understanding son, S., for never complaining, enduring all inconveniences patiently and supporting me wonderfully throughout this period.

Finally, I wish to acknowledge the death of CH, a civic woman participant, whose untimely death is a tragic loss. I also wish to acknowledge that since the Final war some or most of the women combatants who took part in this research may not be alive today, but our differing ethnic identities were not held as barriers by them or by the civic women participants, raising hopes for a better future.

1 Entering a Tiger's Lair

Between the spring of 2002 and autumn of 2003, I visited the Jaffna peninsula in northern Sri Lanka with the aim of gaining a deeper understanding of how three decades of ethno-nationalist war in Sri Lanka has contributed to a major social change for Tamil women in Jaffna. An important component of this change has been the recruitment of women to the Liberation Tigers of Tamil *Eelam* (LTTE), recognised globally as a terrorist group. My aim was to explore the role of combatant women from a gender perspective in order to identify how gender is constructed for women within the revolutionary movement, and the impact that this construction has on civic society.

The fundamental reasoning for conducting a research of this nature is to give a voice to the Other that has been overlooked by masculine-orientated data gathering. The feminist argument is that research conducted under the auspices of feminist research does not merely reflect and validate whatever the interviewees choose to say about their experiences, but also supplies 'a feminist critique and challenge to the way in which women's experience is constructed under (hetero) patriarchy' (Ang-Lygate 1996; Bola 1996; Russell 1996 and Wilkinson and Kitzinger 1996).

This book is therefore about combatant women in the LTTE, an armed resistance group led by Vellupillai Prabhakaran that has been active in Sri Lanka since the early 1970s pursuing the goal of an independent Tamil state named *Tamil Eelam.*[1] During the height of its success, the LTTE controlled large parts of the North, including the central Northern Province known as Vanni, as well as parts of the Eastern Province (although during the period I was in Jaffna, the Sri Lankan government had taken control of all other areas, including the Jaffna peninsula in the Northern Province and the land along Mannar in the North West).

This book addresses the currently limited understanding that exists in relation to the combatant women of the LTTE by forcing the question: how is gender constructed within the revolutionary movement of the LTTE? My findings illustrate that female gender identity is negotiated in complex ways and is transformed as a consequence of women becoming fighters. They become socially constructed images of Armed Virgins (viewed by some as androgynous), female warriors of injustice who protect Tamil nationals. Civic women have also adapted to changing socio-political conditions, although they have retained some aspects of their traditional gender identity. There is evidence that combatant women and civic women both become part of the (re)construction of 'new' women (*Puthumai Pen*), with a new gender identity. This new identity may not conform to Western feminist notions of emancipation, but within the Jaffna Tamil context it represents a profound change.

In addition, two of my findings have more general applications. First, the empirical evidence gathered during this research reveals a previously unrecognised link between those who are internally displaced to the LTTE-controlled area of Vanni, and voluntary enlistment. Due to inaccessibility, or difficulties in gaining entry to both LTTE-controlled areas and to combatant women, this link has previously been overlooked, and the focus has been on forced recruitment. However, this is a key point in understanding the combatant women, as the sense of security that is offered in Vanni (even when living under a tree, exposed to the elements) is preferable to living within the comforts of a home but in a state of continuous fear. The finding that displacement is an important factor in the recruitment of armed combatants may be relevant in other cases elsewhere. My second finding expands the debate on suicide bombings by focusing on combatant women's involvement in the act. Through the empirical research, I have concluded that combatant women view suicide bombing as a selfless act of giving; a view that directly connects suicide bombing to Durkheim's concept of 'obligatory altruistic suicide'. My research findings show that there was a clear gender dimension to the combatant women's involvement. Although at first suicide bombing appears to contradict the traditionally socio-culturally constructed female role of the carer and unselfish giver, in the combatant women's discourse this act symbolizes an extension of a nurturing and giving role. Consequently, the combatant women view it as a willing gift to the Tamil nation—rather than a sacrifice—in order to progress the cause of Tamil *Eelam*.

This book contributes to discussions on the feminist methodology of representing the Other through multiple identities (Sinhalese, Tamil and British) which at once link and separate the researcher and the participants. Issues around multiple identity form recurring themes both in and away from the field, and these identities had to be continually negotiated. These negotiations formed the base of a reflexivity that linked me to the combatant women through our shared identity (Sri Lankan) and yet separated us through the differences of ethnicity (Sinhalese/Tamil and British identities) and language.

Though the conflict ended in May 2009, the safety of all 15 participants still remains paramount to this research, which is based on the narrative life-histories of a group of both combatant and civic women, covering a wide age range and diverse socio-economic backgrounds. The research sample was confined to a small number in order to delve deeper into the life-histories of the seven combatant women, one ex-combatant woman and seven civic women. I was also aware that becoming involved with me might have a detrimental effect upon the participants, as the LTTE could have viewed them as collaborators, and the state-run security forces might have seen them as holding sensitive information that could be of use to them. Therefore, with a view to differentiate the groups of women without compromising their identity, the interview participants have been given anonymity, with alternative names for the combatant women and alphabetic characters for the civic women.

Whilst acknowledging the above, it must also be recognised that researching sensitive topics is fraught with many difficulties.[2] For the purpose of this book, the definition of 'sensitive' is derived from a personal perspective based on the *potential* that the research has for creating a physically dangerous situation both for the individual participants and/or to myself.[3] It must also be recognised that sensitivity does not necessarily change with political or social changes, as physical dangers may continue to exist long after the conflict has ended.

Anxieties on the Field

Both the State armed forces and the LTTE had checkpoints at various border crossings. The Vanni district checkpoints were controlled by the LTTE, as the whole district was under the jurisdiction of the Tamil Tigers. The army had checkpoints along the roads, at jetties and at airports, sealing the northern part of the island. The checks conducted by the state armed forces varied according to the person travelling into or out of the area. At these checkpoints, women and men were subjected to rigorous body searches.

By travelling with LTTE sympathisers and LTTE combatant women, I discovered that my Sinhalese identity, combined with an inability to speak Tamil and an unwillingness to speak Sinhalese, proved to be a hindrance. It was due to this that I attempted to distance myself from my ethnic hegemonic identity in order to be part of a more neutral and accepted identity (for the Tamil nationals and the LTTE) as a British national, but this carried other dangers, and state armed forces often subjected me to a more thorough process of searching than other women. I was aware that I had presented the army with something of an enigma.[4]

I discovered conducting field research in conflict areas where my hegemonic identity made me the enemy in the eyes of one side of the ongoing conflict and a sympathiser with the other gave rise to emotional and personal safety issues. It is considerably easier to reflect on situations away from field conditions with the safety of a few-thousand miles in between. The reality is that, when situated in the field researchers realise that their extensive theoretical knowledge does not prepare them fully to deal with all eventualities that arise, and there is much they need to deal with extemporaneously on their own. This is reminiscent of Sanders' (1980) metaphor of 'rope burns'. My rope burns included the unawareness of when I was being watched, followed or simply informed upon.

I gained first-hand experience of this on the first day in the field, when I had an occasion to change accommodation. As it was getting dark, the need to find another suitable accommodation in a place where there were no hotels prompted me to overlook certain safety aspects. This was a breach of my own security process, whereby I failed to inform anyone in Colombo that I was moving from the address given to them prior to my travel. I was in possession of a list of possible homes that were able to accommodate visitors who had been arriving in Jaffna since the ceasefire in late 2002. These visitors were mostly from the Tamil expatriate community or aid workers, with only a nominal number of Sinhalese; none had been a lone Sinhalese woman, albeit British, wandering on their own in what was essentially a troubled time. Within an hour of being at the new accommodation, I was informed that I was to receive a visit from the LTTE. During the LTTE occupation of Jaffna, householders had to report all visitors staying at their accommodation. This was not the practice during my research period, but I was aware that such practices were continuing covertly during this period of fragile ceasefire. After spending a troubled night waiting for the LTTE to arrive, I was informed that they failed to turn up due to an incident that otherwise occupied them in Jaffna town. This incident made me aware of the ever-present subtext of the unknown and the high levels of vulnerability experienced by researchers on the field.

The researcher's vulnerability in conflict zones is a key part of my own positionality in this research. Emotions that are traditionally overlooked in field research become key factors within conflict zones (Kleinman and Copp 1993: 26-48; Lee-Treweek and Linkogle 2000: 14 and Porter et al. 2005). Whilst there was no sense of danger present on a moment-to-moment basis, there was a continuous sense of being in a very different place, where familiarity and unfamiliarity continuously merged with uncertainty. This changing position was mostly experienced when I travelled away from the relative security of Jaffna to Kilinochchi in Vanni district, which was then held by the LTTE.

The journey often left me feeling physically exposed. This may well be due to the mode of transport: a three-wheeled scooter taxi (an everyday cost-effective way of travelling in Jaffna). The sense of over-exposure was heightened by the journey through isolated jungle areas where there were signposts warning of landmines. On one occasion I noticed a face staring from the undergrowth. As soon as I saw them with their weapons, they blended back into the shadows, making me question the reality of that vision.

Safety and escape routes, therefore, were not an option away from Jaffna and its neighbouring villages. Means of contacting the outside world were also limited, as there was no mobile phone signal and no readily accessible telecommunication service. My limited language skills and local knowledge in a place that was strewn with landmines invariably gave rise to a series of negative thoughts. These thoughts had to be compartmentalised and rationalised in order to retain my focus on the research.

Reflexivity

Researcher Identity, Positionality and Empathy

The researcher's location, positionality and identity have impacted deeply on the research conducted amongst the Tamil women of Jaffna. Throughout this chapter I have identified issues based on my dual identities—Sri Lankan and British. The intricacies of a dual identity based on Britishness placed me outside of the struggle whilst my Sinhalese identity connected me to Tamil women through my hegemonic Sri Lankan identity. This was in line with Anthias' (2002: 512) argument of 'location and positionality [being] more useful concepts for [the] investigating process'. It did concern me that being an outsider with multiple identities but without a Tamil ethnic identity might have made it harder to build trust with the LTTE, which fortunately proved not to be the case.

In 1967, Becker wrote, 'There is no position from which sociological research can be done that is not biased in one way or another' (cited in Hammersley 2000: 61). This highly insightful view became the foundation upon which I thought through my reflexivity. At the preliminary stage of planning I was able to be clinical about how I wished to direct the whole of the research project. However, once I entered the field, relationships and friendships began to develop. Blackwood (1996) states that the word 'friend' is often used by American field researchers to describe their participants. The word 'friend' emerges as a situation-specific word that describes relationships built in the field and the comfort that such relationships offer the researchers who are away from their home environment. Through these friendships the researchers gain a valuable understanding of the conflict they research. I found that the Gatekeeper and his wife located me as part of their family, and I was accepted as a friend. They took it upon themselves not only to act as hosts, but also as teachers of Tamil culture, and even as interpreters for the participants on some occasions.

The relationship between the Gatekeeper's family and myself as the researcher was built upon a common focus, that of the political struggle of the Tamil people, albeit with differing objectives: mine was focusing on an under-researched subject area, and theirs was finding a voice for the suffering endured. This common focus also brought forth an empathy with the participants, as they became the face of the struggle. I had heeded Kondo's (1986) separation of 'knowledge' and 'understanding', in which knowledge is obtained from a certain perspective, and understanding is based on culture, history and biography. My relationship with the Gatekeeper provided me with much-needed understanding. This type of a relationship is referred to in Kleinman and Copp (1993: 29), in which the authors claim that 'participants are the teachers and we are the students'. The understanding was obtained by my constant questions requiring explanations of situations and behaviour that left little room for ambiguity.

I was always very aware that the enhanced status of residing with the Gatekeeper, who was viewed by the LTTE with a great deal of respect, enabled me to have a level of access and trust based on the Gatekeeper's extended connections.

Blackwood (1996: 55) states, 'The ethnographic experience is more than an identification of positionality or subjectivity; we occupy multiple positions and identities that transform over time, forcing us constantly to reconstruct who we are in relation to people we study.' As noted herein, I discovered that self-reconstruction located me within the Gatekeeper's family circle as a 'trusted' person: trusted to live with the family, trusted to roam free in their home, trusted to see their interactions with other civic citizens and combatants of the LTTE. In a way, this kind of trust is historical in Sri Lanka and forms part of its customs where strangers are welcomed and treated as part of a family.[5] However, I was surprised to discover that this custom is still practised in Jaffna, especially after many years of bitter civil war.

It is perhaps inevitable that researchers tend to locate themselves within the research based on loyalties and relationships formed in the field,[6] where researchers are often challenged to ascertain where their sympathies lie in a conflict. The explanation given by researchers generally centres on being neutral in the setting as objective observers rather than engaged participants, as the advantage of being neutral obtains in that the researcher stands outside 'local categorical distinctions and boundaries' (Lee 1995: 23; Gilmore 1991; Sluka 1990 cited in Lee 1995). That said, there are occasions when claiming neutrality becomes problematic, as the researcher's intentions are then questioned–especially in areas of high conflict where social relations have little precedence (Gilmore 1991 cited in Lee 1995). Peritore states, 'Assertion of scientific objectivity or neutrality can be perceived as being naïve or as screening a hidden agenda' (Peritore 1990: 360 cited in Lee 1995: 23). With that in mind, I would argue that complete neutrality is perhaps extremely difficult, as it is impossible to be sympathetic in equal degrees to all parties engaged in the conflict.[7]

There is an issue of empathy that a researcher needs to be aware of where there is the possibility of being drawn into a subject area. This may well be due to romanticising about or empathising with those whom the researcher is researching, which means we are unable to represent those we research without some bias. This danger of romanticism/ empathy can spill over into one's own research. At times I may be guilty of representing the participants in idealistic and romantic ways, and of reclaiming a notion that suits my own social perspective, especially in representing an Other who is involved in danger and violence. Above all, challenging the gender stereotyping of a patriarchal society may cause some romantic awe of the researched where, as Salazar (1991) claims, the participants are aware of their circumstances and actively take up issues to end their oppression. This notion clearly applies to the combatant women of the LTTE.

Kleinman and Copp (1993: 39) state that, 'researchers usually argue that participants' immoral acts stem from a social or structural problem rather than individual failures in moral behaviour'. This statement became quite poignant as the research developed and my feelings became ambivalent. It has become difficult not to empathise to some extent with the women and the harrowing experiences they have undergone, and whilst not agreeing with all of their political ideologies or objectives, I still felt a certain cognitive empathy towards them.[8] I was painfully aware of the need to defer any overwhelming sympathy and understanding of the women's plight—including that of the combatants—and arrive at my own findings. This attempt at distancing myself has resulted in my research being founded on the subtleness between attachment (empathy/sympathy) and detachment (neutrality).

Asymmetric Nature of Power Relations with the Gatekeeper

It is understood among researchers who enter the field through a Gatekeeper that this person invariably holds the power to grant or deny access at will, and that the relationship can prove to be either beneficial or a hindrance (Lee 1995 and Jamieson 2000). This is enhanced when operating within a culture of political distrust. As a researcher from the West, I had a different kind of power and status in comparison with that held by the Gatekeeper, where access to those targeted by the researcher was achieved through bargaining and negotiation. I consider this not to be an equal power status, but an asymmetric form of power that favours one party more than the other.

The asymmetric nature of the power relation was visible from the moment I met the Gatekeeper in order to obtain access. I was able to mention the name of my Contact (whom I have never met) who suggested I meet him. The Gatekeeper questioned, quizzed and watched me keenly to ascertain where my sympathies lay in the conflict. I recall maintaining steady eye contact and trying my best to look earnest. I remember thinking of all the interview techniques I had developed over the years.

The fact that the Gatekeeper was not aware of my visit gave me an advantage in the power relationship by having a space to locate myself directly. I would argue that such direct social interactions have the ability to change the power settings, leaving little room for misconceptions. At the same time, the asymmetric nature of the power relation allowed the Gatekeeper to ask questions and observe my reactions prior to granting any form of access. This power is initially non-negotiable; perhaps the only occasion that it can be re-negotiated is when the researcher has 'earned' the trust of the Gatekeeper.

The asymmetric nature of the power relation is also addressed by Lee's (1995: 123) two categories of 'social access' and 'physical access'. He states that social access may depend on establishing an interpersonal trust with the Gatekeeper, but it is the Gatekeeper who controls the physical access and the levels of trust granted. I would suggest that the trust given or built with the organisation through the involvement of a Gatekeeper involves asymmetric power relations that are exacerbated by ethnicity and a hegemonic identity. The Gatekeeper will only allow access to a researcher who they think will be suitable for the research and beneficial to the revolutionary organisation.

Interestingly, this Gatekeeper was in a position to provide his own interpreter. Though this is far from an ideal situation, as a researcher I was very aware that decision-making in this instance lay solely with the Gatekeeper. The interpreter chosen by an organisation has the potential to act as a filter to stop any undesirable comments from being translated. The field research in Jaffna showed the interpretation to be conducted by civic citizens who were LTTE sympathisers and who appeared at the time to carefully and deliberately construct the language used by the participants (in response to my questions) to express a meaning nearest to the original statement. Upon my return to London, I verified the accuracy and ensured no nuances were missed at translation and transliteration by using a native Tamil speaker of my own choice.

The Participants and the Selection Process

It must be understood that, when conducting research amongst revolutionary organisations or in conflict zones, the option to negotiate over the participant selection process is limited. It can be difficult and extremely dangerous to interview combatant women without the explicit approval of the Gatekeeper (and therefore the LTTE). The Gatekeeper and the Head of the Political Wing selected a suitable group of women for interviewing, the implication of which meant that I only had access to women who were considered by the organisation to be appropriate or suitable. My request for combatant women representing a cross-section of early-to-later recruits was granted. My civic participants were chosen through the contacts of the Gatekeeper and his wife according to my specifications for a cross-section of women varying from the educated socially affluent to the less-educated working classes. Once the selection process was completed, it was clear that the Gatekeeper and the Head of the Political Wing avoided any further assessment.

The seven combatant women from the LTTE were Arasi (aged 30), who was the most senior woman combatant in the LTTE; Kavitha (aged 30), who was then Head of the Jaffna District; Arulvili (aged 23), who was the previous Head of the Jaffna District; Yalini (aged 24), who was the LTTE Political Office translator; Aruna (aged 25), Roja (aged 22) and Mallika (aged 21) who were rank combatants. The ex-combatant AK (aged 34) was married with a child, but had been a section leader and led teams to war. She had to leave active service due to the severe injuries she received during the Elephant Pass battle in April 2000, which was one of the major battles fought against the state's armed forces.

The civic women included married women (with and without children) and childless unmarried women as well. BP, a middle-aged married, former teacher, with no children of her own, was the wife of the Gatekeeper, and she acted as an interpreter on many occasions. CH (aged 26) was the only Christian participant in the interview group, and the only one whose parents were of mixed race (Sinhalese and Tamil). CH died the following year due to a misdiagnosis of cancer and lack of medical care. DK (aged 27) was a professional woman engaged in a highly masculine industry running her family business. GV and HA were both middle-aged professional women from wealthy middle-class backgrounds. GV was married, while HA was unmarried. ES (aged 27) was an academic engaged in higher education, and FP (aged 40) was a married mother of two sons.

The group of civic women were limited to those who were known to the Gatekeeper and his family through their extended social network.

AK also formed a part of this network but was identified specifically because of her previous role as a combatant. They all primarily appeared to be from similar social backgrounds, with the exception of FP who was from the working classes. It must also be noted that, though the civic interview participants appeared at the outset to be independent of the LTTE, some later information revealed their connections to be closer to the terrorist group than previously indicated. For example, one of them was active in the reconstruction of an LTTE graveyard which was destroyed by the state army, and two of them were prominent speakers at various LTTE ceremonies.

Role of the Researcher in Representing the Other

This book contributes to the debate of validating the researcher by identifying the researcher's positionality in the research. I accept that in some situations where difference can enhance the resulting data, it may be appropriate for researchers to come from a background similar to that of the participants. However, this concept is born out of a belief that social research is best obtained if the same ethnic group conducts the research. For example, a Tamil researcher is best suited to conduct research on the Tamil community, as the same ethnic group will be less inhibiting and more forthcoming with one of their own social group.[9] Nonetheless, it must be recognised that social science often deals with the non-ideal world in which the researcher has to manage the participants as given. The interviewer has an effect on the responses received, either by the social characteristics of the interviewer impacting on the results in various ways or by the expectations harboured by the interviewee about the interviewer (Lee 1995; Collins 1980 and Bradburn 1983). Phoenix argues:

> [t]he strategy of matching interviewers and respondents on particular characteristics (such as gender and 'race') does not produce 'better' data. Indeed, since respondents are not positioned in any unitary way, it does not avoid the necessity for analysis of the ways in which wider social relations enter into the interview relationship. (Phoenix 1995: 70)

Following from the above, it could be argued that, had I been a Tamil national, the women of the LTTE may have been more forthcoming with their life-histories. However, I would mitigate that this may not necessarily be true. My status as an 'Outsider' in fact allowed them to 'explain' their experiences in ways that were more self-reflective, as suggested by the primary and secondary interviews with both groups of Tamil women. They might have otherwise made incorrect assumptions regarding my level of knowledge about the issues they were explaining.

The issue of legitimacy directed me to a certain kind of behaviour when dealing with the revolutionary group. I found that I was distancing myself from my hegemonic background and embracing my British identity more, as I believed this would make me appear less hostile to those whom I was interested in interviewing. English language, the language of the coloniser, was perceived as much less prejudicial even though this had to be conveyed through a translator. I found that each single ethnic group I laid claim to brought specific socio-political differences to my research. My British identity helped me to gain access far more easily than my hegemonic origin of being Sinhalese. However, through the latter I had a related identity to the researched Other.[10]

Further reflection on the legitimacy argument regarding my hegemonic identity reveals a strong dichotomy: my Sri Lankan identity ties me to the women combatants, thus legitimising my involvement in the research; my Sinhalese ethnicity within the hegemonic discourse distances us and thereby questions my legitimacy. I would, therefore, argue that legitimacy has no precise definition or standard recipe. Researchers will invariably raise issues of legitimacy, especially when feminists conduct research in representing the Other away from their own ethnic background (see Phoenix 1995). I would agree with Schegloff (1997) that the intersection of class, gender, sexuality and ethnicity does form a more complete picture within this context. Singling out one aspect such as ethnicity creates a risk of obtaining partial data as the "otherness" is only seen through a spectrum of understood differences. This, in turn, made me constantly negotiate my role as a researcher.

Outsider inside the Friendship and Kinship Formation: The Researcher's Positionality within the Combatant Women's Group

I was prompted to look at my own friendship with the combatant women whilst analysing the data relating to the breakdown of the family and subsequent transference of affections to an alternative family within the LTTE (as discussed in Chapter 4). Understanding my own position (as a researcher) in relation to the group meant having to understand the kind of relationship that was practised within the terrorist group. This understanding became heightened once I realised that 'kinship' in this context refers to a deep friendship, unlike a kin identity that is indicative of a familial relation rather than a depth of emotion.

Friendship itself encompasses many levels, such as the friendship that was extended to the outside Other, with many complicated facets differentiating it from the friendship that was practiced within the LTTE's kin group. I was offered friendship as a researcher that overlooked my hegemonic identity and was extended to me because of my British identity and status as a foreigner in their midst. However, I was very aware of being accepted at a different level and being granted the hospitality of a different kind. I partook in meals where good-humoured, casual conversation flourished; I spent time viewing videos with the combatant women laughing and marvelling at images on the screen or going on day trips with them. All of these activities made me conscious of occupying a certain privileged position of friendship with the combatant women.[11] At the same time I was aware that this friendship also removed me to some degree from civic women in Tamil society, making my position fragile and restricted. I was aware that had I been a Tamil national, there would have been the possibility of a putative kinship: being called a *sister*, for example. Such a kin identity would have overridden identity politics, as the relationship would be based on a non-political level. My position stopped short of a kinship identity and affinity of this kind due to the very same Sinhalese ethnic identity and British cultural differences.

As discussed in Chapter 4, these forms of address convey a certain degree of acceptance through kinship and also operate as a mark of respect for the Other. Addressing me by my name placed me in the position of an outsider who did not have a kin identity that can be related back to the combatant group. It must be understood that the lack of kin identity also formed a part of the social interaction within the friendship and its power relationship. My relationship with the combatant women was part of a friendship that was not in the inner realms of kinship. It is also uncertain whether or not the relationships that were made on the field can be maintained in a post-war environment where their former identity and views may need to be kept secret for personal safety reasons.

The aim of this book remains as an insight, albeit a limited insight, into the lives of women who became combatants in the LTTE. Although this book gives an overview of the conflict, the focus remains as a contribution to the understanding of gender and conflict. In order to facilitate this understanding, Chapter 2 presents an overview of Sri Lanka's history that contextualises the conflict. It discusses the historical influences in the social construction of female identity in Sri Lanka, particularly that of Tamil women in Jaffna. Sri Lankans have practised diversity and tolerance of religion and ethnicity for many years. However, within the last three decades their social position has changed; a deeply-embittered and divided ethno-centric split between the Sinhalese and the Tamils has taken place. The chapter describes the construction of a Sinhalese ideology that treats Sri Lanka as a Sinhalese–Buddhist state and views Tamil nationalism as a minority issue. Tamil nationalism argues that only war and the construction of their own state can address Tamil political aspirations, and the way that the government has treated Tamil nationals has enhanced and strengthened that belief. The conflict was defined in terms of ethnic identity based on language and geography, and was intrinsically linked to territory. Both ideologies, therefore, had become further entrenched in war and violence.

Chapter 2 also illustrates that Tamil women's traditional gender roles have evolved to include 'new' social roles which were contradicted by the recruitment of combatant women. A new image of an 'Armed Virgin' was emerging in the combatant woman which contrasted with the civic woman. This image was socially paradoxical, and the newly constructed womanhood was fraught with multiple issues.

Chapter 3 discusses the effects of displacement that impacted on the lives of women who later became combatants. Displacement affected a significant number of people, the majority of whom were from the Jaffna peninsula. The Tamil nationals describe displacement as *Idampeyatha*, meaning a forceful expulsion from home–a term which has now entered into the mainstream language. Home was seen as both a place and a space where women were safe. The break-up of home has a strong symbolic meaning for the displaced.

The chapter suggests that displacement was a key factor in the recruitment of women into the armed struggle, exploring the link between moving to an LTTE-controlled area—where the influence of nationalism was rife—and the decision to join the LTTE voluntarily. I have identified, through narrative histories, a number of contributing factors that had led the women to join the LTTE. These include the loss of home, exclusion from school, the break-up of the family unit, helplessness and above all, loss of agency.

In this chapter, I have looked at the definition of a 'child' as stated by 1983 United Nations Convention on the Rights of the Child Declaration to give a clear understanding of the LTTE's involvement in child recruitment. I have critically examined the issues of insecurities felt by children combined with parents' active admiration and support of combatants within the framework of displacement and child recruitment. From my findings, it became clear that those who were displaced to LTTE-controlled areas with a strong nationalistic fervour voluntarily joined the movement as a place of safety: a kind of safety they felt their parents were no longer able to offer. It must be noted that the chapter is not about child combatants per se, and therefore the research project does not include forced recruits. It is, however, key to the discussions raised in this book as some of the combatant women were child combatants (albeit voluntary recruits). However, all the combatant women who took part in this study claimed displacement to be a catalyst in their decision-making process.

The recognition of female kinship between women combatants had never been at the forefront of war and conflict literature (as opposed to masculine-dominated war literature that discusses male identity, comradeship and friendships in relation to kinship at length).[12] The masculine bias has resulted in a shortfall of documentary evidence in relation to women as combatants and their kinships formed in the battle field. In

Chapter 4, I have addressed the kin identity amongst combatant women and their non-consanguine relationships with the fictive LTTE family.

Young (2001), who has written extensively on women's involvement and participation in the Chinese Revolution's Long March, provides a glimpse in to the kind of kin identity the combatant women may have had with one another.

Young (2001: 246) states:

> **We women cooperated very well, we were united, all of us were one heart. At the time, we women had to be united. We couldn't quarrel or fight. At that time we shared everything from food to clothes—we suffered together, enjoyed together.**

Although there is a lack of documented evidence, one may speculate that a considerable amount of emotional support must have been given to women combatants by their fellow women within different revolutionary contexts. The above narrative may imply that there were strong relationships which outlasted a very difficult time for the combatant women who fought and endured hardship together. The suffering of women was further seen amongst the women guerrillas of various South American revolutionary groups as well as in the Vietnam War.[13]

The friendship-based kin bonding was seen in other revolutionary groups, too. For example, amongst the Zapatista movement, where young combatant women start a very different life from their previous existences in the community, the women state:

> **It gets easier with time, you have to forget the things you left behind. The *companeros* teach you, we talk together; it is like a family again, we learn to love each other because our brothers and sisters stayed on the other side and that brings us together. (Rovira 2000: 41)**

This discourse, in effect, illustrates the transference of consanguine familial affections to the non-consanguine relationships made in the revolutionary family.

The LTTE's construction of a sustainable fictive kinship through friendships amongst combatant women from various socio-economical, religious and caste backgrounds replicating the familial kinships forms the basis of Chapter 4. In this chapter, the words 'kinship' and 'friendship' are used as analytical tools to explore the non-consanguine ties that were built and maintained within the LTTE replacement family. The word 'kinship' is detached from its consanguine roots, and kin terminology is used to describe metaphorically an alternative family unit or 'fictive' kin that was (re)created by the LTTE and founded upon friendships that overrode blood ties. Whilst acknowledging that there is a strong caste-dictated hierarchy that operates in Jaffna, it must also be considered that the LTTE operated on a non-caste-based metaphorical family unit; therefore caste does not form part of this study.

One success of the LTTE's (re)constructed family was its ability to transcend the basic social prejudices that were engrained in Jaffna society; hence kinship in the LTTE successfully rose above social barriers such as caste and religion and had freed combatant women to accept each other. I also critically examine how combatant women (re)constructed an alternative gendered role within the movement that challenged the socially dictated roles for women. The chapter illustrates kin relationships cultivating loyalty regardless of personal circumstances and reaffirming the combatant women's shared experiences that placed them in a valued position within the kinship group.

Chapter 5 discusses the involvement of women in suicide bombings and the gendered dimensions of the motivational forces bchind their participation. From a global perspective, there are two groups that can be the nearest comparison to combatant women of the LTTE. They are the Black Widows of Chechnya and the Army of Roses in Palestine (Herath 2006a).

Brief Overview: The Black Widows of Chechnya

The conflict in Chechnya escalated into open warfare in December 1994 when Russian armed forces occupied the capital city of Grozny from secessionist forces. The cost was high in terms of human causalities and collateral damage to the city. It did not bring peace: five years on, a second wave of the civil war began.

The women of Chechnya took active roles during the first civil war in 1994–1996, and grew from resistance fighters into suicide bombers. In 2003, women performed six out of seven suicide attacks. In 2004, women carried out all 12 of the suicide missions (Bloom 2005: 127). The well-publicised Russian theatre siege in October 2002 included a young woman of 16 years of age. These women were known as the Black Widows, and the status of widowhood in the traditional patriarchal society indirectly creates social outcasts and grants a sense of hopelessness and lack of self-worth to such women.

The Chechen anger was directed at the Russian state and its civic citizens, who were viewed as silent supporters of the state mechanism used against the Chechen nationals. The paying of tax was viewed as supporting the authority's means of sponsoring the war in Chechnya, and the unwillingness of the Russian civic population to protest against the Russian state's atrocities meant condoning the same (Bloom 2005).

One of the aspects of the Chechen women's involvement in suicide bombing is the lead given to other women to be suicide bombers. Although the Russians labelled the suicide missions conducted by Chechen women as 'Palestinisation', it is, in reality, quite the reverse. Letters sent by Palestinian women to Hamas argued that, if Muslim women in Chechnya could become martyrs, then why not the Muslim women of Palestine (Bloom 2005: 130).

From a global perspective, the Chechen women suicide bombers have revealed their catalyst to be the loss of a loved one (Cronin 2003 and Kline and Franchetti 2002). It must be understood that from a Chechen context a woman as a widow has no prospects but a bleak and miserable existence to look forward to, as her identity and agency have always been linked to that of a man. An article in *The Sunday Times* newspaper by Kline and Franchetti (2002) refers to other reports from Chechnya that show women either being *sold* into the Chechen revolutionary movement because of the socio-economic needs of families (where a widow is considered a financial burden) or simply forced into recruitment by patriarchal authority.

There is a lack of empirical research primarily due to the danger and difficulties involved in gaining access to such organisations. It is nonetheless interesting to note the newspaper report on the Russian theatre siege claiming that only the women wore suicide-belts, not the men, thus giving credence to the highly gendered angle of a female's worth to the society being less than that of a man.

Brief Overview: The Army of Roses

On 27 January 2002, Yasser Arafat shifted the focus of suicide bombers from the traditionally masculine role of a male suicide bomber, *shahide* (the male martyr), to a newly created feminine role as *shahida* (a female martyr). This role change was presented to an audience of over a thousand women as equality, selflessness and, above all, a responsibility of womanhood.

Arafat stated (Victor 2004: 19–20):

> Women and men are equal. ...You are my *army of roses* (author's emphasis) that will crush Israeli tanks....You are the hope of Palestine. You will liberate your husbands, fathers, and sons from oppression. *You will sacrifice the way you, women, have always sacrificed for your family.* (author's emphasis in italics)

Suicide bombings conducted in Palestine have increased since the year 2000, with Palestinians claiming that their lives have become more unbearable since the Al Aqsa Intifada. The targets identified by suicide bombers in Palestine are often 'soft' targets against the civic society, and it is said that the cost of a suicide attack can be no more than US $150 in its entirety (Hoffman 2003).

Bloom (2005) and Victor (2004) argue that women's involvement can be theorised as a direct result of the social conditions forced upon Palestinians. Those who live in refugee camps full of hardships, shortages, humiliation and violence, often view life as a transient journey into paradise; thus perceived as a life not worth living. Within these external hardships, the role of women in the domestic sphere is one of subjugation to men in the family. Decisions about their lives are made by men, moving from father to brother to husband. In addition to this patriarchal control, generations of Palestinian women who have been born under Israeli occupation, are not only filled with resentment, but also prohibition. If they wish to attain equality with the men in the community, they must then be prepared to pay a high price for such liberation. In highly gendered societies where there are clearly defined social roles, the use of women as suicide bombers adds a further dimension to the argument. It conveys a message to the men that their masculinity is under threat, and women have become sufficiently politicised to warrant active participation in any armed struggle.

Women's participation in the Israeli/Palestinian conflict is a relatively new phenomenon. The lateness of women's participation in suicide bombing lies in the fact that militant religious political groups (such as Hamas and Islamic Jihad) did not engage women to their ranks. When nationalist groups realised the value of the suicide missions carried out by religious militant groups, they tried to convince their secular members to act in the same way. The reason may well be that, by this stage men who were already pre-disposed to such thinking had joined the religious militant groups of Hamas and Islamic Jihad. When the nationalistic movements called upon women to be active, Al Aqsa Martyrs Brigade stepped in to provide the logistical support for women suicide bombers (Bloom 2005 and Victor 2004).

The first incident of a woman being involved in a suicide bombing occurred on the very day that Yasser Arafat stated that women could be a part of the revolutionary struggle (27 January 2002). A 26-year-old Palestinian Red Crescent worker, named Wafa Idris, carried a bomb in her bag and detonated it in a department store, killing one and injuring some 100 Israeli civilians. The Al Aqsa Brigade claimed responsibility, stating she was a member of the Brigade even though she never left a video message as Palestinian suicide bombers usually do (Victor 2004: 20). This has been viewed by some as indicating Idris had no intention to be a suicide bomber, for she was only directed to carry the bomb to the venue and hand it over to a man. Some believe she arrived at the venue too early and the bomb exploded unexpectedly. The exact reasons will never be known, but she became the first female suicide bomber from Palestine; in that act she became idealised, as shown in her eulogy by the

Fatah movement, as Victor (2004: 54) states, 'Wafa's martyrdom restored honour to the national role of the Palestinian woman, sketched the most wonderful pictures of heroism in the long battle for national liberation.'

The first confirmed Palestinian female suicide bomber may well be Darina Abu Aisha, as her actions (though a few days later) were planned with a recording left for posterity in the usual manner (Victor 2004: 20). Since then, many female suicide bombers have followed her example, including two women suicide bombers from Palestinian Islamic Jihad in 2003 and one from Hamas in January 2004. The Hamas engagement is of interest, as Sheik Yassin, the spiritual leader of Hamas, declared that there is nothing written in the Koran's holy text to say that women should not fight in national liberation wars (Victor 2004: 20). They used their first woman suicide bomber on 14 January 2004. Although Reem Riashi was a wife, mother and grandmother, she undertook a role that had previously been open only to unmarried or divorced women with no nurturing responsibilities.

There are a number of religious-based justifications popularised by the media with regards to Middle Eastern suicide bombers. These include the popularly held belief of many riches in heaven, which expands for women to include gaining a husband in heaven and saving 70 of her relatives, making her the nurturer even in death.

In Chapter 5, my focus is on the argument that the LTTE suicide bombings are part of a collective rational strategy for cost-effective attacks, and that individual motivation is best explained through Durkheim's notion of 'obligatory altruistic suicide'. The chapter also analyses the loss of sexual purity as a motivational factor and reveals a number of politicised issues ranging from body politics to the nation state (Herath 2006b). It discusses the symbolic nature of rape victims using their socioculturally viewed 'polluted bodies' as bombs in a process of purification by immolation. The engagement of women as suicide bombers raises issues about individual agency and autonomy along with gender identity. The chapter argues that social perceptions of women lie behind the sensationalised media reporting of women who commit such acts.

This chapter explores the way in which death was constructed in the LTTE and how it impacted on equality. Combatant women saw the role of a suicide bomber as a career pinnacle and as a 'gift' to society: the ultimate gift to those they care for and the nation. The combatant women revealed that they felt the act of suicide bombing empowering them by reinstating their lost agency. However, the gender equality argument needs to be seen in the context of a violent political conflict, and it is questionable whether women could have maintained the equality gained through self-sacrifice and sustained this particular form of negotiated equality.

Regardless of women's participation in suicide bombings, it must be acknowledged that the number of revolutionary organisations where combatant women have had equality and reached higher levels of leadership is limited. Combatant women mostly appear to gain a certain level of leadership where they become commanders of units but are rarely at the very top of the organisation. These units could be fighting units as well as support units. The Chinese revolutionary combatants create a mixed picture of women reaching the levels of heads of departments that were engaged in providing 'food sacks, straw shoes and clothing for the Red army' (Young 2001: 164) as well as being combatant leaders. Exceptions were seen amongst organisations such as the Zapatista, where the key ideological concept was 'autonomy' rather than 'tradition' or 'progress' (Rovira 2000: 6). By moving away from tradition and progress, they were able to focus on the revolution in an alternative way, whereby socially constructed gender roles were not considered to be of paramount importance over their ability as combatants. By this action, combatant women had an equal opportunity to become leaders based on their own actions. This was also reflective of the Uruguayan Tupamaros revolutionary group, the Salvadorian Farabundo Marti Front for National Liberation (FMLN) and the Nicaraguan Sandinistas (Lobao 1998; and Kampwirth 2001 and 2002).

Thus, in Chapter 6, I critically examine how gender was (re)constructed in the LTTE and the levels of gender equality that women have achieved within the movement and civic society. I argue that the LTTE struggle had accelerated a social change, sweeping women towards a new gender identity. This chapter highlights that the number of combatant women in leading roles was limited, and that their lack of training in decision-making may have contributed to their exclusion from higher levels of the LTTE. I argue against adopting an essentialist feminist view of women as pacifists by claiming that this runs the risk of overlooking the social impact of combatant women on both civic society and civic women. In this chapter, I maintain that women had moved from support roles to active roles and challenged the existing patriarchal views and subordinate roles of women in society. Therefore, the combatant women's (re)constructed identity had granted them a form of equality that must be seen within the historical framework of Jaffna and its patriarchal culture.

In this chapter, I investigate a number of paradoxes that the new gender identity had created, and the levels of achievements are contrasted and compared between combatant and civic women. I also question the role the leader Prabhakaran had played in promoting combatant women to new social positions above that of the women in civic society, and how their active involvement in the LTTE had placed combatant women outside civic society without their realisation. I end this chapter by claiming that the combatant women formed a powerful force for social change and radically altered the perceptions of women in society.

In the concluding Chapter 7, I draw together all the strands that had contributed to women joining the LTTE movement and analyse how gender was (re)constructed in a society that is culturally steeped in masculinity and male dominance, carrying a historically defined, socially marginalised position for women. From the combatant women's perspective they have gained a form of equality, both for themselves and for women in Tamil society as a whole, by joining the LTTE. I identify several catalysts that influenced women in the decision-making process that pushed and pulled them towards the terrorist organisation. These include the non-consanguineous family that the LTTE was able to successfully construct, overriding traditional familial ties and the strong relationship formations between combatant women. These attachments were extended to acts of suicide bombings where combatant women believed that they were giving a gift of self for the greater good of the Tamil nation and for the cause of the separate state of Tamil *Eelam*. I conclude that the reality of both combatant and civic women's emancipation within the confines of war and changing social roles as discussed in this research is complicated. This complication is further compounded by the fact that the apparent gender equality in fact has reinforced, as well as re-constructed, traditional gender ideologies of the self-sacrificing woman. However, the fact remains that the women combatants did become a powerful force for social change and did radically alter the perception of women in terrorist organisations, gaining a world-wide reputation.

The aim of this book is not just to offer a window into the gender equality debate within the LTTE and postulate on the possibilities of *what if*, but to encourage women in Jaffna to take the mantel that has been given to them by the combatant women and move forward; to (re)build their lives knowing the sacrifices that were made and the battles that were won and lost. I acknowledge that, since post-conflict, many who had taken part in this research—and who are still alive–may have changed, some irrevocably. I am unable to say the violent ending of the Tamil struggle was for the best, but neither can I condone a war that had cost so many lives.

One thing I do know for certain is that the women in Jaffna are exceptionally resilient and have the ability to hold long-term goals and aspirations. I am certain that the suffering they had endured during the period of conflict will assist them in moving forward in a positive way in a post-conflict era. Social changes that started with the combatant women have, in effect, paved the way for civic women in Jaffna, allowing Tamil women as a whole a new space to be independent and write a new gender history for themselves.

Notes

1 Tamil *Eelam* means the Tamil part of the *Eelam*. The word 'Eelam' itself is synonymous with the word 'Sri Lanka', and is believed to have been in use circa 200 B.C. to 250 A.D., when the Tamil language word for Sri Lanka was *Ilankai* (pronounced as *Eelankai*), meaning Lanka. Tamil phonetic language does not contain 'la' as a starting sound, thus the vowel 'ee' comes before 'lankai'(Sivathamby 2006).

2 Some authors have written on the subject of sensitivity and danger in fieldwork (see Smyth 2005; Morano 1996; Green 1995; Simons 1995; Nordstrom and Robben 1995;

Schnabel 2005 and Albert 2005). However, it was Lee's texts (1995, and 1999) on sensitive and dangerous topics that I found most useful to my own work.

3 Some researchers such as Farberrow (1963: 1–7) look at sensitive topics through a definition based on themes that are considered to be taboo. Others such as Green (1995: 105) view sensitive topics through elements of fear that merge the boundaries of subjective personal experiences to include collective social memory. Green also claims that experiences of fear and terror are difficult to describe in words. Seiber and Stanley (1998) describe sensitive topics as being any socially sensitive research that may have consequences to either the researched or the group of individuals represented by the research [referred to in Lee (1999: 3)]. Such attempts at defining sensitive research overlook a number of more specific problems that are embedded in conducting sensitive research and deeply rooted in methodological issues (ibid.), not least the risks to the researcher herself. As Lee states, 'sensitive topics present problems because research into them involves potential costs to those involved in the research, including on occasion, the researcher' (1999: 4).

4 I assume that the border guards rarely met Sinhalese people who have adopted a Western nationality and are unable to speak either of Sri Lanka's main languages. I had a difficult time trying to persuade them that living overseas for a lengthy period does result in adopting the native language and that there was nothing sinister about this.

5 The Gatekeeper and his family would organise their day around my needs and safety, as they were concerned about me firstly as a British student of Sinhalese ethnicity, and secondly as a female in a foreign country where the rules of equality are not as defined as in western countries.

6 Related issues include political sympathies that researchers may bring with them to the field. An example here is Moreno, recognised as the only sociologist ever to have played a participant observer role in a political struggle (Whyte 1984: 31). In the late 1960s, Jose Moreno from Cornell University went to the Dominican Republic to research inter-village systems for his PhD study. A few days after his arrival in Santo Domingo, an armed struggle ensued resulting in the city being taken over by the rebel group, to whom Moreno was sympathetic. He volunteered to work with them as a non-combatant, and 'his dedication and abilities in organisation the supply of food and medical and health services for the people of the beleaguered city led him into a close working relationship with the rebel leaders' (Whyte 1984: 31). When Moreno returned to university, he changed his research topic, and 'Faculty members on his committee agreed that a study of inter-village system could always be done, while major rebellions aimed at over throwing a government were relatively rare events' (ibid.). Following his PhD, in 1970 he published a book based on the same, titled *Barrios in Arms*.

7 I presume kindness was previously extended to Schalk when he was conducting his research in Jaffna in 1990. Some view Schalk's (1992) work on combatant women of the LTTE to be biased, as he became sympathetic to the LTTE cause. I do not share this

view, as I found (based on my experience) that Schalk has written quite an accurate description of the women of the LTTE. Many who are critical of the combatant women and of Schalk have never met any combatant women in their own socio-political and geographical location. Not meeting the women in their own space often leads to alternative forms of representations that may not be accurate. One can question whether he was blinded to the harsh realities of the LTTE by being overly involved with his research topic and those who were part of that topic. My own research visits illustrate that he is well-known and highly regarded amongst the LTTE and its sympathisers. Was this 'high regard', then due to his inability to criticise the LTTE as a violent political organisation? Can I criticise those who placed their trust in me and accepted me so readily? These are hard questions, but are recognised by others who argue, '...favouring intimacy over analysis also reflects the value we place on empathy, understanding the perspective of those we study through role taking' (Kleinman and Copp 1993: 27).

8 Kleinman and Copp (1993: 38) define 'cognitive empathy' as 'understanding why people think, feel, and act as they do'.

9 The debate can be extended to intersectionality of class, but the focus here remains as race or ethnicity.

10 Albeit the 'enemy' in the greater context of the political discourse.

11 It is noteworthy that the word 'acquaintance' does not exist in Tamil culture.

12 Leon (2001) discusses Subcomandante Marcos and the Zapatista movement; Davis (1985) discusses the Second World War fought in Burma; Robert Graves a seminal autobiographical text on the First World War; Lionel Sotheby's diaries and letters from the Western Front during the First World War. There is also a vast amount of literature emanating from the Iraq and Afghanistan wars following on the same masculine format of male identity, comradeship and friendships that relates to kinship at length as brotherhood.

13 As detailed above, see Kampwirth (2001) and (2002), Rovira (2000) for South American literature and Turner and Hao (1998) for Vietnam conflict.

2 The Lions and the Tigers

A Historical Overview of the Sri Lankan Conflict and the Role of Women

Historically and culturally, Sri Lankans have regarded themselves as both peace-loving and tolerant, with particular empathy shown to the ethnicity and diversity of religion. However, within the last three decades their social position of 'warmth, hospitality, and good humour … that, amongst other things can laugh at themselves' (Tambiah 1986: 1) has changed to a deeply embittered and divided ethno-centric nation split between Sinhalese and Tamil identities. This division has caused fear amongst the Sri Lankan people, resulting in suspicion, animosity and violence towards each other's community. The unitary State established in colonial times gave way to a war between the State and the LTTE that is reflective of a contemporary conflict constructed in the post-colonial era as a consequence of the state-building process.

The conflict is defined in terms of ethnic identity, and in this chapter I argue that the conflict can be understood as an instrument for constructing an ethnic identity based on language as well as geography. According to the nationalist ideologies of identity politics, ethnic identity is linked to territory (e.g., Tamil-speaking areas must belong to the LTTE). Therefore, extreme forms of violence are a method of gaining exclusive ethnic control over territory. To this end, the membership of the LTTE was formed from disenchanted and frustrated young men, with women being added later.

I argue that gendered relations play a critical role in the construction of identity. In particular, Tamil identity is based on a gendered concept of masculinity, within which women are cast in a female role defined by the hegemonic masculinity embedded in patriarchal Tamil society. At the same time, the realities of the conflict have directly challenged gender construction in Tamil society. According to the cultural perspective of the Tamil society, women play the role of patriotic mother, which is extended during conflict to include their becoming embattled. However, this ideological paradigm of patriotic mother has been contradicted by the recruitment of women as fighters that in turn had created a new kind of femininity which was culturally alien to Tamil women. The newly emerging image that encompassed the roles of female slayers of injustice who protected Tamil nationals is in contrast to the civic women in society.

This newly constructed womanhood was fraught with multiple issues and social paradoxes and was heavily criticised as an androgynous role contrary to femaleness.[1] The next few chapters will address the socially paradoxical issues that Tamil women (both combatant and civic) had learnt to negotiate during a period of heavy conflict and violence.

This chapter is separated into two main sections that focus on the evolution of the conflict and the role of women in Jaffna's Tamil society. The first section provides a chronological political history and outlines the issues relating to discontentment and ethnic separation that resulted in the war with the LTTE. The second section provides an overview of the history of women, covering the social changes that affected all women in Sri Lanka and focusing on Tamil women in particular during colonial and post-colonial periods. It also addresses the gender roles in Jaffna from ancient times through to the modern era that have transformed Tamil society from a matrilineal society to a patrilineal society under the influence of cultural practices that have evolved to include 'new' social roles for women.

The Evolution of the Conflict

Background

According to narratives from both sides, the complexity of the ethnic conflict is embedded in history and mythology; a legend claims that a union between an exiled Indian King and a Lioness created a new ethnic group, the Sinhalese.[2] Though precise recordings do not exist to confirm timelines of the King's arrival in the island (with his band of seven hundred men), it is generally believed that they landed in the north-west coast of Sri Lanka, *Tambapnni*, c. fifth or sixth century B.C. Whilst the legend favours a mythical union with a Lioness, it is most likely that the King and his men becam·· involved with an indigenous tribe known as the Lions that inhabited the island. The Lion tribe were probably the most influential clan to give its name to people and to the land.[3] The 'mythomoteur or constitutive myth of the Sinhalese ethnic polity' (Smith 1986: 15) granted the Sinhalese a space to gain a unique identity that could differ from the Tamil nationals.[4] The word *Sinha* means *lion* in Sanskrit, the language believed to have been used in Sri Lanka during primordial times.[5]

The disagreement on who were the very first settlers in the island still remains. However, in the classic works of G.C. Mendis (1932) and A.J. Wilson (1974) it is suggested that the earliest settlers were perhaps the *Dravidians* from southern India. They have cited a plausible example of the *Veddas*, Sri Lankan aborigines, walking across the 22-mile distance from South India prior to the land between the countries being separated by the *Palk Straits*.[6]

The ancient Buddhist text *Mahavansa*, which chronicles Sri Lanka from the fourth century to the mid-eighteenth century, does not mention the existence of Tamil nationals in the island. While *Mahavansa* is an accepted text amongst historians as a record of the ancient history of Sri Lanka, it is none the less considered a religiously biased document written for the period and 'encrusted with miracle and invention' (de Silva 1984: 3). It is also argued that *Mahavansa* has given rise to an ideology of ethno-centric claims of descent from the Aryans of Northern India. The North Indian culture and civilization is perceived as more advanced than that of South India (Somasundaram 1998 and Sivanayagam 2001). Despite the lack of formal evidence, Tamil nationals in Jaffna claim that they are the original inhabitants of the island, asserting an ancient Tamil presence in the northern part of Sri Lanka (Mendis 1932; Pujangga 1997; Thambiah 1954; Navaratnam 1959 and Rasanayagam 1926). There is, however, historical evidence of a Tamil ruling monarchy during the arrival of the Portuguese invaders in 1505.[7]

The Portuguese found three kingdoms in the island upon their invasion: Kotte, Kandy and Jaffna. Of these, the Kandiyan kingdom retained its autonomy through winning battles—first with the Portuguese (1505–1658), and then the Dutch (1658–1796). The British expelled the Dutch in 1796[8] and made the whole island a Crown Colony in 1802. However, they did not control Kandy, its kingdom and the surrounding hill country until 1815. Scholars argue that the Tamil kingdom in Jaffna had ceased to exist by this time (Mendis 1932; Ram 1989 and Weerasooriya 1970). The British began the creation of modern Ceylon by centralising its administration and economy, which included controlling Sri Lanka's two ethnic groups. 'In their administration the British favoured the Tamils over the Sinhalese, in their typical "divide and rule" policy' (Bandara 2002: 19).

Politics of Nationalism

The violent political struggle between the Tamil minorities and the Sinhalese majority is a relatively recent development. Indeed, these two ethnic groups have co-existed for several centuries (pre- and post-colonial eras) where they had 'developed a reasonable degree of understanding and mutual tolerance' (Wriggins 1960: 231).[9] Such indications of tolerance and acceptance of ethno-cultural variations make the conflict a new war.[10] In her book *New and Old Wars*, Kaldor (2001: 70) states that, 'New forms of power struggles may take the guise of traditional nationalism, tribalism, or communalism, but they are, never the less, contemporary phenomena arising from contemporary causes and displaying new characteristics.'

The emergence of Sinhalese and Tamil national identities based on language and religion was borne out of a reaction to colonialism and the need to provide a political basis for statehood (Wriggins 1960). The beginning of open disharmony dates to when the struggle for independence from Britain was the main objective of both groups. A strong national identity began to emerge amongst the Sinhalese-Buddhists who challenged the Western Christian values of the colonialists. In addition, the suppression of Buddhism under colonial rule became a tool used by Sinhalese nationalists to challenge the existing social order created by the ruling British. The British, in turn, 'devised arrangements and made concessions in the 1870s that, in the long run, evolved into a policy whose central features were a special concern for—if not a special position for—Buddhism within the Sri Lanka polity' (de Silva1998: 4).

Politics of this period formed the backbone of a protracted struggle that took place many years later. The Ceylon National Congress Party of the pre-independence era lacked the required high levels of organisational abilities, resulting in low levels of popularity. This was further compounded by Tamil leaders departing from the party, which created a Sinhalese majority organisation (Kearney 1973: 97). In his book, *The Politics of Ceylon (Sri Lanka)* (1973), he argues that it is these limitations and a lack of communal inclusiveness that forced the Congress Party not to convert into a national political party, but at independence to be incorporated into the newly created United National Party (UNP).[11] This incorporation caused the Congress Party to vanish from the political scene altogether. The UNP was to be a single national party, but it lacked the much-needed popular support and the ability to obtain succour from minority ethnic nationals. They further lacked the post-independent political awareness that compounded them and highlighted their shortcomings (Kearney 1973: 98).

The first Sri Lankan Prime Minister, D.S. Senanayake, from the UNP, had a concept of a utopian state based on an ideological pluralism. He was succeeded by his son, Dudley Senanayake, who was followed in turn by cousin, Sir John Kotelawala. All of them carried a vision of pluralism. However, the 1956 elections changed this political vision with S.W.R.D. Bandaranaike becoming the prime minister. He rejected plurality as prescribed by D.S. Senanayake to embrace a democratic and populist nationalism that was fundamentally divisive because of its determined Sinhalese and Buddhist focus (de Silva 1998: 5).

Meanwhile, the Lanka Sama Samaja Party (LSSP), formed in 1935 as a Trotskyite movement critical of British imperialism as well as the Sri Lankan wealthy social classes, gained mass support both from the working classes and from the lower-middle classes. In 1940, the Stalinists within the party were evicted; they in turn formed the Ceylon Communist Party (CP) in 1943. The LSSP CP and the Mahajana Eksath Peramuna (MEP) later formed a coalition with the Sri Lanka Freedom Party (SLFP), emerging as the main electoral challenger to the UNP. Along with these challenges they also pursued 'revolutionary rhetoric and militant actions' (Roberts 1994: 4) that were popular with the masses (Wriggins 1960 and Kearney 1973: 90–131).

From the mid-1950s and 1960s a number of Tamil radicals actively sought to engage with the LSSP as their idealism was conducive to both ethnic groups in a pre-war colonial state. Post 1964 this position changed as the new generation of young Tamil nationals looked elsewhere to form a new revolutionary organisation 'in search of Eelam for the Tamils' (Roberts 1994: 10).

The elevation of Buddhism continued until 1972, when there were visible signs that Buddhism had marginally failed to become a state religion but had promoted a national identity based on religious status (Roberts 1994: 10). In 1977, the government declared Buddhism to be the state religion, despite much opposition from minority groups. This declaration effectively rendered all non-Buddhist practitioners within the State of Sri Lanka as the Other. It led to the notion that Sri Lankan nationalism was based on Buddhism and Sinhalese ethnicity.

> To be Sinhalese is to be automatically a Buddhist and an Aryan, and to be Buddhist is to be able to make a total claim–territorially and politically–over Sri Lanka. Conversely, to be a Buddhist is to be Aryan Sinhalese by 'race' and 'language', and to be Sinhalese by race gives the right to exclude, perhaps even exterminate, other 'races' in Sri Lanka, especially the Dravidians. (Tambiah 1986: 58–59)

Sinhalese nationalism is then based on the idea that they are the 'sole' indigenous ethnic group in Sri Lanka, and Tamils are regarded as foreigners. It is often argued that 'Tamils have India to go to, but the Sinhalese have only the small island of Sri Lanka'. The view that the Sinhalese are the sole indigenous ethnic group of Sri Lanka is, at its extreme, translated into a feud substantiated by violent conflict.

The majority of the Sri Lankan population is Sinhalese by ethnicity and Buddhist by religion.[12] As Tambiah (1986: 69) states, 'to be truly Sinhalese was to be born Sinhalese, speak Sinhalese, and practice the Sinhalese religion, Buddhism'. The identity politics reflected in this sentence forms the very basis of the nationalist struggle to link religion (Buddhism) with language (Sinhalese) as a single unit that includes the majority and excludes the minority. This linking of language and religion as the basis of the ethnic identity makes the hegemonic group even more powerful.

Tambiah (1986) argues that three main factors contributed to the volatility of the political situation: the language restriction, free education system and the slow growth of the economy during this period. Language has been central to the arguments raised in politics since post-independence, and it is highly relevant to both education and employment.

Under British rule, English was the official language, and it became a tool in the hands of the Sinhalese elite and a large number of Tamil nationals in Sri Lanka. The national languages remained as a 'boundary marker for ethnic groups [...] and a constituent of one's ethnicity' (Roberts 1994: 48). However, the Tamil nationals viewed the English language as a necessity to succeed in daily life, granting them economic advancement as well as social mobility. Advanced academic qualifications opened pathways to professions such as medicine, law and civil administration that were taught and practised in the English language. In 1948 Tamils constituted 10 per cent of the population and 31 per cent of students at universities, which resulted in Tamils gaining a higher percentage of employment in the professional sphere. Though a majority of Sinhalese did feel discriminated against due to their lack of English language skills, this did not become an issue of concern until the 1930s (Ariyaratne 2001 and Ram 1989).

In 1935, linguistic discontent resulted in the development of a new nationalistic ideology. The LSSP was the catalyst, created solely to promote Sinhalese and Tamil languages as *swabasha*, meaning 'one's own language', promoting the idea that Tamil and Sinhalese languages should gradually replace the English language as the nation's official languages for education, legislature and civil administration. This became commonly known as 'parity', implying that both had equal status as official languages. For Tamil nationals it carried a further meaning of 'equality before law; that individual Tamils should have equal opportunity and status with [the] Sinhalese throughout the island' (Wriggins 1960: 250).

The coalition of LSSP, CP and the MEP joining the leading SLFP had a disastrous effect on Tamil–Sinhalese relations. They abandoned their commitment to an equal status for both Tamil and Sinhalese languages in favour of gaining the necessary votes. Armed with ethnicity and religion, the SLFP political rhetoric focused on the prevailing class system by pitching the socially underprivileged classes against the wealthy privileged classes in the country. Amongst the underprivileged were those educated with government assistance who voiced their discontentment at the lack of social progress. They objected to the domination of the coloniser's language, English, and the privileges it parted to the socio-culturally Westernised middles classes. This discontentment in effect formulated the Sinhalese linguistic nationalism and, by that very token, Tamil nationalism (Kearney 1964: 67).[13]

de Silva (1998: 5) claims that language became the basis of nationalism, and this metamorphosis of nationalism affected both the Sinhalese and Tamil population. The SLFP brought in the Official Languages Act in 1956. The minority Tamil representation at the Parliament was unable to influence the Sinhalese majority, who dictated that Sinhalese should become the official language of trade, commerce and education, further sowing the seeds of disharmony.

In 1957, S. J. V. Chelvanayakam, a leading Tamil politician, launched a *satyagraha* (peaceful protest) demanding the repeal of the Official Languages Act (1956) and equal status for the Tamil language, which culminated in the first major anti-Tamil riots in the capital city, Colombo, with many deaths and much destruction of Tamil-owned property.[14] Many Tamil nationals moved to the safety of the northern part of the island, where there was a larger Tamil presence (Sabaratnam 2001: 181; Ram 1989: 39–41 and Narayan-Swamy 2002: 13).

The Official Language Act caused the Tamil language to be restricted to the northern and eastern parts of the island, and those Tamils who lived in any other part of the island were subject to a compulsory requirement of undertaking a Sinhalese proficiency test within three years.[15]

> **In a democratic polity, if the majority community becomes autocratic and the promoter of its own interest at the cost of the minority, it is not only an infringement of basic democratic norms, but also creates a very fertile ground for ethnic violence which will lead to a civil war. (Ariyaratne 2001: 2)**

The Sinhalese Only policy of 1950 was consolidated in the 1972 constitution, granting a secondary position for Tamil language (de Silva 1997: 270). 'The rhetoric not the actual policy had become–to the constituent parties of the government's coalition–the political reality' (de Silva 1997: 270) . This had a further misfortune to be interpreted by the Tamil nationals who judged the incumbent government by what was said rather than what was done. Whilst the rhetoric was elevated to a position of political reality, no further change was made to the language policy in all the three primary spheres of education, administration and public life. The public perceptions, however, remained.[16]

Educational Standardisation

In the education sector, the language related ethnic identity became both strong and sensitive. The choice to study in one's ethnic language was viewed as a group's right, and not an individual's. The politics of language was deeply embedded in the collective ethnic identity that was viewed to be in need of preservation, overriding the individual's choice (de Silva 1997: 269).

Education reforms of the 1930s and 1940s included the use of the student's *mother tongue* as the chosen language medium of study, creating a two-language stream in the process, with an option of an English medium. The Tamil parents had the right to educate their children in the Tamil language as they wished and were not limited to Tamil-speaking geographical locations (de Silva 1997: 269; and Wriggins 1960: 244–245). Those who were educated in the Tamil language had the right to sit for public exams and to enter into the public sector employment in that language (de Silva 1997: 269).

The separation based on language distanced the two ethnic groups in the same educational system through separate language-based schools. The reduced social contact between the young turned 'into enmity and confrontation, [helping] to create distrust, dislike and fear' (Tambia 1986: 76).[17]

The 1960s saw Sinhalese disenchantment over the difference in social status between the Tamil nationals and the Sinhalese that was directly linked to the level of education obtained by the Tamil nationals in securing a superior lifestyle. As Vittachi (1958: 18) states, 'the extent of [Tamil] participation in public life had been far in excess of their numbers'. The increase was a result of the post-colonial promotion of free education creating a 'higher rate of literacy and of the excellent facilities for education in science in the school in the Jaffna district from which many of them entered the universities' (de Silva 1997: 249). [18]

The procedure for entering universities became a political issue in 1970. In 1971, the government reacted to Sinhalese national discontentment by creating a standardisation policy to address this imbalance. The standardisation policy at the beginning involved the language used for conducting the studies to be set in a uniformed scale, enabling those qualifying in each language group to become proportionate to the number who had taken that examination in that particular language. The aim was to counterbalance the higher pass mark achieved by Tamil students in science subjects. As noted by de Silva (1997: 251), 'this was a baseless argument since there were as many such inequalities within each linguistic or ethnic group as there were between them'. This action resulted in the Tamil students aspiring to study medicine or engineering at the university-level having to achieve a higher aggregate mark than the Sinhalese students.[19]

There was another fundamental change introduced during this period which was named the *District Quota* system, and was aimed at redressing the balance in favour of students from rural areas. The concept was 'to allocate university places in proportion to the total population resident in each district (de Silva 1997: 251).[20] However, a group of officials and advisers in the government Ministry of Education deemed it necessary to introduce further changes. They believed that some adjustments in the existing aggregate marking system were necessary in order for the Sinhalese students to compete for coveted studies in sciences. They then became instrumental in creating the controversial *Media-wise Standardisation* at the point of admission to universities in 1973. This action in particular gave both the Sinhalese and the Muslim nationals a decided advantage whilst alienating the Tamil youths from northern parts of the island. The Tamil nationals viewed the new education model as a deliberate attempt at creating a barrier to prevent them from studying coveted science-based subjects (de Silva 1997: 250).

The figures comparing pre-standardisation university entries with the post-standardisation period show the number of entries by Tamil students into higher education was significantly reduced. The Tamil students' entry into science faculties at universities dropped from 35.3 per cent in 1970 to 20.9 per cent in 1974 and 19 per cent in 1975 (de Silva 1997: 252).[21] The results of the employment statistics of 1980 exemplified that, by comparison with Tamil nationals, Sinhalese nationals occupied the majority of civil service, professional and technical positions. This is also reflected in the administration and management sectors (Ram 1989).

In his seminal article 'Affirmative Action Policies: The Sri Lankan Experience', de Silva (1997) argues that there were two main factors underlying the controversies on employment. One was maintaining the same levels of state sector employment enjoyed by the Tamils under British rule, and the other was the Sinhalese insistence on a share of the employment that they perceived was due to them as their right. By the late nineteenth century, it became evident that the rise in Jaffna's population could not be accommodated within traditional agricultural roles. The minimum rainfall made Jaffna a dry zone with harsh living conditions, and education was seen as a way for Tamil nationals to move out of poverty and out of Jaffna. The white-collar employment in the government sector became the ideal occupation for young people in the colonial period. Thus many were engaged in the colonial government employment, albeit at the lower end of the administrative system for '[m]uch of the nineteenth century and the early twentieth century, the most pleasing prospect in Jaffna was the road that led to Colombo' (de Silva 1997: 278).

The ethnic tension started from the beginning of the post-colonisation period when young people dreamt of becoming white-collar workers with middle-class social status and gaining employment in the government sector. In the 1930s, Tamil nationals dominated both the State sector (administration) and the professional sector (doctors and engineers). This period saw the dawn of the competition for employment for Tamil nationals from a newly emerging educated Sinhalese. It is recognised that the post-independence creation of more schools in areas away from cities factored greatly in the rise of an educated Sinhalese population from rural areas. The Sinhalese 'overwhelmingly sought white-collar employment as government servants or school teachers' (Kearney 1973: 206). Invariably, the Tamil dominance in employment sector was threatened by this development, but they 'preferred to believe that it was a matter of discrimination; in fact, it was the national result of an expansion of education at secondary level in the Sinhalese areas' (de Silva 1997: 81). The Sri Lankan economy was not growing at a rate sufficient to accommodate the emerging educated youth with meaningful employment, and, with impending unemployment, a new generation grew up with unfulfilled expectations and bitter views of the future (Tambiah 1986).[22]

Causes of Discontent

The first casualties of the emerging Sinhalese nationalism were the Tamil nationals of Indian origin who were born in Sri Lanka. The Ceylon Citizenship Act no. 18 (1948) demanded proof of eligibility for citizenship through descent or registration. This can be identified as the first instance of State discrimination against the Tamil nationals (Ram 1989).

The rise of Tamil nationalism was a reaction to the rapidly developing Sinhalese ethno-centric policies adopted by the state. Whilst this remains factual, the cause of the discontentment of Tamil nationals needs to be taken in context with other developments during the post-independence era. For instance, the stable birth and death rates changed rapidly during late 1940s primarily due to the use of Western medicines. The increase in population was evident in the urban areas (e.g., Colombo) and the south-west of the island. In order to accommodate the growing population, the government initiated a relocation programme in 1953 to distribute the population evenly throughout the island and avoid any centralised or dense growth in urban areas. The programme was known as the Peasants Colonisation Scheme, which relocated the urban poor of all ethnic groups into dry zone areas of the north-east of the island.[23] The majority of these relocated people were Sinhalese, but the zones to which they were relocated were already inhabited by Tamil nationals, albeit relatively sparsely populated. The Tamil nationals believed that Tamil-speaking areas must belong to them–a notion of regional exclusivity not shared by Sinhalese nationals or the Sinhalese government.[24]

> **The Tamils perceive the influx of Sinhalese as a threat to the integrity of their 'traditional homeland' where they want to retain their voting majority, control over their own affairs, and cultural identity, if not, at least, the names of their villages. (Somasundaram 1998: 32)**

The Sri Lankan economy worsened in the 1970s for two main reasons. First, the government of the day decided to follow a policy of 'self-sufficiency', creating adverse international trade terms; second, there was a decline in the agriculture sector, especially the tea and coconut export markets. This decline was primarily based on Mrs Bandaranaike's government nationalising industries with foreign investment, such as the tea industry, causing a serious concern amongst foreign investors.

'[F]ailure to achieve rapid improvements in employment opportunities and to ameliorate other pressing problems could generate social and political tensions and explosions which would stifle all prospect of economic development (Kearney 1973: 220).' The mismanagement and incorrect economic decisions taken during this period were evident by the 1980s. The economic depression, along with the Sinhalese nation state's anger, were focused on Tamil nationals as the 'nominated enemy', as the Tamils were seen as being gainfully employed and prosperous against a backdrop of rising unemployment (Tambiah 1986: 55).[25]

The 1970s also became an era of discontent for many Tamil youths in Jaffna and saw a rise in revolutionary organisations operating in the Jaffna district. These organisations mostly recruited disillusioned Tamil youths who saw no future prospects and were disappointed with moderate Tamil political leaders who engaged in 'Gandhian' style peaceful agitations for a political recognition that was not materialising. The Tamil politicians were adamant in following the same path of peaceful negotiations with the Sinhalese government that they had relied on for many years, whereas many Tamil youths wanted both a radicalisation of policy and of methods. They shifted the demands from an equal language status to a newly initiated concept of an independent state of Tamil *Eelam* in areas they recognised as their traditional homeland in the northern and eastern parts of the country.

Nadaraja Thangavelu, a well-known smuggler from the Velvetithurai district of Jaffna, an area where Prabhakaran grew up, initiated the use of violent methods and held meetings with other known criminals to plan their campaign of violence (Kalansooriya 2001). Yet, these incidents were of a minor scale when compared with the violence that was to follow in Jaffna. Against this backdrop the Tamil Tiger movement was born in 1972, with Vellupillai Prabhakaran as its leader. At the same time, the Tamil political parties united to create the Tamil United Front (TUF), which changed its name in 1976 to the Tamil United Liberation Front (TULF) by joining with the Federal Party, the Tamil Congress and the Ceylon Workers Congress. They moved away from the equal language demand and promoted a single self-government in the north and the east as the only way out of their predicament (Ram 1989).

In 1977, disregarding the Tamil opposition, the Prime Minister, Sirimavo Bandaranaike not only enforced the 'Sinhalese only' ruling, but also proclaimed a special status to Buddhism as the state religion. This action contributed greatly to sympathy and support of Tamil militancy, as well as creating a fresh phase of communal antagonism along religious lines (Kalansooriya 2001).

The LTTE violence against Buddhism peaked in the 1980s with a number of targeted attacks on Buddhist clergy and religious sites. These included the massacre at Anuradhapura, in which some 146 people, including Buddhist monks were killed, and the bombing of the sacred Temple of the Tooth in Kandy. Notably, this action contributed to solidifying the unitary status of the island as a Buddhist state.[26]

In July 1983, the 'Black July' riots erupted following the response of the LTTE to the death of a close friend of Prabhakaran. The reprisal attack by the LTTE killed 13 Sri Lankan soldiers.[27] Many of the Sinhalese population retaliated with frenzied attacks upon Tamil citizens living in the city. This particular period in history, as described by Bose (1994: 96), 'was [of] crucial significance in exacerbating Sinhalese–Tamil polarisation, and in driving thousands of previously uncommitted young Tamils into armed struggle'. Many young Tamil nationals who were displaced in refugee camps in South India and within Sri Lanka joined the LTTE. McGowan (1992: 182) observes, 'issues such as national self-determination, university admissions and equity in land settlement paled before basic desire for vengeance and the quest for safety in an independent Tamil state'. Balasingham (2003: 76) also notes that in 1984 the LTTE had a 'rapid expansion and growth'.

The early wars fought in Jaffna by various revolutionary groups were factional, with different parties fighting each other as well as the State, but they were unable to maintain their revolutionary status without overseas government assistance. In this instance the assistance came by way of the Indian government, who allowed them to be trained and nurtured in southern India under the auspices of its government ministers and India's secret service Research and Analysis Wing (RAW). RAW performed both a covert and overt role in the training and arming of Tamil youths for guerrilla-type wars against the Sri Lankan government. The LTTE, along with other revolutionary groups, received additional training by the Palestinian Liberation Organisation (PLO). The fractional nature of the Tamil revolutionary groups continued, and by the end of 1986 the LTTE took a strategic view to eliminate all opposition and promote themselves as the sole representative of the Tamil population and the single revolutionary force for the State to deal with. By taking this action, the LTTE was able to radicalise not only their own image as a violent revolutionary group, but also the type of demands they made (Ram 1989 and Narayan-Swamy 2002).

The Politics and Political Interventions

Following the anti-Tamil insurgency of 1983, the Indian government made the first peace interventions with the Indian Peace Keeping Force (IPKF) being based in Jaffna. Indian diplomats organised the signing of the peace accord whilst Prabhakaran was away attending talks in New Delhi, which heightened his animosity towards the Indian government (Narayan-Swamy 2002; and Pratap 2001). The IPKF enjoyed a warm welcome that did not last beyond their arrival, as they became involved in the conflict. Further, the Sinhalese opposed the Indian intervention in what was seen as an internal Sri Lankan political matter (Narayan-Swamy 2002: 248). The unpopular and controversial agreement between the Indian and Sri Lankan governments was finally dissolved in 1989, with the newly elected Sri Lankan government offering a unilateral ceasefire to the LTTE and inviting them to discussions on the future of the island.

Since then there have been many failed peace talks, at times resulting in temporary ceasefires. Often these talks would collapse due to the LTTE being dissatisfied with the progress and actively disengaging from these talks, plunging the country back into civil war. A change was seen with the involvement of the Sri Lanka Monitoring Mission (SLMM) in early 2002, which included the Nordic countries of Norway, Finland, Sweden, Denmark and Iceland. They collectively undertook the role of monitoring the ceasefire agreement signed by the Sri Lankan government and the LTTE.[28] However, the Sinhalese viewed the SLMM as sympathetic to the cause of the LTTE, and within the year a new government agency, titled 'the Secretariat for Coordination of the Peace Process' (SCOPP) was created to facilitate the peace-making process. Its mandate included liaisoning with the SLMM and the monitoring of Cease Fire Agreement (CFA) between the LTTE and the State.[29]

In 2003, as part of the Peace Process, a Sub-committee on Gender Issues (SGI) was created with representation from a government appointed group of feminist academics and a group of LTTE women combatants. This was suspended by 2005 due to the collapse of peace talks and the lack of autonomy of women from both groups.[30]

The major political parties held differing views towards the struggle with the LTTE. Ariyaratne (2001) describes how Chandrika Bandaranaike-Kumaratunga (People's Alliance Party) supported a strategy of a political solution that did not result in a military victory. The political deal was viewed as a tool to isolate and defeat the LTTE, not as a possibility of opening dialogue for peace. Ranil Wickramasinha (United National Party) drafted a framework for a 'unitary state and non-military approach' to be adopted towards the LTTE and stated in 1999 that he would begin discussions with the LTTE even through a third party for a negotiated settlement.

Some seven years later, the incumbent President, Mahinda Rajapaksa, invited the LTTE to the negotiating table backed with a militaristic assault in retaliation to the LTTE attacks upon the army and Sinhalese citizens. By 2006, the situation between the two parties deteriorated irrevocably, and the seeds of a Final War were sown. The ensuing war claimed the life of Prabhakaran's eldest son, Charles Anthony, who became a combatant since 2006. On 18 May 2009, President Rajapaksa made a public declaration of ending the long-standing war with the LTTE. He also claimed the death of the entire LTTE leadership, especially that of Prabhakaran. The announcement contained photo images of Prabhakaran's body lying with a deep head wound. The news then followed of the death of Prabhakaran's family in what was presumed to be an air attack.

An Overview: LTTE

As described in Narayan-Swamy's (2002) book *Tigers of Lanka*, Prabhakaran was born on 26 November 1954 to a law-biding lower middle-class family. His mother, Vallipuram Parvathi, was a deeply religious woman. His father, Tiruvenkatam Velupillai, was a District land officer in the government's civil service. Prabhakaran had four siblings: two sisters and two brothers, all of whom were elder to him. His father adored his youngest son, but was very concerned with his average abilities in education. Due to this concern, his father took Prabhakaran along with him on his various postings around northern parts of the island, including Batticaloa and Vauniya. These trips appear to have given Prabhakaran a first-hand opportunity not only to see the northern parts of the island, but also to understand its socio-economical conditions. As he grew up, he began to identify with the Tamil youths who were disappointed by the lack of state reforms. This experience motivated him to form the Tamil New Tigers (TNT) in 1972 and the LTTE in 1976.

Although animal analogy is steeped in Sri Lankan mythology and is used in the creation of the Tiger emblem, it must be borne in mind that there is a different symbolic meaning to the image of the Lion. I would suggest the striking Tiger image does not represent the creation of a nation, as much it does the (re)creation of an existing nation.

The message of the (re)created nation is to show equal civic status in their own country. However, there are many views regarding the Tiger emblem. Ram (1989) claims that the Tiger emblem portraying a roaring tiger with its paws stretched out in preparation to attack signifies both guerrilla warfare and the rise of Tamils. He also claims the possibility of a historical link with the south Indian Cholai kingdom and its invasions of Jaffna in ancient times. Hellman-Rajanayagam (1986), referred to in Sabaratnam (2001), claims that the function of the symbol represents the coming together of Tamils from Jaffna and Batticaloa.[31] Narayan-Swamy (2002), on the other hand, claims it to be the result of a particular fondness Prabhakaran had for Phantom comics, where the Phantom wears a skull ring whilst fighting evil men and is always one step ahead of his captors.

In Ram's book, *Sri Lanka, the Fractured Island* (1989), he clearly suggests that the LTTE focused on an area where there had not been any previous political dynamism or extreme violence. Somasundaram (1998: 97) also notes, 'the Tamil youth dedicated themselves wholeheartedly and with full force of their youthful energies to the historical task of saving their threatened community, of regenerating the Tamil nation'.

In the initial stages, the LTTE carried out similar guerrilla attacks on the other Tamil revolutionary groups such as PLOTE and TELO. At the time, the revolutionary groups had a membership of some 2,000–3,000 trained in both Sri Lanka and India, and had the ability to mobilise many more should the need occur.[32]

The revolutionaries favoured attacks on police stations and army patrols. In addition, the robberies of state-run banks were greatly favoured, which provided some of the funding for the group's activities. Other sources included a local tax system on a number of goods such as cigarettes and liquor, and combatants further collected money from house to house, known as 'funds'. It is arguable whether the funds were given willingly or under fear and duress. However, many civic citizens supported and assisted the rebel groups and by doing so, incurred the wrath of the armed forces, which often resulted in their deaths.[33]

The LTTE used a method widely known as *Lamp Posting*, a method of public execution to eliminate individuals among the civil population who were believed to be informants of the State, which was very effective in instilling fear into the civic citizens in Jaffna. The act of lamp posting also conveyed a message of deterrence to others who may have considered being disloyal to the LTTE.[34] The LTTE mastered suicide bombing and soon gained notoriety as a deadly revolutionary group. The LTTE also filmed and photographed their major operations, which is characteristic of contemporary revolutionary groups.[35]

Often funds for the LTTE were raised through the Tamil diaspora living in the West, especially France, Canada, England and Australia. However, the Anti-terrorism Legislation (2001) in Britain outlawed the LTTE, and its funds were frozen. Though the LTTE no longer raised funds openly in the UK, Canada and other Western countries, they devised a new system whereby extremely polite and well-mannered young Tamil men visited homes of the Tamil diaspora and requested that a large sum of money should be given to the LTTE as a bond to develop war-torn Jaffna. The sum of money was negotiable up to a point, and assurances were given that the bond would be repaid in full by the future LTTE Tamil State (information received through a Tamil contact; details withheld for safety reasons). The LTTE was also involved internationally in credit card fraud, which became the headline news in the UK in April 2007. The change in legislation also changed the face of the conflict between the LTTE and the Sri Lankan government from a national to a global level of conflict. The LTTE was essentially involved in a nationalist struggle, but they were aware that in the future they would be dealing with the international community and were increasingly aware of the international dimensions to their conflict (Uyangoda 2003).

In her book, *The Will to Freedom*, Adel Balasingham (the wife of Anton Balasingham, the political theoretician of the LTTE) refers to the complex nature of the LTTE's revolutionary struggle: 'The national liberation organisation conducts its struggle on the politico-military level. In an armed revolutionary struggle for political freedom, the military and the political aspects are inextricably interlinked. The military struggle becomes the very instrument to achieve the political cause of liberation' (Balasingham 2003: 75).

Within these issues she discusses how the social dynamics based on repression were able to attract people to the LTTE revolutionary movement.[36] One such person, grounded in both Marxism and Leninism, was Anton Balasingham. Narayan-Swamy (2002) argues that though Anton Balasingham was invited to join the LTTE in 1979 to teach ideological classes, the LTTE was neither a Marxist nor a Leninist organisation. After joining the movement he became the LTTE's theoretician and chief negotiator. Although Prabhakaran was a practical man with no interest in political ideologies of Marxism, he shared with Balasingham a passion for Tamil nationalism.

The LTTE's major tactic was 'hit and run'. They often justified their actions through the claim of acting in self-defence. This argument was frequently used for revenge-killings against the State's armed forces. Pratap (2002: 94–95) claims that Prabhakaran once stated, 'We don't want Eelam on a platter. We will fight and win Eelam... 'Thousands of my boys have laid down their lives for Eelam. Their death cannot be in vain. They have given their life for this cause, how can I betray them by opting for anything less than Eelam?'.

The use of violence thus appeared to be a tool with which Prabhakaran intended to achieve the objective of a Tamil nation state of *Eelam*.

The LTTE had a respectful view of death in battle, which one could argue was manipulative in its portrayal of such deaths as martyrdom (as discussed in detail in Chapter 5). In the LTTE movement there was a pragmatic approach to killings and assassinations, for these were considered part of the revolutionary process. The very first LTTE political assassination, in 1975, is credited to Prabhakaran, resolutely carried out with an old rusted revolver and bullets made out of matchstick tips.[37]

In the early stages the LTTE only targeted the Sri Lankan armed forces, but it then spread to Sinhalese villagers in rural farming areas in the northeast.[38] The attacks began to spread to Colombo, and the targets became more high profile with then President Premadasa in May 1993 and a number of cabinet ministers assassinated in successive suicide bombings.

The greater claim for notoriety by the LTTE is in the assassination of Rajiv Gandhi on Indian soil.[39] The act, committed in 1991 by a woman suicide bomber, had until recently been denied by the LTTE. For many years the only admittance was made in private by Anton Balasingham, who referred to the incident as a 'historical blunder' (Pratap 2002), and a public apology was made in 2006. However, the attack on Rajiv Gandhi prompted India to close down and outlaw the LTTE operations in India. The attack further led Indians to view the LTTE as a dangerous and untrustworthy group of militants rather than a desperate collective of innocent victims (Pratap 2002).

Women in Jaffna's Tamil Society

Background

A few English language texts reflect on Tamil ethnic identity in ancient Jaffna, but these often overlook the roles played by women. In her book, *Ideological Factors in Subordination of Women*, Thiruchandran (1993) focuses on the historical roles of Tamil women. However, the specifics of gender discussed focus more on Tamil women of southern India rather than Jaffna. This was not problematic, as the related identity between the two groups of women has made the text relevant to both. With such limitations, it was exciting to discover literature relating to a matriarchal society with a matrilineal social structure in Jaffna c. 2000 B.C. Within this socio-cultural structure, Tamil women had a great deal of autonomy and social freedom, and were free from the moral sanctions that were to follow a few centuries later.[40]

> Women enjoyed great freedom and liberty. Young men and women met each other freely in pleasure gardens, in groves and in the fields where the girls were engaged in guarding the crop. They fell in love and later married with consent of the parents.[41] (Rasanayagam 1926: 170).

The period in reference to this text is claimed to be the *Sangam* period c. 2347 B.C., a time of enlightenment in ancient Jaffna where women were encouraged to develop their minds and engage in education.

However, the matrilineal cultural practice may have predated the records of the *Sangam* era.[42] It is not known what precise social changes occurred that ended the matrilineal socio-cultural system and gave way to the patrilineal society that is seen to date.

After the *Sangam* period, a clear division was seen separating women into two groups: those who stay within the confines of home, *Kula Makal*, meaning 'women of the family'; and *Vilai Makal*, those who are 'available for a price' (Thiruchandran 1998: 23). The role of the *Kula Makal* became more focused then, with an added dimension of religious fervour elevating women to a pious social role and, at the same time, reducing their sexuality to procreation purposes and a passive submission to the domination of males (ibid.). The issue of this social separation creating moral social hierarchies amongst women is not addressed in texts. I would argue that the piety attributed to the female body at the cost of its sexuality was the beginning of the perception of women in the domestic sphere as morally virtuous, meaning 'good'–as opposed to those women engaged in sexual activities being seen as morally decadent and as 'evil'. Therefore, women who were engaged in sexual activity fell into the category of *Vilai Makal,* women who were seen as being available for a price, and were viewed as evil temptresses set against the good and pious wife.[43]

Colonial and Post-colonial Eras

The separated social roles played by women in the domestic sphere and the public sphere continued until colonisation by the Europeans. The male consciousness and the masculinity of colonisation contributed to Tamil conservative ideology, forming a new social identity for Tamil women in the community in the nineteenth century. Thiruchandran (1998: 109) claims that female roles were idealistically feminised, and rigid moral behaviour was considered the only acceptable social norm for Tamil women. Interestingly, much of the prescribed normative behaviour imposed on Tamil women was drawn from Victorian morality, with the bodies of women being turned into sites of male moral consciousness.

Female gender construction in Sri Lanka is full of paradoxical complexities. On one hand, women of high socio-economic status have made considerable strides towards emancipation; on the other, lower-class women are defined by cultural boundaries that have not changed for generations. Women from middle or upper classes backed with a strong English education provided a fertile ground for creating a women's movement in Sri Lanka during the latter part of colonial rule through to the early post-colonial period. Jayawardena and de Alwis (2002: 246) describe the women's movement as being 'a broad based movement that encompasse[d] a variety of organisations and groups that [had] arisen out of different struggles and conflicts, at different historical moments'. For example, women succeeded in winning the right to vote in 1931 despite adverse male comments such as, 'Do not throw pearls before swine, for they will turn and rend you ... what suits European women will not suit us' (Jayawardena and de Alwis 2002: 10).[44]

The women of the Women's Franchise Union (WFU)[45] were particularly remarkable as they were not militant (in comparison to British and Indian women's movements), but were part of the conservative elite in Colombo. Their role should be recognised not only for their active participation in obtaining the vote for women, but also for the fact that they were 'the first autonomous, multi-ethnic women's organisation in Sri Lanka that was founded with the sole purpose of claiming *their* political right' (Jayawardena and de Alwis 2002: 247; my italics).[46]

The Donoughmore Commission (1927) made recommendations to engage the 'population in the election of Ceylonese to the Legislative Council, as well as to devise a constitution that would give substantial power to the Ceylonese representative in the council to govern the country' (Manogaran 1987: 34). It recommended that the vote be given to all women aged 30 and over, but upon implementation this became 21 years of age in order to broaden the base of political power across both ethnic groups (Jayawardena 1992: 128–129 and Tambiah 2002: 427).

Women have generally entered politics in Sri Lanka because of the death of a male relative such as a husband or a father. The best example of this is the political engagement of the world's first female Prime Minister, Mrs Sirimavo Bandaranaike, who succeeded her assassinated husband, S.W.R.D.

Bandaranaike. Jayawardena (1992: 129) refers to this pattern of female entry into the male world of politics as 'inheriting, as it were, the male mantle of power', which could be argued was the only way of entering the masculine world of politics and State governance in a post-colonial era.

Mrs Bandaranaike victory gave many women confidence to enter the patriarchal public arena. This dynastic approach was further seen when Mrs Bandaranaike's daughter, Chandrika, also entered the political arena. This is reflective of many other countries (e.g., India and the Nehru family; Pakistan and the Bhutto family) where elite women have spearheaded political change.[47]

Tamil women with influence all resided in Colombo, a progressive and modern society when compared to Jaffna, a city still steeped in patriarchal culture and values. As noted by Tambiah (2002), and Jayawardena and de Alwis (2002), the concept of modernity was embedded in Sri Lanka's socialism. It is the privileged and educated minority of women that have led social change. Their very education and idealism 'contributed to the socializing of women into roles that were only superficially different from those of traditional society' (Jayawardena 1992: 136).

It is unfortunate that those most in need of pragmatic social change were overlooked in the march towards progress. Women of rural areas, and the non-elite who lived in urban areas (both Tamil and Sinhalese), were committed in their demands for social change and female recognition, but their lives were still dictated and controlled by hegemonic masculine practices:

> Sri Lanka is thus an interesting example of a society in which women were not subjected to harsh and overt form of oppression, and therefore did not develop a movement for women's emancipation that went beyond the existing social parameters. It is precisely this background that has enabled Sri Lanka to produce a woman prime minister, as well as many women in the professions, but without disturbing the general patterns of subordination. (Jayawardena 1992: 136)

The number of Tamil women who have entered politics since the post-colonial era is limited. Tamil women have historically been supporters of their husbands or sons, who were the carriers of the cause. During the early post-colonial era, Tamil women in Jaffna had never been in leading positions of any political struggle, which is reflective of their social position and their relationship to the struggle, or the cause was through their secondary roles to masculine politics by way of engaging in peaceful protests known as *satyagraha* (Maunaguru 1995: 160).

However, a number of Tamil women c.1920 made political statements with public criticism of the patriarchal state system.[48] de Alwis and Jayawardena (2001: 56) describe these women as 'professional independent women [who] were able to speak out loud and clear'. Tamil women conducted their activities through writing articles to national newspapers on gender equality (de Alwis and Jayawardena 2001). This kind of non-confrontational but effective activity is reminiscent of the maxim *the pen is mightier than the sword* because they were forthcoming with their approach and criticisms.[49] The first Tamil woman to enter the State Council, in 1932, was a popular figure who lasted a decade in that role.[50] From 1942–1980 there had been no Tamil female representation in the government; 1994 saw the first Tamil woman as a government minister in charge of the Education Department. These culturally imposed limits were exacerbated by the assassination of Sarojini Yogeswaran, the mayor of Jaffna, in 1997 (believed to have been carried out by the LTTE), which reduced the number of political appointments of woman.[51]

According to the Human Development Report, women in Sri Lanka are a 'model for developing countries' (Tambiah 2002: 428); they have some of the highest level of literacy (83.1 per cent) and female life expectancy (74.2 years) among developing countries. The same report records that the female fertility rate has dropped due to the number of females entering higher education and also due to a rise in the average age of women at marriage (25.2 years).[52] These figures reflect the State's commitment to welfare issues during the post-colonial era, including the creation of a Women's Bureau and a Ministry for Women's Affairs together with a constitutional guarantee of equality and the adoption of a Women's Charter.

Nevertheless, these achievements 'do not necessarily mean empowerment of women in terms of greater participation in the decision-making process' (Tambiah 2002: 428). Tambiah argues that it is still difficult for women to enter public spaces; hence, women's representation in the labour market is still half than that of males. This significant difference can be explained by the gender construction in a society that sees women's roles as primarily of being wives and mothers and is central to the nationalist discourse of the late colonial era with its heavy reliance upon the post-colonial female identity (de Alwis 1998a cited in Jayawardena and de Alwis 2002: 258).

Women of Sri Lanka (regardless of ethnicity) act as primary carers in families for the children and the elderly, as is common of many other societies. In addition to these roles in the domestic sphere, many women are compelled to seek employment that may not be in the formal economy and would not be recorded in official statistics (Tambiah 2002: 428). Women are tied to a moral code of conduct which unites all women in Sri Lanka and overlooks their ethnic identity.

> The do's include chastity, modesty, servility, self-sacrifice, and confinement to home, preoccupation with children, husband, relations, and husband's friends, not to mention looking after his property. There were also several don'ts including loud talk, laughing, running, idling and keeping the company of independent (therefore bad) women. (Jayawardena 1986: 23 cited in Tambiah 2002: 249)

The women's socialisation process that takes place at home constructs a culturally acceptable female identity. 'These ideas are then internalised and reproduced from generation to generation. Education has done little to change these attitudes and perceptions, and all along had been a powerful reinforcing factor operating as an agent to socio–cultural reproduction, legitimising gender-role stereotypes' (Jayawardena 1986: 23 cited in Tambiah 2002: 249).

This reinforcement of gender roles also restricts women's activities in public spaces, where women's representation in decision-making roles or in political activism is often thwarted and, at times, discouraged by the men in their families.

During the past two decades there has been a notable change in women's social recognition with the ratification of the Covenant for

Elimination of Discrimination Against Women (1981) and the Women's Charter (1992). In 1994, the existing colonial laws regarding the age of consent and marriage were changed, and incest was criminalised (Jayawardena and de Alwis 2002: 255). It is clear that the influence of a few progressive women changed much in society for all women.

An anti-feminist backlash was seen in the mid-1980s. Women who wished to change discrimination were accused of being culturally misguided due to their Westernised views and of failing to understand the freedom that women in civic society have always had (Jayawardena and de Alwis 2002: 257). Some feminists claim that the reason behind society's change of attitude was the intrinsic tie of the role of women to masculinity.

Consequently, 'one of the reasons all males, including those of the left, refuse to support women's liberation is that they do not want to lose the benefits of participating in their homes as well as in society' (Jayawardena and Kelkar 1989 cited in Jayawardena and de Alwis 2002: 257).

The gap has widened since the ethnic violence of 1983, prompting feminists to criticise the military and its handling of Tamil civic citizens. This action has further enraged the men in the society, whose views are supported by the media portrayal of Sri Lankan feminists as 'dishonouring their country by publicising "private" and "local" problems internationally' (Jayawardena and Kelkar 1989 cited in Jayawardena and de Alwis 2002: 263). They accused the feminists of Sri Lanka of not collaborating in the 'nationalist' agenda and of exposing the 'private' matter of ethnic violence to the world.

An Overview of Modern Tamil Women in Jaffna

Jaffna has a strong hierarchical caste-based social structure. The landed gentry known as the *Vellala,* for example, are defined by a higher social position by the caste system.[53] Although there is a social link between the women of Jaffna and southern India, there are some major differences between the women of Jaffna, the community in which they live, and South India. One such difference is seen in the hierarchical roles played by Brahmins. Whilst they are respected in both the communities, the roles of the Brahmins of Jaffna are limited to attending to rituals in temples, whereas the Brahmins of South India hold a great deal of power in the society and have imposed a very strict code of conduct for women (Subrahmanian 1996; and Thiruchandran 1994 and 1993). Due to this hierarchical variation, the women of Jaffna have not suffered the same extreme socio-cultural conditions, and this has afforded some freedom, albeit marginal, within the patriarchal social structure.

Women within the domestic sphere hold either an elevated social position as *auspicious* women (married with children) or a lowly position as *in*auspicious women (widowed and/or childless). In modern Jaffna, Tamil women have enjoyed a great deal of power within the confines of the home, but are dependent on their male family members whilst in public spaces. A woman who behaves in an assertive way in public spaces may be criticised for her immodest behaviour. However, women with a lack of social capital are restricted to seeking employment away from domestic boundaries and are aware of and negotiate their roles in public spaces. At the onset of war, Tamil women in Jaffna re-negotiated this identity without straying too far from its core patriarchal values. Thiruchandran (1998: 79) states that those who do not follow the existing norms are seen as the Other, which includes women who practise various forms of Christian faith. Such women, though seen as the Other, are not totally excluded from the society due to a shared hegemonic identity based on ethnicity, language and culture. This invokes a sense of belonging to the Tamil nation state and, as a consequence, a nationalistic identity. This has prevented the creation of an exclusive religious value-based subculture for Christian-Tamil women. The absence of any politicisation of religion had assisted the LTTE in demanding a traditional homeland rather than a Hindu-based identity.

The opening of a university in Jaffna in 1974 contributed to the development of a political consciousness amongst Tamil women. The women of the university were the founding members of the 'Women's Progressive Association'.[54] Their aim was to raise awareness amongst both their male and female peer groups who met up for weekly meetings to discuss feminist literature. They also included those outside the campus and introduced a 'Women's Study Circle' to engage with a wider peer base in Jaffna. The Association and the Study Circle, with the support of the faculty, were immediately successful.[55] Unfortunately, there is no clear information in the public realm since the early days of the Association and Study Circle, but through my research interviews I am able to confirm that the groups were forced to dissolve under escalating violence that made it impossible for them to meet and discuss social issues. The group is now scattered around the world, barring a very small number who remained in the country to pursue an alternative form of activism amidst the ongoing political changes.

Women and the LTTE

The Tamil women of Jaffna found themselves highly exposed during the periods of war as the LTTE guerrilla style of fighting made it difficult for these civic women to be distinguished from the combatant women (Ram 1989). This also meant that many civilians were tortured, raped and murdered as suspected LTTE combatants or supporters; under these circumstances, the women who suffered sexual violence often committed suicide (Thiranagama et al. 1990). This has particular resonance when considering the IPKF statement claiming that they could not differentiate between the civic and combatant women. As one officer stated:

> We are not checking women deliberately. You see, one day, when one of our officers was going on an open vehicle, there were two young women on the roadside. One waved while the other raised her skirt and fired an automatic gun at our officer and Jawan. Don't you think we have to check women? It is women who are carrying weapons strapped to their thighs and in their blouses. (Thiranagama et al. 1990: 316)

It was apparent that women were targeted due to their vulnerability, and there was a clear disregard for the social norms concerning civilians and women in particular.[56]

As discussed later in this book, the reasons for women joining the movement were both varied and complex. The LTTE policy of recruiting women brought criticism from some feminists. They claim that it was the need for human resources within the LTTE that prompted them to recruit women rather than the promotion of women's social involvement and equality during a period of political conflict. This debate is analysed at length in Chapter 6. In 1984, the Tamil language magazine *Thalir* stated the following in their editorial:

> **Women are half of our population and hence their participation in various levels of armed struggle is extremely necessary. Women are the internal revolutionary force in any national movement. The level of participation of women in the Eelam struggle including armed combat will prove the revolutionary potentialities of Tamil women. (Thalir 1984: 21–31 cited in Maunaguru 1995: 163)**

Coomaraswamy (1996) argues that Tamil history does not have any militant female figures to draw upon.[57] I suggest that this is a result of the dominance of patriarchal religious culture in Tamil society, as discussed earlier in this chapter. The LTTE based its women combatants on the image of a masculine warrior in a feminine guise and placed her in a role of a protector, combining the cultural ideology of the auspicious mother and the modern concept of the female warrior/combatant (de Mel 2001; Jayawardena and de Alwis 2002; Maunaguru 1995 and de Alwis 1998b). The LTTE recognised Tamil women's potential beyond the narrowly constructed gender roles of reproducers to include them in a wider social context of a combatant: '...woman was not only considered to be a reproducer of male heroes, but also a fighter herself' (Maunaguru 1995: 163); and women were trained to the same skill levels as men in guerrilla warfare. The paradoxical nature of this role is discussed throughout this book to establish the precise role that the women combatants now hold.

Summary

The Sinhalese and Tamil ethnic groups have co-existed for centuries. Post-colonial Sinhalese and Tamil national identities were based on language and religion. The basis of nationalism was language, and this affected both the Sinhalese and the Tamils. The suppression of Buddhism under colonial rule became a tool used by Sinhalese nationalists, and Sri Lankan nationalism was based on Buddhism and Sinhalese ethnicity.

Nationalist identity politics connected to religion and language in a way that favoured the majority and excluded the minority. From the Sinhalese perspective, the issue of Tamil nationalism was viewed as a minority issue, not a question for the whole nation. The Sinhalese ideology has assumed Sri Lankans to be Sinhalese-Buddhist, a view that excludes all other inhabitants. The view that the Sinhalese are the sole indigenous ethnic group of Sri Lanka translates into an ethnic polarisation that is substantiated by violence. The radicalisation of Tamils shifted demands from an equal language status to an independent state of Tamil *Eelam* in the context of growing discontent of youth and romanticism about armed struggle.

The LTTE had developed a vision of a secular autonomous geographic state and responded that Tamils are a nation and not a minority. The fundamental belief amongst Tamil nationalists was that Tamil political interests could only be addressed through war and the construction of their own state, and the way that the government treated Tamil nationals only strengthened that belief.

Since the late 1970s, Sri Lanka has endured a civil war, several failed peace talks, and distrust, hostility and violence between the ethnic communities. The LTTE targets changed from military personnel to Sinhalese nationals, with the elimination of anyone who criticised or disagreed with its practices. Thus, the use of violence appears to have been a tool to achieve the objective of a Tamil nation state of *Eelam* and the dominance of the LTTE within that state.

Many civic citizens supported the rebel groups and incurred the wrath of the armed forces, which often resulted in their deaths. The State, the peacekeeping forces and the LTTE itself have all committed acts of violence that have targeted civic society—beatings, rapes, disappearances and murders. One notable story is that of the IPKF claiming not to be able to differentiate between civic and combatant women.

The entry of women into the political sphere did not challenge the patriarchal social fabric. Tamil women's historical autonomy changed to domesticity and subservience. In modern Jaffna, civic and combatant women are inextricably linked to a patriarchal society constructed through hierarchies of caste, class and masculinities, which they have to continually negotiate.

The emphasis on women who stay within the confines of home, *Kula Makal*, elevates domestic women to a pious social role and reduces their sexuality to a passive submission to the domination of males. The women's socialisation process takes place at home and constructs a culturally acceptable female identity that is idealistically feminised to the point where rigid moral behaviour is the only acceptable social norm for Tamil women. Further, domestic women are viewed as either auspicious women (married with children) or inauspicious women (widowed/childless).

Tamil women do not actively participate in decision-making, which is still in the hands of men (as discussed further in Chapter 6), and it is difficult for women (who are also reluctant) to enter public spaces, including the political arena. This significant imbalance in female representation can be explained by the construction of gender by a society that sees women's roles primarily as that of wives and mothers.

The LTTE combatant women had an image of a masculine warrior in a feminine guise: a role with the paradoxical nature of the protectoress combining the cultural ideology of the auspicious mother and the modern concept of the female warrior. By this action, the status of Tamil women was raised from their traditional role of subservience. Against this backdrop, the combatant women of the LTTE were critically important to the success of the revolution. But did this promote female equality and empowerment? That remains the central question of this book.

Notes

1 The androgynous argument is explored in detail in chapter 6. Also see Coomaraswamy (1996).

2 The conceptual notion that the Sinhalese are an Aryan ethnic group is portrayed by Bose as a 'racist myth that made its first appearance during the second half of the nineteenth century' (1994: 14). The use of the term Aryan to describe a race of people is further argued by the German indologist Mueller to be a scientific-descriptive term unsuited to application to a race (Bose 1994: 41).

3 In the classic text *The Early History of Ceylon*, Mendis (1932) notes that there were a number of tribes in addition to the *Sinha* (Lion) tribe such as the *Taraccha* (Hyena), *Balibhojaka* (Crow), *Lambakanna* (Hare) and *Moriya* (Peacock). He argues that the clan names may have originated from worshiping totems, emblems and animals.

4 Smith (1986), referred to in De Votta (2007: 6).

5 The king Vijaya arrived with 700 'fair skinned' Aryan men (Ram 1989: 32). The colour of the skin also forms part of the ethnically divisive discourse. There is a claim by Navaratnam (1959) that earlier forms of language were a mixture of Tamil and Sinhalese. Also see Mendis (1932).

6 See Wilson (1974: 1–9) and Mendis (1932) for a detailed description of the early period in Sri Lanka.

7 Tambiah (1954) refers to a number of scholarly works including Rasanayagam (1926), *Ancient Jaffna* (English edition); Fr. Gnanapragasar, *Yalpana Vaipava Vimarsenam* (Tamil edition); Sivanathan, *Early Settlement in Jaffna* (Tamil edition); Muttutamby, *Jaffna History* (edition not known). Detailing a number of regency periods in The Laws and Customs of Tamils of Ceylon, which includes fifteen kings and the periods in which they reigned in Jaffna (1954: 10–16). Further, see Mendis (1932) and Ram (1989). Also see Wriggins (1960).

8 The Dutch expulsion and British acquisition of the country came via the British take over of the Dutch East India Company in 1796, of which Sri Lanka was a part.

9 Also see Mendis (1943).

10 Also see Mendis (1932), Bose (1994) and Weerasooria (1970) for further references to the multi-ethnic society.

11 Also see Wriggins (1960).

12 This is based on the last conclusive census carried out in 1981: the non-Sinhalese minority was 26 per cent and the non-Buddhist minority was 30.7 per cent (of the total population). Also discussed in Hyndman (1988).

13 Also see Wriggins (1960), de Silva (1986).

14 Ram (1989: 41) claims that over 10,000 Tamils were evacuated from Colombo to Jaffna, and another 12,000 were kept in camps 'for their own safety'. Also see Wriggins (1960: 265) for detailed description of *satyagraha* and its effects.

15 This policy not only affected the Tamils but also other minority nationalities in Sri Lanka such as the Burghers (European descent), Muslims and those Sinhalese who were educated in the English language. The language policy in Sri Lanka started during the colonial period as English only rule was changed in the post-colonial period of 1944–1956 to Sinhalese and Tamil. From 1956–78 it went on to claim *Sinhalese Only* policy which subsequently changed back into all three languages from 1978 onwards (de Silva 1997:272).

16 It also maintained Chapter IV of 1978 constitution whilst operating the status of Sinhalese as 'the' official language under Article 18. Under Article 19, Tamil language was formally recognised as the national language. Chapter IV, which was

an elaboration of Article (1) (f) and 27 (6), gave a guarantee under state policy for the individual freedom to use own language: 'no citizen shall suffer any disability by reason of language' (de Silva 1997: 271).

17 It must also be noted that special provisions were made for Muslims who were Tamil-language speakers from 1940s onwards. Until 1974, Muslim children had the right to study in any of the three languages. They also had special schools set up by the state. de Silva (1997: 270) argues, '[t]he establishment and expansion of these schools, it must be emphasised, vitiates the principle of non-sectarian state education that has been the declared policy of all governments since 1960'.

18 It must also be noted that the best schools in the island were set up by the British in and around the capital Colombo and other major towns but not in climatically harsh areas such as Jaffna. Schools in Jaffna were set up by missionaries, with a strong academic focus producing many generations of educated Tamils, qualified to undertake civil service administrations (de Silva 1997: 278).

19 'To weight the marks of the candidates so that those qualifying for admission form each language group would be proportionate to the number who sat the examination in that language' (de Silva 1997: 251).

20 A secondary caveat defines this as Sinhalese and Tamil students being given the location of the school from where the exams were taken, but Muslim students were given the place of birth. The system failed to acknowledge those who had won scholarship to schools in cities from rural areas (de Silva 1997).

21 Also see Ram (1989) and Kearney (1973).

22 Also see Samarasinghe (1984).

23 The island of Sri Lanka is divided into dry and wet zones based on rainfall. The wet zones are fertile land easy to irrigate unlike the dry zones, where water is often difficult to obtain. The government has addressed this issue by building a number of irrigation facilities and man-made lakes. See Manogaran (1987) and Somasundaram (1998).

24 Repercussion of this belief resulted in the second and third generations of Sinhalese and Muslim peasant farmers and their families living in these areas being targeted by the LTTE, who see them as outsiders, and brutally murdered.

25 Also see Wilson (2000).

26 In May 1985, the LTTE attacked and killed some 146 worshippers in the sacred area of the Sri Maha Bodhi tree in Anuradhapura. Amongst the dead were Buddhist monks, nuns, children and elderly pilgrims. In June 1987, the LTTE killed some 33 young Buddhist monks and their mentor, Hegoda Indrasara Thera, at Arantalawa in Amparai district. In January 1998, the LTTE bombed the Temple of Tooth in Kandy (De Votta 2007: 38).

27 The significance of this particular death was due to the close relationship Prabhakaran had with the deceased, Charles Anthony. In fact Prabhakaran's eldest son was named after this person. The incident of torture and killing of the 13 soldiers (all under the age of 21) happened in Tinnevely, Jaffna. Also see Narayan-Swamy (2002) and Hyndman (1988).

28 The SLMM website claims 'The cease-fire in Sri Lanka is not a result of a memorandum of understanding (MOU), but that of The Cease-fire Agreement (CFA), signed formally by the GOSL and LTTE' (accessed on 24 January 2004).

29 Global IDP (2002) and <http://peaceinsrilanka.com> (accessed on 10 September 2007).

30 See Del Viso (2005), Harris (2004) <http://www.peaceinsrilanka.com> (accessed on 20 October 2007).

31 Amongst Tamil nationals, those from Jaffna district are generally viewed as superior to other Tamils in Sri Lanka. This view has lead to a split in the LTTE between the leader of the Batticaloa region, Col. Karuna and Prabhakaran. The cause for its separation is believed to be the Jaffna combatants being treated more favourably within the organisation than those of Batticaloa. The Sri Lankan army has used this situation to their advantage by providing support to Col. Karuna and his breakaway group to cause further disharmony against the rest of the LTTE. After a bitter battle, Col. Karuna joined the government and is currently in charge of the Batticaloa district and enjoys the privileges of a civic citizen.

32 Narayan-Swamy (2002) discusses this at length. Also, see O'ballance (1989), Manogaran (1987), Hellman-Rajanayagam (1994) and Wilson (2000).

33 Narayan-Swamy (2002: 187)'s text was agreed by some of the civic women I interviewed as confirming that their assistance was interpreted by the state-run army as an act of collaboration with the revolutionaries.

34 Lamp posting as discussed in Thiruchandran (1999) and Narayan-Swamy (2002) is a form of punishment meted out to collaborators and criminals by the LTTE. The suspected person is tied to an electric pole (lamp post) and shot in the head, usually with a single bullet.

35 The LTTE video recorded all their achievements to be used as propaganda material, which was readily available to be purchased along any of the high street stores in Jaffna and Vanni.

36 Also see Bose (1994).

37 The first recognised political assassination is that of Jaffna's Mayor, Duraiyapah, on 27 July 1975 (Narayan-Swamy 2002).

38 These areas also form parts of the government's redistribution of population to north-east sector of the island, which the LTTE viewed as their land. The LTTE is known to have used knives to commit murder, especially in Sinhalese villages. This may be because it is easier to kill unarmed and untrained civilians (children and babies included) with a knife rather than wasting expensive bombs or bullet to accomplish the same result of taking lives (Kalansooriya 2001).

39 Dhanu, a woman combatant from the LTTE suicide squad known as the Black Tigers, killed Rajiv Gandhi. She detonated the bomb whilst bending down to touch the feet of Rajiv in the accepted customary manner of showing respect among Indians.

40 Rasanayagam (1870–1940) wrote *Tamils of Ceylon* in 1926. Since then his work has been criticised for inaccuracies. With such criticisms in mind, I have only included

his work where I can corroborate it against other works, such as Navaratnam (1959) or Thiruchandran (1998). However Rajsanayagam's work must be recognised for the elements of nationalist ethics in Tamil historical literature produced at a time when there were none written.

41 Marriages of this type were known as *kalavu* and were widely practised amongst Tamils during early historical times.

42 The *Sangam* period described by Rasanayagam (1926) refers to c. 2347 B.C., and Thiruchandran (1998) refers to the same period as A.D. 100–300. Whilst the accuracy of dates for their period has been debated, Thiruchandran (1998: 37) states this debate has now been settled, which reflected in her writing as A.D. 100–300 and in Rasanayagam as 2347 B.C. This variation may be due to Rasanayagam book published in 1926, prior to the debate being resolved. The first preserved literatures of Tamil areas are known as *Sangam* literature, also spelt as *Cankum*. The poems themselves were written by citizens of varying social backgrounds with 28 women and four queens amongst women writers, and kings, chieftains, carpenters, blacksmiths and artists amongst the male writers (Thiruchandran 1998: 37).

43 The separation of women in society into either good or evil further created new words to describe women who are engaged in the sexual appeasement of men. 'Prostitution had become institutionalised with a stigma on the women who were socially marginalised with derogatory names' (Thiruchandran 1998: 24). Also see Kersenboom (1987). Names such as *Paratai* meaning prostitute; *Vilai Matu* meaning women available for a price; *Porudpendir* women who are paid materially with goods; *Kanikaiyar* meaning courtesan and *Potumakal* meaning morally loose common women. Within these sexualised groups of women there emerged a secondary group containing *Ill Paratai*, the concubines, and *Seri Paratai*, meaning women from slum dwellings that accommodated any paid customers (Thiruchandran 1998: 24).

44 This comment was made by Sir P. Ramanathan as cited in Special Commission on the Constitution, Oral Evidence, Vol. 1, 30 November 1927, pp. 248. The full reference of which is St Mathew Chapter 7 Verse 6, 'Give not that which is holy unto the dogs, neither cast ye your pearls before swine, lest they trample them under their feet, and turn again and rend you' cited in de Alwis and Jayawardena (2001: 10).

45 More information on the movement can be found in de Alwis M. and K. Jayawardena, (2001) *Casting Pearls: the Women's Franchise Movement in Sri Lanka*, Colombo, Social Scientist Association.

46 Their confidence was reflected in their conduct as seen by Agnes de Silva, the leader of the WFU delegation who remarked, '[w]e went in the spirit of crusaders and answered the questions in an inspired manner. Lord Donoughmore asked if we wanted Indian Tamil women labourers on the estates to have the vote. I replied certainly, they are women too. We want all women to have the vote' (Tambiah 2002: 427).

47 Also see Minault (1989).

48 A journalist named Mangalammal Masilamany, a doctor Nallama Sathyavagiswara Aiyar and a writer Meenachi Ammal Natesa Aiyar. Of all of these women, Masilamany

was the most vociferous, for instance in regards to the issues of women and marriage she stated, and 'Marriage is not the end result of a woman's life'. Dr Nallama Sathyavagiswara Aiyar became the first Tamil woman to practise medicine in Sri Lanka (de Alwis and Jayawardena 2001: 57).

49 The maxim *the pen is mightier than the sword* is legendary in Sri Lankan history with a story of E.W. Perera, a nationalist minded lawyer from the 'National Congress Party', carrying a letter to the Queen of England requesting independence from Britain. The letter is believed to have been hidden in his shoe for the fear of it being confiscated by the governing authorities in Sri Lanka. Since independence the school children have always been taught that the *pen is mightier than the sword* and much can be achieved through non-violent means.

50 Naysum Saravanamuttu joined the State Council from Colombo North Seat that she kept for 10 years. After many years, Ranganayaki Padmanathan was appointed as a replacement for her dead brother in Pothuvil district in 1980. In 1989, Rasa Manohari Pulendran was nominated in place of her murdered husband. From her re-election in 1994, she became the first Tamil woman minister in Sri Lankan government, in charge of the Ministry of Education.

51 Sarojini Yogeswaran was a widow of a former Member of Parliament in Jaffna who was assassinated. Her own assassination was allegedly committed by the LTTE for her calling for an ending to the culture of violence that was taking place in Jaffna and for her election affiliation with the Tamil United Liberation Front (TULF), whom the LTTE considered as one of its enemies. (Tambiah 2002: 434).

52 Women and Men in Sri Lanka, A Report, Department of Census and Statistics, Colombo (1995), cited in Tambiah (2002: 428).

53 Also see Pfaffenberger (1982).

54 BP, one of the civic participants in this research, was one such person.

55 Jayawardena and de Alwis (2002: 255) in reference to Maunaguru's unpublished paper.

56 Male soldiers were giving women full body checks at sentry points manned by the IPKF soldiers (Thirangama et al. 1990). The continual targeting of women is cited as a contributing factor that led women to join the LTTE due to the lack of safety they felt as discussed in later chapters.

57 Whilst globally it has become a familiar sight to see women combatants in the twentieth century armed forces, it is still a new concept for Tamil nationals to see Tamil women in this role. See Carreiras (2006), Elshtain and Tobias (1990), Enloe (1988), D'amico (1998), Elshtain (1990) and Klein (1998). In other countries there have been clear examples of women warriors, such as the Trung Sisters of Vietnam (Eisen-Bergman 1975) and the Dahomey women warriors of West Africa (Edgerton 2000).

3 Displacement and Contributing Factors to Joining the LTTE

Idampeyatha is a word in the Tamil language that means a 'forceful expulsion from one's home'. During the pre-war era, this word was considered a formal/academic word, but has now entered the mainstream language of Tamil nationals. The home represents a symbolic space 'frequently articulated through nostalgia, a form of melancholia caused by prolonged absence from one's home or country' (de Alwis 2004: 216). This is the basis from which GV explains her own self-discovery through an analogy of her relationship with her home.

> I want you to tell [her] this. Tell her that for a Jaffna woman her house is her soul. The house could be a small hut. So, for a woman who has been living like this, to leave her home was a very difficult matter. Whether we had problems with our parents or had problems with our own thoughts, or if we loved someone or went out to do a job, we never left our homes we always came back to it and we wouldn't do anything without our parent's approval. We, who were never able to break up our home were ordered to leave the house within an hour and break up the house that were never able to do before ... At this time the rain that came down also played an important part. In that rain what can I carry and take. As far as I can remember I have tried to be a good example in the society and there is this house to which I was bound to and was never before able to break away from it and I have put all that I possessed in it. The sad part was that I was unable to get away from this house before all this happened.... All these years I could not break away from this house because of all that I have put in it my relationships, my happy memories, my softness, my possessions I couldn't leave these things and go. Though there were many opportunities and many chances where I could have achieved more and

> **never left the house. But now in a moment's notice I had to leave this house for a small reason. To me it felt like a small reason because I missed out on achieving a lot in this world because of being unable to leave the house and when asked to leave it didn't affect me at all. Even if I had to die I didn't want to leave the house. I was in Nallur [home region] and I refuse to go. I told even if I die I don't want to go. When I think back I was a typical Jaffna woman culturally bound to her house. (GV) [*sic*]**

The house as described by GV is in essence relevant to all participants of the research. The concept of the house is more than a mere building of bricks and mortar; it is, in effect, a space of self-location. When GV also explains that 'the thing called "Jaffna culture" is always kept in the house', she means that the cultural role of women is linked to the house, which provides women with security, stability and modesty. Thus, the house not only gains an identity and a personality of its own but also a gendered dimension with cultural representations for female moral virtue, modesty and social respectability.

As discussed in Chapter 2, from a historical perspective women were divided into categories based on the house (*Kula Makal*, good women; *Vilai Makal*, evil women). Thus, the links with the house for Tamil women are constructed in the gendered terms of space and place. de Alwis (2004: 214) describes a space to be an 'area of safety and security' and a place to be an 'area of uncertainty and unfamiliarity'. The act of leaving a known 'space' and moving into an unknown 'place' proved to be a deeply emotional experience as it is tied to the multiple positions that women occupy. Massey (1994), cited in de Alwis (2004), argues that 'space' is a 'site of interaction' and 'place' is a 'site of enclosures'; that, there are no 'pure' places, and both the place and space are, in essence, products of human interaction, means that the gendered dimensions in the interaction make displacement a disruptive and life-changing experience. The conceptual notion held within the space of the house provided the same kind of respectable stability for civic women and combatant women alike. The continuous displacements forcing women into various 'places' have eroded the security that is provided by the house (the space) and have damaged (irrevocably, in some cases) the relationships contained within the boundaries of that space known as the house.

The women whom I have interviewed, and others I have met in the course of this research, have spoken about the deep emotional impact of displacement. In order to gain a fuller understanding, displacement needs to be seen in the context of the highly gendered traditional Tamil culture that identifies the home as a culturally confined and socially dictated personal space for women, both young and old. Therefore, any disruptions to this traditional environment would create an artificial space, with drastic consequences. In this instance it did contribute to the nature of displacement that made women break away from the narrow confines of their traditional roles, whether by re-evaluating their own views or by being pushed into becoming armed combatants.

Changing Roles and Family Structures

Displacement can be easily linked to the LTTE's major wars with the State and ceased during its periods of ceasefire agreements.[1] Such displacement, whether it occurs once or more than once, or is short- or long-term, causes a considerable amount of damage to intra-familial relationships.

My research revealed that the continual displacements which occurred in Jaffna had created circumstances that resulted in the deterioration of both the cultural norms and the social hierarchy of the family unit. 'Before displacement there was a chance [an opportunity] to join [the LTTE]' (Yalini), but for many women in this research (except AK) it was an opportunity they did not take because of their strong familial ties. The prolonged war challenged the stability that formed the foundation of the family, where the father acts both as protector and provider as the 'male' head of household. There are also many families that are no longer headed by men, shifting the gendered dimensions within the confines of the concept of home/house. The disrupted familial structure invariably leads to a social transformation, which under violent political conflicts means a constant contest for available social space. The boundaries of social interactions that were erected during non-war periods, such as respect for elders in the immediate family and/or the greater community, were obliterated when displacement took place. The elders in the community found it hard to maintain discipline and authority, for the stable structure within the set boundaries of home no longer cohered. Adults were often unable to articulate their feelings of helplessness due to depression, which in turn resulted in an inability to care for children, and they lost their cultural and moral authority as an elder or head of a household. The breakdown of the family unit extended to the relatives and reduced the control men have over the unit, which included the women in particular. When this formula was applied to the society as a whole, it was seen to produce an extensive reduction in social control over Tamil women as a collective (Brownlees 2004: 117–119. Also see Schrijvers 1999).

Under the circumstances of displacement, the decline in importance of the head of the household, and the decline of that control adults have over children in a domestic sphere, made these experiences equally hard to deal with for the young. This is particularly pertinent to young children who no longer saw the family as a functioning unit. As Roja says, 'My mother was very sad when Akka [elder sister] left home to join. But Akka was very unhappy with all the displacements, and being at home without going to school must have made her join [the LTTE]. She was 12 years old'. Roja raises three key points in this extract: first, her sister no longer viewed the family unit as a place she could be happy in; second, the unhappiness caused by being displaced could not be changed by the family; and third, the ability to leave the family environment to attend a different school was no longer an option. The combination of all these appears to indicate that Roja's sister felt a sense of futility at being with her parents and family who were unable to provide for her needs in the displaced environment.

The Vanni Influence: An Ethno-nationalist Revival?

I further suggest that there may be a high-level of revival of ethno-nationalism in geographical locations controlled by the LTTE where women's roles were varied to include changes. Szczepanikova (2005: 283) refers to this as the women taking 'the essentialised role of biological reproducers and cultural cultivators of the boundaries of ethnic–national collectives and their ideologies'. This view is shared by Korac (2004), Yuval-Davis and Anthias (1989) and Moser and Clerk (2001): women who were displaced during ethnic conflicts became the symbolic embodiment of the conflict.[2]

I would assert that displacement should be seen within the context of the war in order to fully understand the women combatants' decision to join the LTTE. Through ethno-nationalism, the women were granted a new kind of gender identity, one that differs vastly from the socio-historical positions of pre-displacement times, when space and place were at odds with one another.

> **I am from Alavetty. At the age of 12 I was displaced. We were displaced six times. First displaced from south Alavetty to North Alavetty. Then Innuvil, then Kondavil, then Kaithady, and then Vanni, and then Jaffna. When I was in Vanni I joined the movement. (Roja)**

Whilst the age that Roja gave as the time of her initial displacement (12 years) does not add up correctly with the subsequent events—a continuous displacement for four years; joining the LTTE at the age of 14 (or younger)—it can nonetheless be said that she was rather young when her displacements took place. Her continuous four-year displacement ended when the family moved to Vanni, where she joined the LTTE as a child combatant.

In Jaffna, displaced women have emerged to play a social role very different to that traditionally expected of them, and they articulate their interests beyond the confines of the family unit (Schrijvers 1999 and Zackariya and Shanmugaratnam 2002). In a culture where there have always been defined private and public spaces, women found that 'there are no family secrets anymore and there is no such thing as a private life' (Shanmugaratnam 2001: 30). The impact of the lack of private life is reflected in the interviews of all participants but is particularly poignant in GV and Kavitha's narratives. In Kavitha's life, displacement became an important influence on her decision-making process, and GV used the displacement to re-evaluate her whole life and existence.

It is interesting to note an emerging pattern of those who were displaced to the LTTE-controlled Vanni area joining the movement. The pattern of displacement to Vanni and subsequent enlisting in the LTTE was also reflective of Kavitha, Yalini, Aruna and Arulvili's experiences. They all moved from various parts of Jaffna to Vanni for safety and security. The exception was Mallika, who was a resident in Vanni and did not experience displacement. However, she was acutely aware of the hardships of others through conversations heard at home. It was unclear from which particular geographical locality Arasi decided to join the LTTE; AK, due to her long-term role of a logistical supporter, joined the movement by invitation. In comparison, none of the civic women who also encountered displacement joined the LTTE, but interestingly neither were they displaced to the Vanni area. The connection between Vanni and the women's recruitment is significant here. However, it appears that due to the prolonged war there has been no research conducted on the connection between the Vanni region and women's enrolment in the LTTE.

I would argue that the displacement to Vanni combines space and place through a network of social interactions with a collective of displaced women. These interactions (with the collective of women) transcend the limited spatiality of secluded personal spaces that separate caste and class through the confines of home. By joining the LTTE, the space changed to that of place. The place in this instance was Vanni, the heartland of the LTTE-controlled area. This created a definitive sense of safety, belonging and, above all, some semblance of normalcy under violent conditions.

Although displacement was not the sole cause for women joining the LTTE, it appeared to be one of the more prominent reasons. I put this to the test by asking Kavitha if she would still have joined the movement had she not been displaced, to which she answered:

> **As with anything, when you want to do [something] you need some inducement. So displacement was the final push. Maybe if I had lived here [in Jaffna] there would have been something**

> **else that happened here that would have induced me to join like the problem with Rajani.[3] Incidents like that would have made me want to join. I am sure if I had lived here, some of the incidents that took place here with the army would have made me join the movement. (Kavitha)**

For Kavitha, her displacement acted as the final catalyst for her joining the revolutionary movement, along with other incidents she had witnessed over a period of time. Although in this narrative she did not admit to experiencing violence directly, she nonetheless recognised it as a similarly influential force. Therefore, it can be said that the experience of displacement was perceived in the same way as other forms of more direct violence.

The spatiality aspect of displacement further lends itself to the issue of having to live with others such as relatives, friends or total strangers for long periods of time. Though communal living (same as living with extended families) is accepted by the Tamil society, there are issues of class and caste that make this unacceptable for many in this situation.

> **Being displaced and living in somebody else's house was a problem. Also this was our first time in Vanni, and it was not comfortable and suitable to me. I felt that there was no point in living a life in fear which I didn't like, and it was better to have a good life without fear. (Kavitha)**

Both civic and combatant women mentioned fear as part of their daily existence under war conditions. However, in Kavitha's narrative she ties fear to displacement pushing her and her family towards homelessness and an uncertain future. Kavitha was not alone in making life-changing decisions based on displacement, as others such as Yalini and Aruna also revealed similar examples. They both were displaced many times, which resulted in their families being forced to find refuge under a tree in Vanni, away from Jaffna's war areas.

Aruna narrates, 'I faced three displacements. During the Kilinochchi battle. [and] During Sothiya operation I faced another displacement. Our family, also I, live[ed] under the tree … we were unable to do anything. So I felt'.

> Yes. In Jaffna Fort and in 1995 the military occupied whole of Jaffna Peninsula. At that time we were displaced to Vanni and we settled ... not that we were really settled ... we had a home under a tree in Kilinochchi. Then we made a temporary cottage [mud hut] in Kilinochchi. Then I went to school in Kilinochchi only for ten days. (Yalini)

Both women describe being forced to live outside under a tree, but Aruna in particular strikes a keynote in voicing the helplessness she felt. When taken together, these examples create a picture not only of dissatisfaction, but also of fear, helplessness, and a lack of agency and empowerment. These issues will be discussed later on in Chapter 6 with an analysis of the roles of equality. These emotions were strong during displacement, especially when a considerable percentage of the people who disappeared in Jaffna peninsula were children.[4]

Positive Aspects of Displacement

Much of the research relating to displacement and refugee studies shows that it is women who are far more affected by wars, and it is women on the whole who take positive steps to change their social positions in times of displacement (Brownlees 2004; Szczepanikova 2005; Kirk 2006 and Gardner and El Bushra 2004). The interviews revealed that a number of women have embraced the changes as a positive move in their lives, rendering displacement the catalyst for an alternative life which they may otherwise have only contemplated in passing. Being uprooted from their comfort zones of 'space' and being pushed into the 'place' had changed the gendered role of women. This change was particularly visible among the financially affluent, educated middle-class women such as GV and HA.

> I was so used to my life in my home enjoying the nature that surrounded it, the people and my own thoughts, and I always thought there was no other life than this. But now because of this displacement I felt I could live anywhere and in anyway. I felt that had I lost my life earlier, I could have done all this [other activities] before all this [displacement] happened. I even started to cycle everyday. Before all this happened I had friends

> **in other places, but I never went to see them [except] on a motorbike, or a car or a bus, because they were far away places and I didn't want to stay there. I had to come back to my own home as I didn't like staying away from it....These are places that I never wanted to go, but now I [can] tie things on the back of the bike and cycle to that place. (GV)**

> **Survival....So there are so many places to meet [people], things to discuss, so many things to face. I can't worry now. I can ride my bicycle even ten kilometres, I can carry so much. This is [the] main advantage of this war for Tamil women. (HA)**

Removing the private space and opening the public place have resulted in these women reflecting on the social changes that had taken place due to displacement. In displacement, home no longer represented gendered values of previous times. GV and HA were particularly able to identify and relate to the positive aspects these changes brought to their lives, such as riding a bicycle, which was synonymous with women's independence to move around unchaperoned.

Another notable positive aspect of change due to displacement was that women of high caste and/or the financially affluent middle classes were confronted with sharing their living spaces with other social classes and castes. This shared physical space was described by GV as 'multiculturalism', even though there was no other ethnic group apart from Tamil nationals present.

> **[At] this time we had to go and live with four families: a total of 25 people in a small house with two bedrooms and a veranda. Only here I came across the multi-culture society. All these days [previous to displacement] we lived an independent life in Jaffna, and now we had to live with 25 other people. This is where my independent life broke. (GV)**

The mixing of different social statuses, castes and classes caused GV to adjust to living with others in a communal way, thus, merging the certainty of space with the uncertainty of place. For the first time in her privileged life she realised that she had to learn to live with others, and that she no longer held the same position of power as she had within her own home. Displacement forces social groups to share personal / physical spaces that the traditions of caste and class would not have permitted before.[5]

Effects of Displacement on Education

School is recognised in displacement literature as being a stabilising factor in children's lives. Machel (2001), who compiled global evidence on child displacement as part of the impact of war on children, claimed education to be the 'fourth pillar' in displacement, alongside food and water, shelter and healthcare. The breaking of routines such as attending school was often found to be particularly destructive for young children who thrive on stability, as suggested by many of the narratives discussed in this chapter.

Herringshaw (2000: 1) states that education in displacement bears the same high-level of need as food and water. The young were keen to learn, but upon displacement they were denied such an opportunity, as reflected in the discourse of both the civic and combatant women alike. Arasi narrates, 'One of my dreams was to go to the university. The circumstances and the war environment that we were living [in] at that time didn't permit us to study'.

> In 1995 we [were] displaced. For six months we can't [couldn't] come to Jaffna. We are in the Thenmarachi area out of Jaffna. We have no books, nothing. For about six months we studied nothing. Stay like this in the house and playing games and like that. Even we can't study anything. That time was six months' waste....I think about if I can enter the medical faculty and I became a doctor no problem no.... (ES)

One of the main disruptions in the displacement period was that many people sought refuge inside school buildings, causing those schools to close for an indefinite period of time. Arulvili comments, 'Displaced people were [living] there [in the schools]...'

It must be understood that schools were not necessarily recognised as official refugee sites, but people often felt a sense of safety in being together during periods of violent army attacks which included aerial bombardments of homes and villages. However, the schools were often the targets for bombardments. Yalini describes, 'Here you can see. Many schools were destroyed by the Sri Lankan government. In Kilinochchi also lot of schools....Not because school was not there but not function[ing]...'

The reasons for non-functioning of schools were not limited simply to the occupation of schools by refugees or IDPs; the State's armed forces also used the buildings for military purposes. Before the 2002 ceasefire agreement it was assessed that there were some 150 schools in the northern part of Sri Lanka that were used either as army camps or as sentry posts by the Sri Lankan State Army.[6] This position changed after the ceasefire agreement, as one of its conditions was for all public buildings occupied by the armed forces to be vacated immediately.[7] Interestingly, when the armed forces moved out of school buildings they generally erected their camps adjacent to the school. It must also be recognised that it was not only the State that was monopolising schools; the LTTE, too, were erecting their camps next door to schools, as noticed in Kavitha and AK's interviews. Thus every time the State attacked an LTTE camp it inevitably destroyed adjacent schools.

The number of children walking many miles to a functioning school underlines the importance of education. One such person was Yalini, an academically bright student who was prepared to attend school whilst being forced to live under a tree, then in a temporary hut erected in the same place. Though the cost of sending a child to school becomes hard for displaced parents to bear, they often try to make adjustments to allow this to happen, strongly believing in education being the only way out of their problems. The State provides free education and gives a form of allowances for school uniforms, but the cost of textbooks and other material must be born by the parents. Furthermore, the displaced children who attend schools are outsiders to the community and tend to become stigmatised (Smith 2003: 24–33).

Displacement can again be seen as a catalyst that pushed young people to pursue alternative lives. As Aruna says, 'Already I know about the movement ... but I didn't decide to join. After displacement I cannot [attend school]....I was unable to continue my studies....I decided to join the movement.' Education was seen as the sole route to a better life; when denied, the LTTE was seen as the only remaining pathway open to the young. It was clear that the State was either unaware of, or simply did not care to recognise, the importance of schooling during the periods of conflict and displacement. The complacency of the Sri Lankan government with regard to children's education was pointed out by Sri-Jayntha (2002: 6), who states that the government was sending alcohol by ship to Jaffna (the only mode of transport to Jaffna other than by air) far more regularly than much-needed textbooks for schools.

What Is a Child?

To define precisely what or who is a child has been problematic to many policy makers. Therefore, many rely on the 1983 United Nations Convention on the Rights of the Child declaration, which states that 'a child must be a human being below the age of 18 years' (Goodwin-Gill and Cohn 1997: 6). On the surface, this appears to be a sensible approach to a difficult problem of definition. However, it overlooks cultural practices that are inherent in certain societies, as well as the biological development of physical maturity and mental capacity that is present in the 15 to 18 year old age group. Goodwin-Gill and Cohn (1997: 6) argue that the identification of children between the ages of 15 to 18 perhaps need to be referred to as 'youths' or 'young adults' rather than children. Breaking the age group down into these categories will allocate some leeway for the cultural norms and practices to be pursued within the greater definition. It also allows the young person to take some responsibility as dictated by their individual cultures (Goodwin-Gill and Cohn 1997: 6).

There are some 300,000 children involved in 30 separate conflicts globally, and many are under the age of 16 (Brownlees 2004 and Machel 2001). It is interesting to note that during periods of violent conflict both lawgivers and politicians have an opportunity to utilise the lack of clear theoretical definition for the benefit of the state. For instance, Usher (1991: 15) notes, 'the Israel military's definition of the legal criminal age had been remarkably fluid. In 1987, it was 16; by 1988, 14; more recently it has been 12' (cited in Cairn's 1996: 9). This grants a space for the State to prosecute children as adults. In Sri Lanka, criminal responsibility starts at the age of eight years (although those who are between the ages of 8 and 12 have a defence of 'maturity' that will be taken under consideration by a court of law).[8]

The extensive research conducted by Goodwill-Gill and Cohn (1997) on the global use of children as soldiers by the State-run armed forces and militia revealed that, out of 185 countries only 103 had documentation on child soldiers. Seven countries recruited from under 17 years of age, and 24 others accepted volunteers from under 17 years of age with parental consent.[9]

Child Soldiers of the LTTE

In a global setting, displacement has been linked to children wanting to join revolutionary movements as a result of the insecurities felt in their lives (Cairns 1996; Machel 2001; Stedman and Tanner 2003 and Brownlees 2004). This, however, is not widely debated in the available literature focusing on the LTTE and its combatants. The literature does little to emphasise upon the issue of displacement being a catalyst for many children and young adults wanting to join the revolutionary movement as an alternative to the instability of continuous displacements and life in refugee camps but discusses it under the theme of forced recruitments or abductions (Smith 2003 and Schrijvers 1999).

The recruitment of children into the LTTE can be traced back to around 1987, at a time when the LTTE suffered heavy defeats resulting in the deaths of many male fighters. This was a period when the immediate enemy was the IPKF, not the Sri Lankan armed forces.[10] This drastic shortage of combatants forced the revolutionary movement to reassess what alternative human resources were available to them (by this stage women had already started to join the movement). The recruitment of children as combatants was recognised as a low-cost and efficient way for revolutionary organisations to increase the strength of their force (Slinger 2005: 38). However, there is literature that reveals the creation of a children's unit known as the *Bakuts*, meaning Baby Brigade, in 1984. Their training was limited to primary education and physical exercises as there was no need at that time to use children in combatant roles. By 1986, some of those children emerged as 16-year-old combatants (Gunaratna 2003: 2 and Bandara 2002).

However, with time the situation regarding child combatants differed greatly from earlier periods, as illustrated by the National Child Protection Authority in Sri Lanka. The Human Rights Watch Report (2004: 16) states, 'In 1994, I found that one in nineteen child recruits was abducted. Now, in 2004, the reverse is true and only one in nineteen is a volunteer.'

There are a number of reports prepared by the Human Rights Watch, UNICEF, the Coalition to Stop the Use of Child Soldiers, UTHR (Jaffna) and others, on the subject of forcible child recruitment by the LTTE clearly indicating that such malpractice happened in the LTTE, including going into refugee camps to recruit children who were orphaned in the December 2004 tsunami.[11]

The enrolment patterns have changed over the years, with a notable decrease in children 'volunteering'. Whilst the precise cause for decreased enrolment was not specified, it can perhaps be attributed to a number of reasons, including the children becoming less romanticised about the role played by combatants, and the families and children themselves being less naïve of the realities of war. This in turn resulted in an increased forced recruitment through abductions and demands made from households to provide a child for the cause.[12] It must be said from the outset that this chapter is not actively seeking to address the issues of forcible child recruitment as the women combatants of this research were willing volunteers.[13]

The debate on child recruits continued with various agencies such as the Human Rights Watch, Amnesty International and UNICEF demanding an end to the practice. The LTTE had not openly claimed the use of child combatants, but had given assurances since 1998 that they will discontinue the practice and release all children engaged within the organisation. In 2003, the Sri Lankan government and the LTTE signed a formal document titled Action Plan for Children Affected by War, which gave assurances to end child recruitment and release existing children from the organisation. Needless to say, this did not happen in the way that was expected, and only a handful of children were released. Human Rights Watch Report November 2004 states that those who were in fact released were of no use to the LTTE due to their physical conditions. Therefore, children were seen as armed combatants right up to the end of the LTTE's Final War.

The most comprehensive study that is currently available on the gendered aspect of child soldiering in the LTTE is by Keairns (2003). *The Voices of Girl Child Soldiers* was part of a larger study that included four separate countries and 23 female child combatants. The part concerned with female child combatants in Sri Lanka revealed three contributing factors to a child's decision to become a combatant: the first is personal circumstance and environment; the second is abduction and financial hardship; and the third is a means of contributing to something meaningful with their own lives. There is also a perceived assumption that respect will be granted by the civil society to those who become combatants of the LTTE.

Some authors, such as Gunaratna (2003), argue that it was the uniforms of the combatants that attract children into the movement. Gunaratna (2003: 3) states, 'Interestingly, the appearance of the young recruits was a strong factor in attracting youngsters to the movement. Tiger-striped uniforms, polished boots and automatic weapons acted as magnets to the children.'

The exact numbers of child combatants recruited by the LTTE are unknown. In 2002, President Kumaratunga stated in an interview to CNN television that there were 1,000 child combatants serving in the LTTE (CNN Television, 16 May 2002). Sri-Jayantha (2002) argued that when this figure is compared against the estimate of 10,000 total LTTE combatants it reveals that 1 out of every 10 combatants was under the age of 18 years. Basu (2005) claimed the total numbers of children in the LTTE to be 40 per cent. As with all data relating to the LTTE, this too, was an area where there were no means to obtain accurate data. Therefore, a crude method had been devised by the State that involved counting the number of dead bodies of children found after various battles. The Sri Lankan Government's Directorate of Military Intelligence claims that a figure of 60 per cent of combatants killed were under the age of 18 years (Gunaratna 2003: 1). Gunaratna (2003) argues that, even if the State's intelligence has over-estimated the number of child recruits, the battlefield deaths show a figure of 40 per cent being children (of both sexes) between the ages of 9 and 18 years, a notable number of whom were between the ages of 10 and 16 years. There is no information available to ascertain how many combatants of the Final War were children.

Whilst acknowledging that many publications by various international organisations collate and publish details on child recruitment, it is only a very limited number that discuss the role of female children who have either been forced into the LTTE movement or become willing 'volunteers'. The numbers involved vary between authors and their sources, often with a gender-blindness that fails to distinguish male children from female children, although Gunaratna does acknowledge that both male and female children's bodies were included. One exception to this has been Smith (2003: 23), who added to the debate by focusing on the battle at Ampkamam (in the northern part of the island) in which 140 LTTE combatants' bodies were recovered. Of this number, 49 were children, 32 of which were female children between the ages of 11 and 15 years.

All of the female combatants in my research stated that they were willing volunteers. The majority of them were at least 18 years of age at the time of joining the LTTE. The exceptions are Arulvili, who had just turned 17 (she joined after her seventeenth birthday), and Mallika and Roja, who claim to have been 15 years of age at the time of their recruitment. However, there was a one-year age gap between them, which indicated that either Roja was 15 and Mallika 14 years, or they were both younger than they stated. During this research it proved very difficult to obtain the precise age of combatant women at the time of their joining the LTTE. Therefore, the ages were ascertained by linking their recruitment to a time of a major event in their lives, such as during key exam times (e.g., ordinary level and advance level exams). Whilst I would not say it was a deliberate ploy to confuse the researcher, it does go some way to suggesting that the LTTE may have instructed those who joined under the age of 18 to be economical with precise details of their age at the time of recruitment. It nonetheless confirmed that they were young enough to be classified as children based on the United Nations Convention Declaration definition of a child being under the age of 18.

It must also be noted that, as with many other revolutionary groups that use children as combatants, the LTTE openly values parents who have sacrificed their children to the movement by granting them material advantages.[14]

Slinger (2005: 63–64) states, 'In Sri Lanka, parents within LTTE-controlled zones who lose a child [as a combatant] are treated with special status as "great hero families". They pay no taxes, receive job preferences, and are allocated special seats at all public events.' I would argue that there were a number of reasons why the LTTE used this tactic. On one level, a clear message was sent out to the community that all was not lost in a family due to the death of a child who chose to be a combatant, as the family will be cared for by the LTTE. On another level, it sent a message to the child that their demise will not force the family to endure hardships in the future with no one to care for them, as the LTTE will look after them. It also encouraged the children to join and the parents not to discourage such interests in children. Further, it also publicly overlooked the Tamil society's deeply ingrained caste and class system by promoting such families to a socially elevated position, bypassing their caste and class. This in itself was an interesting phenomenon: to some extent, class can be changed by education and wealth; caste remains with a person from the time of their birth to their death. Being recognised as a 'great hero family' is thus an honour that a low caste family would never encounter under normal conditions.

There is one aspect that makes the LTTE very distinctive from other revolutionary groups, which was their issue of cyanide capsules to *all* combatants *regardless* of age or sex, as mentioned in Chapter 2 (Keairns 2003; Schalk 1992; Narayan-Swamy 2002 and Bose 1994). A female child combatant cited in Keairns (2003: 15) reveals, 'The day I was given the cyanide (capsule) I was very happy because no one would catch me alive—abuse or harass me. This was for *my safety*. I felt good to carry this round my neck.' By issuing child combatants with cyanide capsules, the LTTE instilled a sense of confidence that the enemy would not be able to capture them alive. The LTTE told the children that death by cyanide is considerably better than being captured and tortured by the Sri Lankan armed forces, and thus the children believe that the cyanide capsule is for 'their' own safety, issued by a *caring* organisation (Keairns 2003: 15).

The Politicisation of Children

Cairns (1996: 124) argues that the family holds a stronger influence over the development of a child's political conscience than previously recognised. This is mostly noted among families in divided ethno-nationalist societies, where ethnic identity is re-created to fit in with the political situation. He argues that these views can be divided into three main areas that implicate parental influences: parents sharing the same political ideology, eliminating any political confusion; the importance of politics to both of the child's parents and the child's own perception of the importance of politics to the parents.

During my research it transpired that the women combatants developed their initial relationships with the LTTE combatants while still living at home. 'Through my father I came to know more of Prabhakaran and the Tigers' (AK). Thus AK's view of Prabhakaran and the LTTE was formulated by her father and was unconsciously and unquestionably adopted by her.[15]

Arasi described the influence of the family in a child's political awareness:

> During this time, at night my parents, my uncle and neighbours will sit and talk about these things [LTTE activities] very softly....After that only I started reading the newspapers that were in the house. I read about the problems that were going on here and there. Sometimes I used to ask my mother about all what was happening and my mother would explain things to me. (Arasi)

As with AK, Arasi's political awareness was directly gained through the process of listening to parental views and thoughts, which in turn influenced her to choose the same political views. These views and thoughts were additionally confirmed as the 'correct' thinking in the external environment of school.

> Also I heard stories [at school] about the fighters who were fighting for us. We have heard it at school. And also we have seen our parents giving them food and treating them kindly when they came home in the night. When we went to school the next day we found that all my friends' parents were also doing the same thing and we discussed it amongst ourselves. Then we began to like them. (Arasi)

As can be seen in Arasi's narrative, children discussed the issue of the LTTE and its combatants. They then realised that not only their own family, but also many others, held the LTTE in high regard. These views were reinforced by her school (both by her teachers and fellow pupils–her peer group), formalising a righteous belief. Further, the discussions conducted at school about the LTTE and the political situation meant that the LTTE combatants were seen as fighting on behalf of others, thus creating a certain veneration of acts of selfless bravery.

The combatants' active visits to the homes of civic citizens to collect food and/or medicine also allowed them to get closer to families that were sympathetic to them as individuals.

> Even before the IPKF came all of us liked the Tigers very much... I liked the Tigers very, very much....My family also liked them very much. Because they go through a lot of hardships, and go on without food. At times they come to our house in the middle of the night asking for food....When ever they came, even if it was in the middle of the night, we would get up and cook for them and feed them. At home, when our mother ask us to do some work around the house we will give excuses not to do, but when the Tigers came at any time of the day we will do everything very eagerly. At home everyone will say that you are ever ready to do things for them. When you see them you don't mind doing any work for them. Whenever there is a celebration or festivities at home and when we prepare nice food and eat we think of the Tigers and wonder what hardships they are going through at this moment and whether they had any food to eat.

> They are people who are fighting for us. The thought that army might be hurting them upsets us. (Arasi)

Arasi, who sees the combatants through the eyes of a child and was captivated by the tales of hardship, appeared to have a sense of guilt that she articulates as, 'they are people who are fighting for us'. As a child with few resources available to her, she was able to express her admiration to the combatants by eagerly awaiting their nightly visits to her home, where she could actively take part in the preparation of food for them. Further, the concerns expressed illustrated that the LTTE combatants were no longer seen as outsiders but as an extension of the family.

The fact that Arasi was 'ever ready' to assist the LTTE goes far deeper into the personal fears she felt as a child. She stated:

> [b]ecause with the army they will just come and shoot people at random without saying anything. Then I realised that they [LTTE] are the only people who can save us from the army. Then as we were growing up we began to like them very much and wanted to talk to them. We felt that we would be safer if we go with them [the LTTE combatants] and was scared to stay at home. (Arasi)

Arasi's narrative highlighted children being shifted from one safe space to another. Her description described a shift from home to the LTTE as a safe space when the home is threatened. In effect, the shift in perceived safe spaces (home and the LTTE) feeds the childhood fantasy of the LTTE as a safe space, but in reality recruitment was a clear path to danger. Therefore, the LTTE combatants were inevitably seen as selfless beings that were not only committed to the cause but also to the community and especially to the young, who were seen as the future of the nation.

> So at times I have asked them take me with them. But they always told us 'you must study well and be good, then only you can look after our people later on'. 'If tomorrow we get our land you are the people who are going to be in charge, so don't come with us but study well'. They emphasised on us studying well. We were very much inspired by them so we studied hard to please them. And it was like our goal to study well. (Arasi)

As illustrated above, Arasi accepted their advice, which was given before the LTTE started to recruit children into their ranks. It was also a time when parents still welcomed the combatants, and children openly admired them. Quite often they were also seen as part of the family. In a culture that is known to accept and obey parental views unquestioningly, it was easy to see how the older combatants became heroes in the eyes of the desperate young adolescents.

> When we started helping the Tigers, he [father] never stopped us. So by that time I started to help in projects, which the Tigers had started. Also I used to go and collect food parcels for the LTTE and take care of the wounded. He [father] allowed us to go and do all these work without any objections. (AK)

AK's father was known to be a strict man with an authoritative style of parenting who saw no need to curb AK's involvement with the LTTE. By this token, her father conveyed his acceptance of her involvement with the LTTE. Along with such admiration, there was also an inevitable obligation felt by the individual child and their family, who perceived that their own safety and well-being rested upon the protection provided by the selflessness of the LTTE combatants. Slinger (2005: 64) claims, 'Parents may also drive children into war indirectly by their own admiration of combatants.' This was highlighted in Yalini's family when her father pointed out that her freedom depended upon the sacrifices made by the combatants.

> My father told us they are fighting for us; they are fighting in the jungle without having food. Like that my father will talk [to] us; you studying, you are living freely because the Tigers are fighting for us. My father will talk with us. (Yalini)

Such parental statements often made a child feel that they were indebted to the LTTE. The child 'owed' her life and daily existence to the non-selfish commitment and self-sacrifice made by the LTTE on behalf of the child and her family. Many have overlooked the cultural context, in which children accept these parental ideologies unquestioningly as the 'correct' belief. However, based on my own findings, I agree with Cairns that there is strong evidence to suggest that the parents' political views do foster the child's own political socialisation.

It must also be noted that the civic women did not discuss the same kind of admiration and appreciation as seen amongst combatant women's families. The civic women supporters of the LTTE in their adult years did not get involved with the combatants that visited them. Although their parents, too, offered food, medicine and at times money, their aim was to ensure that they did not antagonise or get noted in any way.

Whilst acknowledging the feelings of admiration for the LTTE that the women felt through parental influence when young, there were also non-parental influences that instilled or reinforced these feelings of admiration. One such influence that encouraged women to join the LTTE was the visual imagery on the billboards along main roads that depicted the glamour and excitement of being a combatant. During the research, I noticed a number of billboards depicting many 'storyboards'. One such board illustrated a group of girls in school uniform talking with a group of women in combatant uniform. There were also other storyboard sketches, clearly aimed at girls, illustrating the violence committed by the army upon civilians, and how young girls were retaliating by becoming combatants and confronting the injustices committed. In a society where age, caste, class and gender identity all play a recognisable role, continuous environmental imagery can be a powerful form of an incentive.

Power Relations in the Family

During the times of displacement, the amount of control able to be exerted by the parents is reduced, and the children are often exposed to a harsh and cruel environment where they have to learn to survive. The displacement camps became fertile grounds for finding new recruits for the LTTE, as discussed above. The inadequate facilities (including lack of educational facilities) in camps made the LTTE appear a very alluring alternative. Brownlees (2004: 119) and Cairns (1996) both argue that in such environments children begin to develop an additional political conscience, which may have some of its roots in parental political ideologies, but could also have a stronger influence based on their own feelings of 'having nothing to lose'. This in itself is a direct result of the 'desperation and dispossession' that is generally felt in displacement. On such occasions armed resistance was viewed by the young people as granting them some form of 'empowerment' (Goodwin-Gill and Cohen 1997: 41).[16] The LTTE, too, offered such an empowerment to these young people, enabling them to regain a certain level of control that was lost to them.

This was reflected in my interviews with Roja and Mallika, who revealed that, once a child recruit reached the age of 18 years, they are given an option to remain with the organisation or return home.

> **Mallika:** Her sister [referring to Roja's elder sister] studied for nearly five years. And we studied for three years. According to LTTE rules, only after you are 18 years old you are allowed to go for fighting. But the youngsters were all the time wanting to go into fighting.
>
> **Translator:** After the age of 18 they will ask again [whether they still want to be with the LTTE and do battle]. They can decide if they want to go home they can go home. Isn't it so?
>
> **Roja:** Yes. We can go home. But not many go home like that. (Mallika, Roja and Translator)

The analysis of the narrative indicated that there was a stronger sense of voluntarism felt by young combatants than coercion. It may be that many young combatant women do not return home because of the empowerment they gain, or the alternative family they create, within the revolutionary movement. The issue of many children deciding to stay with the LTTE rather than return home is discussed in Chapter 4 under kinship in friendship.

Research relating to relationship interactions within families during periods of violent political conflict is riddled with contradictions. Parenting styles tend to change during conflicts because of reasons that include displacement, financial and domicile instability, and a heightened sense of parental responsibility. There is a tendency to develop an authoritative style of parenting to compensate for the fear of being unable to protect the children, as seen among those that were displaced.

However, during the interviews it became quite clear that the relationship parents had with the LTTE combatants, which was both cultivated and developed by the combatants, was in fact strained when the women (as young adults) decided to join the movement. It appeared that, though the parents were fully prepared to openly admire the combatants and their endeavours, they were wholly unprepared to face their children's desire to become combatants. There is a notable distinction between children discussing their desire to join the revolutionary movement with their parents and actually obtaining parental blessings. The children's own desire to join may stem from their desire to be accepted in the same way as combatants, having seen their parents' admiration for them. Or, the children may think that by becoming combatants they are actively protecting their parents.

However, the relationship between the women combatants and their parents was not as clearly defined as it first appeared to be. Together, the cultural normative and gender dimension had created a highly complex social interaction within the family unit during times of war, displacement and violence. There were new forms of power relation being born within the family unit itself. The power used by the children to negotiate their own position and determine their own views (based on the internal domestic sphere through politics discussed by the parents or/and the external sphere of school, peer groups and the greater society) had effectively distanced them from their parents.

Most of the combatant women who took part in this research admit to their parents' grief at discovering their child had joined the LTTE. None of the participants in this research had informed their parents of their intention to join the LTTE before leaving home. The excuses given by the women combatants in order to leave the house without raising their parents' suspicions were wide and varied. Roja explains, *I told them [parents] I was going to the temple*, while Mallika reveals, *I told my mother I was going for tuition*.

> [a]s we were going we passed the school in which our younger brother and sister were studying and they were just coming out of school. They asked us where we were going. They knew

> that we often went to Morris's [local LTTE leader's] meetings so we told them that we were going to the meeting and we went. (AK)

None of the women combatants viewed these excuses to be significant deceptions; they simply viewed the excuses as a means of getting themselves out of the home with the least resistance from their parents. If the parents did discover what they were doing, it was very likely that they would prevent their daughter(s) from leaving home. AK related the story of her friend 'Navamany', who was active with AK in providing logistical support to the LTTE until they were both invited to join the movement. When Navamany went home to gather her belongings, her mother became suspicious, locked her in the house and prevented her from leaving with AK. However, the action taken by her mother did not prevent Navamany from joining the movement on a later date and subsequently dying in battle.

Yalini sums up the emotional anxiety that was felt by her parents upon her enrolment in the LTTE. It also shows a definitive decision being made by Yalini to join the revolutionary movement.

> Many times I talked with my mother about joining the LTTE. Everyday I will talk. My mother told me that if you go to LTTE you have to face many difficulties. You will be without food. How can you survive? I told my mother, yeah, there are lot of cadres in the movement, and they are fighting, why can't I fight? My mother didn't believe me; I am only talking about this but not joining. But one day I joined on my way to tuition class. I went to a LTTE men cadre, then he left me in a women's cadre base. I was in the women's cadre base for five days, and then I went for training. So later, when I met the man cadre, he spoke to me about my mother. My mother went to that cadre's place and my mother was crying and lying down, and my mother said 'I will not go back to my home without my daughter', and just lied down and that's it and refusing to get up again. Then my father came to that place. And my father talk with my mother and both of them went back to home.... After five months I saw my mother. They came to my base. (Yalini)

Once the parents overcame the initial shock and disappointment, they eventually came to accept their child's choice to join the LTTE. In this situation, the child altered the power relationship she had with her parents to gain her own wishes. The fact that the child was not going to leave the organisation, regardless of the emotional trauma caused to the parents, was a new kind of relationship dynamic that was not seen to the same extent before in Tamil culture. Parents have fewer agencies within the changing relationship dynamics and are left to deal with the situation in an alternative to the traditional way they have been accustomed to.

> At the beginning any parents find it difficult to see their child leave. Our culture is that always the family stays together. Usually we don't leave the parents until we get married and go. But as time went by when they too experienced lot of difficulties during the war and they felt that it was ok for one to join the movement and fight for the cause....Until they met me for the first time after I joined they were not happy. There was a certain period of time when we were under training I couldn't meet them. But once they saw me after the initial parting they were happy. (Kavitha)

The word 'happy' was used by Kavitha to describe her parent's acceptance of her into the revolutionary movement, but this needs to be looked at in a broader sense of the word as it was used to describe a situation where parents had neither power nor control. The usage of the word also makes the situation a lot more congenial and devoid of conflict. Kavitha's description is without any of the sentiments attached to that of Arulvili's: 'At first when we say we are going to join they [parents] *don't like* it but after we joined they [parents] *accepted* it.' This statement also illustrated the disempowerment of the parental authority practised in Tamil culture. The acceptance of a female child's action as irreversible by disempowered parents challenged the gender normative in a society that grants more freedom of choice to a male child than a female child. The male child was viewed from the beginning of his life to be part of the world outside, spending his adult life in the public spaces and making his mark. The female child, on the other hand, was seen from the time of her birth to be a part of a family, confined to the domestic space, away from anything that was public. The only time she can truly *leave home* is when she is married. If she does not get married then she will *always* live within the confines of the parental home, as discussed in Chapter 6.

Summary

There is a universal acceptance that children have no place in wars, either as victims or as perpetrators. Whilst the LTTE used children, justifying it as an operational need, the children themselves were driven by circumstances towards the revolutionary organisation, which of course welcomed them with open arms. Within these circumstances displacement is one of the key factors.

The claim made in the Human Rights Watch Report that there were more child volunteers in 1994 indicates that during the first decade of war, with multiple displacements, children themselves had actively sought an alternative life with the LTTE.

Education in displacement was recognised as a key factor that provided a certain sense of stability and normalcy for a young person. Education was disrupted during displacement, with many school buildings closed because of people seeking refuge or because they were the targets for bombardments due to the proximity of the LTTE camps or occupied for military purposes by the armed forces. It also gave hope as a central factor in everyday existence, linked to the longer-term betterment of an individual's life that extended beyond the times of displacement. Therefore, education was seen as not only a short-term means of providing immediate stability but also as a form of providing long-tem opportunities for the future where none was seen.

Children's roles were generally moulded under the watchful authority of the consanguine relationships of elders. However, the role of the elders was obliterated by displacement when the terrorist group stepped in and took control under the same cultural normative of a 'watchful' elder. The involvement of the terrorist group as the nominated elder in time restored the disempowerment felt by the young person, as the new kinship developed and became stronger than the consanguine genealogical relationships.

The prolonged war challenged the stability that forms the foundation of the family and, together with displacement, caused further damage to intra-familial relationships, especially affecting the male roles (including that of head of the household), altering the traditionally gendered dimensions of the concept of home.

The combatants were seen as a righteous group of people with no moral corruption, and their reputation was such that parents openly encouraged their children to associate with the LTTE. The admiration of the young person towards a serving older combatant, therefore, was often fuelled by parental involvement and support for the rebel group displayed in the presence of that young person. By joining the LTTE, the young women gained a powerful protector whom they had admired for some time based largely on the politicisation they received at home under the guidance of parents or from non-parental influences without the knowledge of their parents. The exercising of agency by young Tamil women needs to be recognised in a cultural context as a challenge to the parental authority within a patriarchal culture where women (regardless of age) do not usually take the main decisions that effect their lives and do not leave home other than in marriage.

Displacement both contradicts and questions an individual's agency and the control they are able to exert over their lives. It raises questions about traditional values of caste and class. The displacement allows an individual to break away from traditional holds that keep them subjected to set roles in society. They are able to make some decisions regarding their own lives and those of their family but are unable to carry out the decisions made, which creates a paradoxical position in their lives.

Those displaced to LTTE-controlled areas felt a sense of safety and a stronger sense of ethnic identity even without proper accommodation. From their perspective it was better to stay under a tree in Vanni with some degree of safety than to live in an area with comfort but no safety. The LTTE stepped in where the family had failed to provide stability or address the insecurity that was felt within the immediate biological family.

I would argue that displacement cannot be dismissed as a mere oddity in the women's decision-making process, and, when combined with the safety and security felt when under the protection of the LTTE in the Vanni district, was a common theme that appears to have attracted women to the movement. Again, as with the issues of lack of control and empowerment, this was indicative of the LTTE replacing the lost agency of the individual, which was lost to all victims of displacement.

Notes

1 These were the First *Eelam* war on 27 November 1983 to 13 May 1987; the Second *Eelam* war 11 June 1990 to 13 October 1994; the Third *Eelam* war 19th April 1995 and the Final War May 2006 to May 2009.

2 'In the context of violent conflict over ethnically homogenous territories and states, uprooted women have become symbolic and strategic sites of nationalism and the quest for the destruction of a multiethnic-national society' (Korac 2004: 252).

3 Rajani was a school girl who was raped and murdered by the State army. The army also killed her mother, brother and a neighbour who came into the army camp looking for her.

4 Somasundaram (2002) claims that out of a total of 600 who disappeared in the peninsula 15 per cent (90) were children.

5 As discussed in Brownlees (2004: 118), such mixing of social groups appears not to be unique to the Tamil displacement but happens in a global context.

6 It is difficult to ascertain the precise number of schools that were operational during periods of conflict and displacement. However, an overview of the situation just before the ceasefire period reveals that in the Jaffna district alone only some 85 out of 402 schools were functioning. It has been noted by a World Bank official that there were 128,000 students in Jaffna, with only 862 teachers (Sri-Jayantha 2002: 5–6).

7 'The letter of this agreement has been followed in the main, yet in many cases the camps have been moved directly adjacent to the schools, so intimidation still occurs' (Sri-Jayantha 2002: 5).

8 Only children under the age of eight are considered incapable of possessing *mens rea* (the 'Lectric Law Library).

9 The seven countries are: Afghanistan, Iran, Lao Peoples Democratic Republic, Mexico, Namibia, Nicaragua and South Africa. Those who accept volunteers from under 17 with parental consent included many Western States including the United States and the United Kingdom. However, it is difficult to know precisely which of the revolutionary groups started the recruitment of children to its ranks.

10 Child Soldiers Global Report (2001: 34), Coalition to Stop the Use of Child Soldiers, cited in Human Watch Report November (2004: 5).

11 Human Rights Watch: 14 January 2005, Refugees International: 21 March 2005, BBC News: 13 January 2005.

12 Each household was ordered to give one child to the cause. These instances have been detailed in Human Rights Watch, Amnesty and UNICEF documents (various dates).

13 That said, I do recognise that international law has explicitly prohibited the use of children under the age of 18 from being recruited into armed revolutionary groups and partaking in hostile activities. I also acknowledge that under the same law (since 1998) it is a war crime to recruit children under the age of 15 years (see <www.humanrightswatch.org> or UN Document A/CONF.183/2/Add.1 for fuller details).

14 Afshar (2004: 53) states in relation to mothers of Iranian child combatants who died in battle, women who had many martyred sons were offered pensions for their achievements, given prizes, hauled up at Friday prayers and praised for offering their sons to the war and helping them achieve martyrdom.

15 Cairns (1996: 125) observes this to be an indirect way of parents politicising the children: 'This is of course not to suggest that parents necessarily give direct political instructions to their children. Instead, what probably happens is that children overhear parental conversations or that they informally learn of their parents' political views. Also, parents are required to answer questions about politics just as they are asked to answer a thousand and one other questions as children grow up'.

16 This is an agreed view amongst psychologist and child care workers who worked amongst Palestinian displaced children (Goodwin-Gill and Cohen 1997: 41).

4 The Tiger Family

Kin Identity amongst Women Combatants of the LTTE

As discussed in the previous chapter, the family unit and its loyalties were tested to the full under conditions of war. The effects of displacement created instability for some women and left many of them with no alternative but to break away from their culturally defined roles of womanhood. Such acts can be seen as attempts at re-establishing an individual's sense of lost agency and a need to be in an environment where they feel they have some control. In order to feel a sense of empowerment, some women had actively sought out and joined the LTTE movement, which embraced them as a part of a substitute family unit.

The definition of kinship according to the *Concise Oxford Dictionary* (2009) is a 'blood relationship; similarity or alliance in character'. Within the anthropologically defined social understanding of kinship, the term breaks down to describe three forms: a strong bond created within the 'consanguine' (blood-related) social groups; the 'affinal' kinships that extend to include familial ties made through marriages to non-consanguine others in the society; and finally, 'fictive' kinships that include those who are attached to a family unit but are neither connected through blood line nor marriage. Kinship terminology in this chapter is used in reference to the Tamil culture to describe the relationships that traditionally exist in a consanguine family. In this chapter, I have to a greater an extent, taken the word 'kinship' away from its consanguine roots and used it to describe the alternative family unit recreated by the LTTE. This family unit can be described as a fictive family unit founded upon friendships that in turn imitate or replace the kinships of a consanguine family.

The word friendship is defined by the same dictionary as 'being friends, relation between friends; friendly disposition felt or shown'. It also describes the word 'friend' as 'one joined to another in intimacy and mutual benevolence independently of sexual or family love'. In this chapter, fictive kinship is based on the friendship that occurred among the women in the terrorist movement. My argument that friendships form a major part of the fictive kin family will assist when using the words 'kinship' and 'friendship' as analytical tools to explore the use of familial ties that are idealised, built and maintained within the confines of the substituted LTTE family. In this chapter, I look in detail at how the LTTE succeeded in constructing a sustainable fictive kinship through the friendships amongst women combatants who were from various socio-economical, religious and caste backgrounds.

The Concept of Kinship

Schneider (1984) has challenged extant assumptions about the measurement of kinship through consanguine ties, arguing that relationships are practised in socio-cultural groups in his seminal text *A Critique of the Study of Kinship*. Here, he states that biological relatedness is not the sole factor in forming kinships in society. While consanguine ties are an important factor in determining relationships, there are other influences that need to be acknowledged as key considerations in kin relationships, such as socio-cultural influences. However, the literature that addresses the issue of developing friendships as part of solidarity between consanguine kin members is limited (Contarello and Volpato 1991). Many kinship studies were conducted from a primarily Western point of view, focusing on the formation and social interaction of consanguine relationships at a cost of overlooking valuable cultural practices (Schneider 1984; Rezende 1999; Reed-Danahay 1999; Bell and Coleman 1999 and Carsten 2004).[1]

Carsten's research *Heat of the Hearth* (1997) addresses the issues of consanguine and socialisation in kin groups, which she further explores in *Culture of Relatedness* (2000). She argues that cultural practices external to conventional anthropological research must be taken into consideration when trying to understand kin relationships. An awareness of cultural practices may distinguish fictive kinship from the real thing. However, a recognisable change did occur in kinship studies with the rise of feminism, which challenged the way in which kinship was depicted in anthropology, where it was often difficult to separate or identify metaphorical kinship from other forms (Carsten 2004 and O'Conner 1992). An example of this can be seen in the work of White (2004), where women refer to one another using consanguine kin terminology in fictive kin relationships due to economic circumstances, creating a 'webs of indebtedness'. It must also be noted that, amongst the literature on friendship, there is no direct link to kin relationships except under sexual orientation (Carsten 2004).

The focal point of the LTTE's kin relationships appeared to promote metaphorical kinship as a temporary substitute for consanguine kinship. As the women of the LTTE faced many difficulties in their lives, the notion of kinship is significant to the understanding of the relationships that were formed with one another. The success of the LTTE's newly (re)created family, and the security and stability that the LTTE family provides, was very much dependent on the promotion of a fictive kin identity that was devoid of blood ties. This also resonates with the wider literature on 'families we choose' or chosen kinship, as opposed to families based on blood ties or formal marriage (Weston 1991).

Though feminism has changed the way in which Western thinking affects traditional kinship studies, the research conducted amongst combatant women on an international scale is also limited. Within this limited literature the relationships that women combatants have with each other are neither discussed at length nor critically analysed or debated, but have to be inferred as part of the text that discusses the women's involvement in various armed revolutionary struggles. Often these discussions emanate from a strong gender perspective based on changing social roles for women with occasional references to the metaphorical kinships within the individual revolutionary group.[2] This is also reflected among authors who focus on the LTTE and the women's involvement in the organisation but have not delved deeply into the positive development of familial identity encouraged within the movement. The exceptions to this are Balasingham (2003 and writing as Adele Ann) and Schalk (1992), who do discuss to some degree the combatant women's involvement with the LTTE from a perspective of a friendship. These discussions are referred to throughout this chapter.

Kin: The Chosen Family?

When the LTTE created the revolutionary family, it was required to maintain a respectable and socially accepted format, which was achieved in a number of ways. Firstly, the LTTE adhered to the strict moral code expected by both civic society and the women combatants themselves. Although the LTTE enforced the authority and responsibility of a consanguine family, they also provided opportunities for women combatants to (re)negotiate and challenge their gender roles, as discussed in later sections. Secondly, by using linguistic expressions that suggested familial ties, the male and female combatants avoided any sexual connotations that could be misconstrued when addressing one another. This, in turn, introduced a form of respect that was shown by a consanguine family unit through a trusted and familial set of kin terminology. Lastly, the women were given a sense of belonging to a family through both consanguine and non-consanguine ties, along with a sense of loyalty to the family unit, and especially to its patriarchal head of family, Prabhakaran. The LTTE relied on the loyalties of the combatants to a higher degree, as illustrated by the combatant's oath, in which they pledged allegiance not just to the LTTE, but also to Prabhakaran directly. As Arasi reveals, 'The movement has high moral values and is a *very sweet family*.'

The above statement by Arasi is reflective of the view held by combatant women regarding the LTTE and its re-constructed family unit. The high-moral values were often seen as part of the LTTE's strength and granted them a great deal of respect from those in civic society, where women's behaviour was often critically observed. The 'family' that was actively promoted within the LTTE reproduces many of the social values of the broader patriarchal society. The gender-based social controls within civic society, which restrain women's social interaction with men, are seen in an alternative guise that does not necessarily restrict but expect conformity.[3] As Balasingham suggests:

> [t]he LTTE upheld a rigid code of moral conduct amongst the cadres. Premarital separation between the sexes is a well-entrenched cultural norm amongst the conservative section of the Hindu Jaffna society, and Mr Pirabakaran [Prabhakaran] was sensitive to the importance of this sensibility amongst the Tamil people. He demonstrated considerable political acumen by identifying this socio-cultural factor as critical if he was to continue to enjoy the widespread support of the people that the LTTE did at this stage and sustain the recruitment level into the organisation. (Balasingham 2003: 79)

The organisation was aware that women's acceptance into the LTTE family meant that there must be a way to include them along with the men without being criticised by the civic society as morally decadent. This was an important factor, as the LTTE relied heavily upon the support of the civic community not just for its logistical support but also for new recruits. As Arulvili comments, 'Just like the normal women we are also working with men in the movement. We are with them together everyday but we don't think like that. *We think we are all brothers and sisters of one family.*'

A great emphasis was placed on the kinship aspect of the revolutionary family even though the combatant women saw parallels between themselves and the women working in the greater civic community. The emphasis on the kinship aspects worked to allay the fears derived from the social taboos concerning women's close association with men. This also distanced the notional view of women who spent time with men as having a bad character, as pointed out by Balasingham:

> [a]spersions cast on the moral character of women is a death knell to her maintaining or establishing any kind of credible friendships and respect amongst people in the community. Once a woman is labelled as a 'bad' character in the Tamil society she loses her moral authority...[...]... The concept of 'bad' character is loosely used and is broad in its application. The social perimeters around which a woman can operate before she

> is considered as [having a] 'bad' character are indeed narrow by western standards. For example, an unmarried girl seen frequently talking to boys runs the risk of being considered a 'bad' character. Balasingham (2003: 85)

With a strong understanding of how society constructs women's character, the women combatants maintained a familial kin identity and an intimacy that was never displayed publicly other than with a well-trained and completely composed interaction between each other. The very nature of being in a terrorist organisation meant that women combatants needed to be both private and secretive, which in turn formed part of the cultural constellation of friendship in the LTTE.

A closer examination of the family unit revealed that, when women from the civic society joined the LTTE movement, they were, in fact, joining a group of people they had already had some contact with over a period of time and have become friendly with, although they may not be friends. As discussed in Chapter 3, all the women combatants in the research knew a number of active combatants in the LTTE prior to their enrolment. The significance of this information is that, when they leave home and take up residence with the LTTE, they are not considered to be amongst 'complete strangers' but are with known people whom they are already used to calling *Annay* (elder brother) or *Akka* (elder sister). This type of address forms the basis of the LTTE's (re)construction of a non-caste based family unit, which is reflective of a consanguine family unit using familial references.

From a cultural perspective, it is respectful to refer to one another as elder brother, *Annay,* and elder sister, *Akka,* or younger sister, *Thangachchi,* and younger brother, *Thambi.* This usage of kin terminology amongst the combatants encouraged both men and women to overlook, to some degree, the power relations that exist between the sexes by focusing directly on the relationship aspects. (The issue of gender and power relations will be looked at in more depth in Chapter 6). The relationship aspects create levels of authority that an elder sister *(Akka)* would gain over a younger sister *(Thangachchi)* by recreating the natural hierarchy of a family unit. The socio-familial interaction was further discussed by Balasingham upon her first meeting with Prabhakaran in 1979 at Chennai, South India:

> **He was obviously concerned as to how to address me. In Tamil culture the titles Mr. and Mrs. are not generally used to address people. Titles of address are linked to social hierarchy and social and familial relationships. Since our relations were not familial or familiar he couldn't address me as 'akka' (elder sister) and at the same time he couldn't be so formal as to address me as Mrs. Balasingham. Since I was older than he was it would not be culturally correct to address me as an equal by using my Christian name either. 'Thamby' [Prabhakaran's familial name given to mean younger brother] found a solution to his dilemma by christening me with the affectionate compromise and comprehensive title 'Auntie'. Apart from Bala [husband] and one or two others, Tamil people of all ages have come to know and address me as 'Auntie' many, I think, unaware of my real name. Balasingham (2003: 43–44)**

What is particularly interesting in the description given by Balasingham is the fact that the English word *Auntie* in reality makes her an outsider inside the family unit of the organisation. The English words *Auntie* and *Uncle* are generally given to outsiders who are older to denote a mark of respect. As stated by Balasingham, it is not acceptable for younger people to call elders by their given names (forename). The word *Auntie* carries both an external distance and a closer kin identity within a context of friendship that Balasingham is still a part of.

On extremely rare occasions, the familial hierarchy of a younger brother may change to accommodate him as an elder brother based on his merits if they are perceived to go beyond those of a younger person. For instance, Prabhakaran was referred to as *Thamby* during the early stages of the revolutionary struggle when he was based in Chennai. The affectionate form of addressing him as a younger brother changed to a respectful elder brother, *Annay,* with the battle of Elephant Pass, 10 July 1990.[4] Though Prabhakaran lost the battle, he nonetheless proved to the world that he was a formidable combatant and a revolutionary leader of considerable standing.

> **It was a crushing military blow to the LTTE. But Pirabhkaran's [Prabhakaran] spirit was far from crushed by the debacle. It actually blossomed and crystallised into a new persona. Gone was the boyish guerrilla. Instead, there was a man who moved and behaved like the Big Boss ... nobody called him Thambi anymore. Everybody now referred to him as Annai, or elder brother.... (Pratap 2001: 92–93)**

In addition to the created kin terminology practices, Tamil culture views the extended family as part of the greater familial system. This reaches beyond the immediate family of elderly parents and other relatives to those of distant blood relatives, and also to friends and neighbours. Though Balasingham (2003: 47) discusses social relationships and interactions in the daily offering and sharing of food from one household to another, or amongst neighbours and friends, she fails to mention the caste boundaries that operate within Tamil culture, particularly in the Jaffna province. In *A Special Caste? Tamil Women of Sri Lanka*, Skjonsberg (1982) illustrates ways in which the caste system is perpetuated and legitimised by the community itself but appears not to apply in the same way to a non-Tamil national. (Adele) Balasingham, being an Australian, was an outsider; hence the customary practices of caste-related prejudices within the greater Tamil community would not affect her in the same way. Her marriage to Anton Balasingham, the highly respected theoretician of the LTTE, granted her a certain trusted, respected and secure position amongst the combatants and amongst the Tamil civic community in Jaffna. Further, neither was she not looking for an alternative, nor for a substitute family unit, and so was not dependent on cultivating the same level of kin identity as others. Therefore, I would argue that from the very beginning her kin identity with the LTTE revolutionary family was somewhat different, but she was nonetheless tied to the familial relationships of the extended LTTE family.

As the LTTE was founded amongst a small community, having some consanguine kin amongst the combatants was inevitable. For instance, Arasi, Roja and AK all had sisters in the movement, some of whom joined up at the same time as they did. Both CH and Aruna had brothers in the movement. In addition to the immediate family members in the movement, both Roja and Kavitha had cousins enlisted in the movement. Thus, connections within the LTTE organisation included both close consanguine kin members and extended family members.

Knowledge of blood relatives within the organisation was not necessarily disclosed to me until I directly posed the question.

> **Aruna:** My brother joined.
> **Me:** He has joined as well? How old is he?
> **Aruna:** Same age.
> **Arulvili:** [***shouts***] Twins!
> **Me:** Oh really! Identical? Do you look alike?
> **Aruna:** Yes ... yes.
> **Arulvili:** A little bit different. He's got a beard.
> [Laughter][5]

The conversation at that moment appeared to be light-hearted with a close knowledge of one another's family. Allen (1979: 36) claims that being a friend 'involves some degree of personal knowledge and mutual communion', as opposed to being friendly, which Burns (1953) calls 'polite fiction', meaning a polite interaction, which can happen between individuals even with a dislike of one another. I was aware of the usage of the word 'friend' amongst the women combatants, with its primary variable of socio-cultural construction and the secondary variable of nuances. Clear examples of the two variables are seen within the revolutionary group's kin relationship with Adele Balasingham and the titled reference of 'Aunt' (as discussed previously).

Kinship in Friendship

In addition to consanguine relationships, the women combatants often had a large number of peers who had joined the revolutionary organisation. Updegraff et al. (2002) acknowledge that friends in this context offer the same emotional support and intimacy as siblings do in adolescent years, meaning that women who joined at a young age formed their kin relationships with more ease, an instance of which was seen in the relationship between Roja and Mallika. They were approximately of the same age (as discussed previously in Chapter 3) when joining the revolutionary movement and undertook their training together. During periods of training they endured many physical hardships. Once training was completed they went in different directions: Roja becoming part of the ceremonial musical band and Mallika an active front-line combatant. They were reunited during the ceasefire period, when these interviews were being conducted. The relationship identity of the strength of kin relationship was recognised by Reed-Danahay, who observed kin relations:

> ... in peer socialisation, and in the formation of social bonds that persists throughout adulthood, cutting across household ties. Moreover, the strength of peer friendship is connected to the adaptation of the community to social change, in that age–mates provide forms of social support for new adaptations and changes. (Reed-Danahay 1999: 138)

The 'new adaptations and change' discussed by Reed-Danahay (1999) was seen amongst the close bonds built between women combatants. Within the LTTE there was a definitive peer friendship that replaced blood ties. This adolescent familial support was received unconditionally from peers who have had similar life experiences since joining the revolutionary movement.

LTTE in a Parental Role

During the interviews with the combatant women it became apparent that there was a great significance attached to friendship that was understood as part of the acceptance into the LTTE kin family. The individual's personal differences were not held against them as an obstacle but were accepted as part of their personal disclosure of 'true' self. The diverse upbringing may be revealed to chosen friends within the kin family of the LTTE. The similarities identified may be of schooling or home life prior to joining the terrorist organisation.

Kondo (1986) argues that the narratives and the reality in a friendship relationship may vary due to the values and ideals it expresses. She further claims that these ideals are constantly reviewed due to the power they hold in directing an individual's behaviour towards others. Based on this argument, I examined the power relations within the LTTE family and its negotiations, which from the first instance were revealed to be set in a (somewhat) complex format. The relationships were conducted through a set style of familial structure as well as the disciplined hierarchical militaristic structure of the revolutionary organisation. In other words, the LTTE family used both the familial hierarchical powers of an elder sister (or an elder brother) in combination with the militaristic seniority style of senior combatants directing those under their command. Employing both these methods granted them a certain position of power to negotiate both an authoritative kinship along with a (somewhat) complex friendship within the overall relationship. This identified kinship through friendship based on the traditional familial structure, and through the militaristic structure.

However, it must also be recognised that both these relationships (kinship and friendship) were also tied to a highly disciplined structure that superseded all the other relationships within the organisation. The exclusivity of these kinships forms a tighter relationship within the kin group. Also, it must be noted that the exclusion of women combatants from the wider society, both socially as well as physically, make them dependent on one another for safety and well-being, alongside other daily demands during times of war and conflict. Therefore, the kin and friendships were both subordinate to, and a facilitating factor in, the militaristic frame that superseded them.

The younger women combatants who have grown up in the revolutionary group placed an implicit trust in the organisation to attend to their needs justly, in the same way that they might expect a consanguine parent would. This was reflected amongst the women combatants by their view of the organisation as the 'mother': one who will not only protect them but will do their best for the combatant women, which extended to decisions that were made on behalf of the young women combatants, and which encompass their future and welfare.

> **I will work for the political side. But in the movement they know which skills we have and what we are good at. *Just like a mother knows her child is good at something,* they [the LTTE**

> **movement] also know and give us work according to our skills. (Roja)**

In this discourse, Roja had placed the LTTE family in a position of a mother—a person who cared, provided and protected those that were born of her. She also placed herself as a child who depended on all that was given by a mother in order to survive. The familial relationship shown in this instance was a strong bond between a mother and a child. The individualised knowledge akin to that of a parent, generated a belief in Roja that the organisation was able to recognise the skills and qualities that the combatant woman possessed. This belief granted a form of symbolic trust built between the individual combatant woman and the organisation. This trust was a metaphor for the relationship between a mother and child.

The strong parental role was particularly visible amongst the combatants whose kin roots have been in the LTTE-maintained children's homes. My research revealed that the LTTE actively avoided using the word 'orphanage' and insisted on using the word 'home', which reframes the residence as a space where the LTTE representatives take a parental role. This was reflected in the kinship that was formed between Prabhakaran and the children, which was also steeped in the familial structure of a father and sons/daughters.

Prabhakaran regularly visited the two main children's homes, *San Cholai* (beautiful garden filled with trees and flowers), which mainly housed female children, and *Kantha Ruban* (the meaning of *Kantham* is magnetic, and *Ruban* may have been given in memory of a dead combatant closed to Prabhakaran), housing male children. During these visits he developed personal contact with the orphaned children, becoming an alternative father figure to them. Members of the elite squad, *Siruthai Padai* (Leopard Brigade), were mainly recruited from these children's homes.[6] The squad was known for their fierce fighting ability as well as their unwavering loyalty to Prabhakaran; however, there has never been sufficient information to identify if the children were voluntary recruits or were compulsory conscripts. The identity of Prabhakaran as the kin father replacing the biological father had resulted in an enhanced loyalty that reaffirmed the relationship built on the familial kinship developed in childhood. 'Most see him [Prabhakaran] as a father figure and equate a request from him to a directive from heaven' (Gunaratna 2003: 6), meaning that Prabhakaran's non-consanguine paternal role had, in fact, risen to a level of patri-centric veneration of godliness in the eyes of many young combatants. This veneration can be seen as a part of the nationalist patriarchal cosmology of the LTTE. However, it nonetheless illustrates Prabhakaran's close interactions with the young as confirming a systematically-cultivated kin identity.

It must also be noted that, whilst Prabhakaran was actively involved with the children of the LTTE, the rest of his family were not. It was a widely held belief that his wife, Mathivathani (known as Mathy), actively discouraged Prabhakaran's own children from being involved in the movement to such an extent that they opted to reside in an unknown location somewhere in Europe rather than live in the LTTE-controlled parts of Sri Lanka. A change to this long-standing position was made later in 2006, when Charles Anthony became an adult and joined the movement. However, keeping with the tradition of the LTTE, Mathy supported Prabhakaran by naming their eldest son Charles Anthony after his friend who died in battle; his youngest son, Balachandran, was named after Mathy's younger brother who was killed in combat with the Indian army; and his daughter, Dwaraka, was named after one of Mathy's bodyguards who died in battle. This indicates that within Prabhakaran's own family they adopted the same custom that was practised within the LTTE of naming the children after dead combatants as a way to keep the names alive (Balasingham 2003: 89).

Marriages

Initially, romantic relationships were strictly forbidden in the LTTE on the basis that it would be a distraction to achieving the key aims of the revolutionary organisation. As Narayan-Swamy (2002: 66) says, 'When Prabhakaran drew up the LTTE constitution, he had made it very clear that he considered family life [marital] and love affairs as an impediment to revolutionary politics.' These restrictions on marriages between combatants changed with Prabhakaran's own marriage on 1 October 1984, when he fell in love with a Jaffna university student and arranged her kidnap (along with eight other students) in order to prevent her from fasting to death in protest against the government's injustices on education.[7] Prabhakaran's intention to marry caused a considerable ruction within the movement that had up to that point been extremely inflexible in regards to romantic relationships and marriages, especially in reference to the previous bitter separation between Prabhakaran and Uma Maheshwaran (the former Chairman of the LTTE). Adele Balasingham wrote:

> [W]e were never comfortable with the lack of flexibility of the [LTTE] rules in regards to love and marriage as practiced in the LTTE [...] If Mr Pirabakaran [Prabhakaran] had retained his chaste status he would have had to live up to the image of a saint and all the cadres then and now, would have been condemned to emotional sterility and frustration. (Balasingham 2003: 80)

Balasingham's introduction of a human element into Prabhakaran's desire to marry Mathivathani (Mathy) in effect paved the way for a great deal of change within the movement. Interestingly, Anton Balasingham placated the bitter combatants who had renounced their own love interests due to the commitment they had made to the LTTE. Balasingham brought in an argument that the former moral code needed changing in order to keep up with changing times. He further claimed that 'romance and heroism were values upheld in Tamil culture' (Balasingham 2003: 81). He convinced the combatants that this was a positive move needed to improve the image of the movement (ibid.).

> In political terms Mr Pirabakaran's relationship with Mathy was [a] crucial, healthy and progressive element in perceiving [him] as a leader. The Tamil community, which views unmarried people as not fully mature adults, would be more confident in the judgement of a leader who has been mellowed and matured by the profound emotional experience and responsibility of marriage and family life. (Balasingham 2003: 80)

Marriage was seen as having its rightful place in society, and as such those in the LTTE had a set format that they needed to follow in order to achieve this end. Though the rules were changed, granting combatants the right to matrimony, they still contained a prescriptive formula for an accepted minimum age for marriage. For women combatants the minimum age of marriage was 25 years, and for a male combatant it was 30 years. Arulvili explains, 'Once we are over 25, if a man and woman like each other they have no restrictions in getting married.'

There was also a service caveat that required a five-year minimum period of service prior to being considered eligible for marriage. The women combatants informed me that there were dispensations for those who had served less than five years, but the minimum age for marriage was generally upheld, and those who were under 18 years of age and wished to get married were actively discouraged.

The change brought into the LTTE by Prabhakaran's marriage was still based on a system similar to that practised in civic society, with a notable difference of women having a say in the choice of the proposed marital partner. By being able to contribute their own views about whom they wish to marry, the women combatants actively controlled acceptance or rejection of the proposals brought to them. When a man (either from civic society or from the ranks of the LTTE) was interested in marrying a combatant woman, or vice versa, a proposal of marriage was sent to the leader of the woman combatant's unit seeking the woman's views.

> **The boy will approach the [team] leader in charge of the girl. She [woman combatant] will make her own decision. It is not for her [the team leader] to decide whether they should get married or not but when the marriage can take place. She [the team leader] will ask the girl whether she wants to get married to this particular person and if the girl says yes, she will decide on the date etc. The [team] leader will come to the Central Committee and then they decide on the date. (Kavitha)**

The combatant woman had the option to accept or reject the proposal (unlike in civic society) and was not compelled to marry by a certain age or constrained within caste and class. If the combatant woman was unwilling to accept the proposal sent, as Kavitha clarifies, 'Then of course the leader will tell the man I am sorry but the girl is not interested in marrying you.'

Within the LTTE family, the leader of the team acts in place of a consanguine parent who was responsible for the welfare and the future of the women combatants under her care. The Central Committee acted in place of the greater family, which was traditionally involved in the planning of the marriage, and attended to the ceremony.

Combatant women were also allowed to marry men from civic society, as seen with AK. Within the LTTE, romantic relationships and courting rituals are not practised. Pre-marital relationships, especially those of a sexual nature, were strictly forbidden. It must also be recognised that, within the cultural parameters, sex is always seen within a hetero-normative framework, with sexual connections between a man and a woman permitted only after marriage. Any other forms of sexual activity (be they pre-marital or extra-marital sexual liaisons) are unacceptable for women both within civic society and amongst the LTTE.[8] Arasi explains, 'It is the same as how the society treats pre-marital sex, it is the same in the movement.'

As stated in Arasi's discourse, the LTTE movement reflects the moral values of civic society and their cultural expectations when she states that:

> We didn't have any problems regarding sex. Our women's leadership and male and female leadership made sure that we didn't have to face any such problems. Also [we have] very strict moral codes. But we had the permission to love some one and get married. Say, for instance, I love someone and he also loves me then we let the leadership know about it. There are many cases like that. Then they [are] allowed to get married. Oh yes. They are given separate home and monthly allowances. But they can have sexual relationship only after marriage. Before that if they love each other they can talk to each other with the permission of their leaders, they can write to each other but they are barred from going out alone together. (Arasi)

The implication made in Arasi's discourse suggests that women combatants did not have to face any predatory sexual approaches within the movement. She clearly indicated that both men and women in leadership roles were entrusted with ensuring that women combatants were not sexually violated within the movement, and a high-level of sexual morality was preserved (it is also noteworthy that the LTTE was not known for any sexual aggression/violence against any Sinhalese women). The preservation of female sexual morality was, in effect, a mirror of a consanguine family protecting its females in the family unit.

Romantic relationship that developed between man and woman continued under the watchful eyes of the leaders, who granted permission for the couple to communicate with one another. It was interesting to note that, though the combatants were trained extensively in codes of conduct which included modes of behaviour and were sent on missions together (unchaperoned by the leaders), the leadership would not allow a female and a male combatant to meet each other if they were romantically linked. The restriction on male and female association has intrigued many authors, playwrights, novelists and academics alike.[9] According to Coomaraswamy (1996: 10), the lack of freedom to associate with each other is due to 'sexuality [being] seen [within the LTTE] as an evil debilitating force'.

Within the LTTE, the combatants who were engaged in pre-marital relationships were expected to behave in the same way as they would in civic society. The women combatants were upheld for their sexual morality and overall good behaviour in regards to the opposite sex. According to Arasi, 'We feel that person who is morally good only can be a brave fighter … [a] good fighter … [a] good leader … [and a] good cadre.'

By linking fighting abilities with moral conduct, the LTTE reinforced society's dominant view of patriarchal control over feminine virtue and modesty, along with their own view of moral conduct being linked to ability to perform as a fighter. I would argue that this was also reflective of the way in which gender was constructed within the LTTE. Its roots were deeply embedded in a patriarchy that conflicts morality and physical virtue with ability to perform, all neatly packaged as Armed Virgins who had risen above social decadence.

Many of the women combatants did not see a need for marriage and socially accepted normalcy of family life. This was often against the wishes of the biological parents but not the wishes of the LTTE. Unlike women in civic society, the combatant women were neither frowned upon nor penalised within the LTTE for being unmarried, even if they were of mature age. Interestingly, this reveals both a replication of patriarchal views of civic society and a questioning of those same ideologies and norms.

The women combatants who harboured views different to those of their consanguine family (with regards to marriage), mediate these expectations by positioning themselves as children. This was highlighted by Arulvili, who stated, 'we are the children', meaning that they were too young to be considered for marriage and thus had no need to be in a matrimonial relationship. They were unanimous in saying:

> **Arulvili:** We don't like it [marriage]. We don't need to have boy friends. We don't need....
>
> **Yalini:** We don't need to have a boy friend. But they [female combatants] don't like to [get married]....In our movement they [female combatant] don't like to get married before 25. We don't like (laughs).
>
> **Arulvili:** We joined young and our mind is still like small children. We are the same now as the time we joined the movement. We are quite happy at the moment, so we don't have the desire to be married.

Close social interactions between the sexes were frowned upon by the civic society. Though the LTTE may not take into consideration all of civic society's moralistic views, they nonetheless needed to rely on the support given by the civic society, especially on the issue of sexual morals. It can be argued that the creation of the 'Armed Virgin' with her pure sexual morals did feed into this mindset. Therefore, justification for the 'dislike' of marriage given by Arulvili, as in 'we like our work', and the lack of a 'need' for a boyfriend, needs to be seen in the context of the environment in which they lived. Female combatants lived in separate compounds to male combatants, with little interaction between the two sexes except during certain types of training or in the battlefield. Social interaction was virtually non-existent. That is not to say that they did not speak to each other outside of field conditions, but that there was a definite lack of male–female social interaction. This was viewed as part of the discipline that was coveted in the organisation and the civic society.

The separation of the sexes effectively preserved the sexual morality of the women combatants within the confines of the LTTE movement but overlooked the possibility of same-sex relationships forming. An individual woman combatant's sexuality away from the hetero-normative understanding of sex and sexuality was a taboo topic that was not discussed with the combatant women. Whilst reflecting on the individual combatant woman's sexuality, I became aware of the stringent nature of morality linked to homosexual interactions as viewed by the society in general and the LTTE in particular. It must also be understood that the society (regardless of ethnicity or religious persuasion) not only abhors same sex sexual-relationships, it is viewed as a criminal offence under Sri Lankan Penal Code 365A.[10] It is interesting to note that, whilst the LTTE did not prevent women from moving away from their traditionally constrictive gender class/caste roles, they did not condone any aspect of sexual liberation. As stated previously, the LTTE relied heavily on civic society's support and was unwilling to isolate themselves over the valued issue of sexual morality.

The complex nature of same-sex interaction is highlighted when society is observed as a whole, where single sex friendships of women (and men) tend to be very tactile. This is often seen by the very close physical proximity in which women conduct their interactions with each other as well as holding hands with other women in public places. This form of behaviour is perfectly acceptable in a society where women's sexual morality is regularly scrutinised and criticised. It must also be noted that a woman keeping company with another woman is far more socially acceptable than a woman keeping company with a man. As sexual morality is held in high esteem for both men and women, I am unable to confirm or deny with any certainty whether the strict claims of sexual morality and chasteness as depicted by women combatants in fact were a true indication of their sexuality.

However, when discussing (hetero-normative) marriage, it became evident that the combatant women saw marriage in a way different to that of the civic women I interviewed. This difference can be seen in two main ways: first, as the combatant women questioning patriarchy; and second, seeing male partners as equals, and thus, expecting domestic chores and responsibilities to be shared equally with a male partner. According to Yalini, 'After they get married ... men and women are both doing their housework they take turns.'

The equality of sexes within the domestic sphere is quite a novel idea within the Tamil culture, where there are clearly defined boundaries between men and women regarding their roles both within the house as well as away from it. Men do no laundry, cooking, cleaning or childcare, which are strictly the duties of women. The women combatants, however, saw their male counterparts in a different light to men of civic society. As Arulvili clarifies, 'Our cadres are different. Our cadres do the sweeping and all other work ... cooking, sweeping.' Yalini also voices the same as she says, 'Our cadres are unique ... LTTE men are all the same. They won't expect us to do all house work. They are also prepared to do anything....They can cook.'

The gender implication raised in Yalini's statement positions both male and female combatants firmly within the LTTE's own gender construction. It is interesting to see that women combatants saw the male combatants as progressive in comparison with men of civic society. The male combatants were viewed as 'unique' and 'prepared to do anything', meaning any domestic chores that have historically been in a female domain. The combatant women's comments give a clear indication of male combatants being comfortable with a masculinity that required no boasting or approval from the society and embraced a moderate social role that was quite alien to Tamil culture. This kind of alternative masculinity within the LTTE may be a direct result of the familial structure that was cultivated within the LTTE, where hyper-masculinity was not visible within its overall gender construction or through a militarist context where the discipline of combatants was partly enforced due to sex segregation and the regulation of everyday tasks.

The female combatant's view of male combatants being more suitable marital partners was not reciprocated by male combatants. Stack-O'Conner (2007: 51) claims that in 2006 there appears to have been a preference amongst the LTTE male combatants to marry women from the civic community, who were more 'traditional' over those within the LTTE family. The reason given by male combatants for this preference was the stark division between combatant women and civic women's conduct and expectations. As I discuss in Chapter 6, combatant women had been separated from the women of civic society by being able to do anything that a man can do, in effect removing themselves from the matrimonial eligibility criteria by being independent of male assistance. Added to this, the interviews revealed that the women combatants did not view marriage as the life-changing experience that many of the women who remained in civic society did. If marriage was to happen, it was accepted in a very pragmatic way, but not as a means of distancing one's self from the movement. This is clear when Arulvili remarks, 'Even after getting married the women cadres carry on working. Not change....' And then Yalini complements and says, 'After the LTTE women cadres get married they also doing their work within the LTTE movement as normal.'

The commitment made to the LTTE can continue after marriage, as seen in AK's narrative; she only considered marriage to a civic man on the condition that he would not interfere with her work in the movement. AK was discharged from the LTTE at the time of her marriage (due to injuries received in combat) and moved back to living in the civic community, but she continued to work in LTTE-related areas. It must be noted that this is in direct contrast with civic society, in which a married woman is expected to be totally committed to her husband's family since she is seen as belonging to her husband's household, and not her parents'. The combatant women do not necessarily hold this view, as their fictive kin relationships and responsibilities to the LTTE must be able to co-exist with the marital relationship. The active combatants who decided to marry one another were provided with housing by the LTTE. Married combatants with children were given an option to opt out of battle engagements. If parents do decide to engage in battle activities, there was a choice to leave the children either with the maternal or paternal side of the family. There was also a care home in the Puthukuddyiruppu area that was provided by the LTTE for the children to stay in until their parents returned from war. In the event that both parents die in battle, care would be provided by the grandparents or other family members. If there was no one to provide such care, the LTTE steps in as an alternative family, making provision for the children to be housed with them in one of the LTTE's own children's homes and continuing to provide a familial structure based on kinship as discussed throughout this chapter.

Kinship and the Nation State

The LTTE's use of kinship was reflected in the narratives that were extended to link kinship, the individual and the nation state. The women in the revolutionary group invoked a metaphor of family and kinship that was tied to the nation state. Arasi expanded on this use of kinship linked to nation state by defining the symbolic role of the protective mother in the guise of a hen rising to protect her helpless chicks (the Tamil civic citizens) from being attacked by a mighty Hawk (the State-run armed forces):

> I will give you an example. In our homes we all have poultry. The mother hen looks after her chicks with love and care. When you look at the mother hen she looks gentle, soft and very loving. But if a hawk comes down to catch one of the chicks, the mother hen will immediately jump up and fight with the hawk to protect her chicks. So the strength she gets to fight with the hawk comes from her gentleness and her motherhood. We love our community and we want to protect them because we felt the responsibility to protect our community we had to become fighters. (Arasi)

The first reading of the above discourse revealed a narrative that was straightforward, discussing the weak rising against the strong regardless of their inabilities, incapability or inadequacy. However, underneath the veneer of strength and weakness lies a whole plethora of kin and nation state complexities which were mixed with female roles in society based on theories of biological essentialism that required women to be 'givers'. The 'givers' were seen in multiple roles as givers of life and givers of self, always rising above their own needs to provide for others. It also portrayed women as mothers who were seen as the 'good women' in society and expected to harbour a maternal instinct that had a 'need' to protect others (Enloe 1993; Yuval-Davis 2000; Narayan 1997 and Puri 1999). The 'others' in this instance were seen to be kin relations based on an understanding of the ethno-national Tamil nation state and its collective identity. It also reveals an awareness on Arasi's part of the combatant women's role of being the protectors of the Tamil community, and through this a stronger part of the nation-kin group. The narrative further addressed the combatant women's own awareness of the 'difference' in kin ideology between the greater Tamil community and the combatant women. This particular aspect will be discussed at length in Chapter 6.

The awareness by women combatants of their differences with women of civic community was the result of combatant women having stepped out of the consanguine family that forms part of the community, that Arasi claims to 'feel' a responsibility to protect. In order to protect the civic community she had to step out of one community (civic) into the other (LTTE) community. With this transition, she in effect moved from one family to another, but never stepped away from the family structure *per se*.

The idea of the nation as part of the kin group is claimed by Ryang (2004: 763) to be an aspect of war when morality of the nation as family emerges as a dominant ideology. She further argues that the non-consanguine familial identification is achieved through the usage of language such as 'our sons and daughters' (2004: 763), which in Arasi's discourse was highlighted as the 'protective mother'. By such references, those who have gone to war as part of ethno-nationalistic bidding become metaphorical mothers, fathers, sons and daughters as directed in kinship, making linguistic expression important in constructing the alternative family unit.

The 'fictive kin' concept as discussed in anthropology describes non-consanguine or non-affinal individuals treated as members of one family. The ethno-nationalism related to kin identity has the same ability to create a fictive kin identity amongst a whole community without any kind of blood ties, illustrating that within the nation state the kin identity of individual combatants blends with that of the civic society during periods of social unrest and mass protests. This was particularly visible during the hunger strikes carried out by LTTE combatants and their sympathisers. On such occasions, a kin identity develops on a non-consanguine basis which identifies the individual as part of a blood-related family.

> **In 1987 Thileepan Anna [elder brother] had a hunger strike, but the Indian government or Sri Lankan forces [did nothing]....And in 1980 one Amma [mother] had a hunger strike for a month. She died. They [government] did nothing. Almost everyday the cadres attained martyrdom everyday during the battle. (Yalini)**

The very identification of Thileepan as *Annay* (a brother) and the elderly woman Poopathy as *Amma* (a mother) illustrated a kin identity with those of civic status who are joined together by a single cause.[11] This narrative clearly identified the martyred dead as members of the same non-consanguine family through the use of familial kin terminology. The shared cause and related identity lays the culpability for their deaths with the state and also absolves the LTTE of their responsibility in supporting an act of this kind solely to gain attention from the wider public.

The sense of injustice that was felt by the wider society in turn becomes a stronger and more forceful part of the ethno-national consanguine identity, leading to the development of a notional fictive kin (in this instance, civic citizenship). This in turn has the potential to move towards a greater nation state based on kin identity. The wider concept of such kin identity runs parallel to the sociocultural ways of addressing those who are respected in the community as dictated by age and caste.

Summary

One of the catalytic aspects of displacement was the breakdown of the consanguine family structure causing women to actively seek alternatives away from home where they may feel safe and secure and be part of a family. With the limited options open to women, they often ended up with the LTTE, which had re-constructed a form of metaphoric or fictive family unit that was both culturally and socially integrated with the ideologies of the Tamil society with its attendant hierarchical familial relationship structure. The LTTE's use of the metaphoric family facilitated the building of strong interrelationships that can be used to serve the aims and objectives of the revolutionary organisation. It also maintained the socially accepted moral values as part of its own discipline procedure, causing the familial structure created within the organisation to be further in line with the civic society.

The interview discourse also revealed that the friendships formed amongst women revolutionaries were different to other forms of friendship. In the LTTE, warm and fluid friendship was often illustrated through kinship terminology. I would urge that Western notions and understanding of kinships must not be used to measure friendship in a non-Western cultural setting such as the extent of the LTTE women combatants' relationships with one another. The subtle ways used by women combatants to describe their own roles or their relationships with fellow combatants (including Prabhakaran) from an ambiguous yet identifiable process of social distinction was very much based on the culturally accepted family structure. Within this structure there was a great deal of respect given to fellow combatants who were identified as elders within the group.

The kinship provided by the substituted family feeds a need and fills the void that had been left open by the absence of a consanguine family. The consanguine families are unarguably patriarchal in Tamil society. The LTTE created a fine line between the civic society's expectations of a family and the LTTE family provided to the combatants. There was a degree of replication of a patriarchal family unit, with its morality and behavioural codes but without the rigidity that was seen in the gender divisions in consanguine families. Prabhakaran had been actively involved in the (re)creation of that familial unit by his personal involvement in the LTTE's children's homes, where he was seen very much as a father figure. He had further developed fictive kinships by naming his own children after those who were close to him who had died in battle. This practice served the purpose of keeping the names and memories alive to venerate friendships that were built within the LTTE's kin family. Similarly, the combatant women showed the same kind of respect for their dead comrades, which can be likened to that shown to dead family members (as discussed in detail in Chapter 5).

The combatant women's marriages within the LTTE can be seen as perpetuating the values of a society that dictated all women be married at a given age and become mothers. The fact that the women combatants did not see any need for marriage can, however, be argued as their own way of reconstructing an alternative gendered role within the organisation that challenged the socially dictated roles for women, which included marriage. The combatant women have stated an apparent lack of need for marriage and the companionship a marital union offered, which could be seen as a direct result of their strong friendship ties within the kin group.

The non-consanguine uniqueness of the relationships was particularly reflective within the fictive kinship formation amongst women combatants who have adopted a friendship-based kinship that was a replacement or mirror to the familial structure in civic society. It is imperative to understand that the metaphorical kin relationships that were formed between the women combatants of the LTTE were deep and significant. As such, these relationships were a result of not only a shared commitment to the political cause, but also extended to include socially formed kin relationships with the wider community.

The kinship in the LTTE discussed in this chapter critiques the use of fictive kin relationships to rise above social barriers such as caste, class and religion, and has pushed combatant women into accepting one another. I would argue that the success of the LTTE's revolutionary family had been in its ability to transcend the basic social prejudices that had been engrained in Jaffna society for generations. I would further argue that the kin relationships created within the LTTE cultivated loyalty and trust amongst individuals regardless of the similarities or differences in their personal circumstances. It was also an affirmation of relationships conducted in private spaces of public arenas within the terrorist group. The strength in fictive kinship formed a foundation that reaffirms combatant women's shared experiences. Such affinities translate into being valued and placed in a familial position within the kinship group.

Notes

1 Also see Collier and Yanagisako (1992).

2 Taillion (1999) and Ward (1983 and 2001) both wrote about women revolutionaries in the Irish struggle in the 1900s. Hillyar and McDermot (2000) focused on women revolutionaries in Russia during 1870–1917. Kampwirth (2002) wrote about women guerrilla fighters in South America. Young (2001) and Young (1998) concentrated on women's involvement in the Chinese Cultural Revolution, including women's active participation in the Long March. Wilson (1991) wrote about the women fighters in the Eritrean conflict. Eisen-Bergman (1975) and Turner and Hao (1998) discuss the role of women combatants in the Vietnam War.

3 When the LTTE have celebrations it is noticeable that there is no male /female mixed dancing. The men dance in their own group and women within their own group.

4 The Elephant Pass battle was of great significance as a vast number of combatants were killed in a short period of three weeks. It is estimated that over 600 LTTE combatants died in this battle—a large number by comparison with the 800 combatants who died in a period of two and half years battle with the IPKF (Pratap 2001: 90–92).

5 This was a group interview conducted with Yalini acting as the main interpreter as well as a participant. However both Kavitha and Aruna were able to understand some English and give some responses in English without the assistance of Yalini. This particular piece relates to such an occasion.

6 *Siruthai* is pronounced as *si-ru-thai*, meaning leopard; *Padai* means brigade. See Gunaratna (2003) and Bandara (2002: 547).

7 Prabhakaran kidnapped her and eight others who were fasting, stating that fasting and other peaceful methods of protest are long over. The kidnapped students were taken to Tamil Nadu, and the four girls of the group were kept at Balasingham's residence, the LTTE women's wing during its early stage of creation.

8 Conversation with Tamil nationals in Sri Lanka and in London reveal that the men in civic society have some sexual freedom that does not involve homosexuality or freedom to engage in such activities. The kind of sexual freedom I mention here may be limited to visiting brothels. However, this is not publicised. Furthermore, brothels in town were closed during the period of the LTTE control in Jaffna. The interview participants (both combatant and civic) informed me that in the LTTE the male combatants are tied to the same sexual and moral code of conduct as the women combatants.

9 The Play *Forbidden Area* (2000); films *Kalu Sudu Mal* (2005) and *The Terrorist* (2001).

10 Section 365A of the Sri Lankan Penal Code prohibits homosexual relationships and carries a maximum penalty of 10 years of imprisonment. It must also be noted that the law is directly aimed at male homosexuality rather than lesbianism. However, attempts were made in 1995 to include lesbianism into homosexual laws. It is also

noteworthy that no prosecution has been attempted for homosexuality in the past 50 years. See WSG (2002).

11 Thileepan was a male combatant of the LTTE in charge of the male political wing in Jaffna during the 1980s. He began a fast unto death on 15 August 1987 at the Nallur Kandaswamy temple in Jaffna. He refused food and water until his demands of withdrawing the Sinhalese army camps and Sinhalese government colonisation of Tamil areas, etc., were met. Thileepan died on 26 August 1987. Kanapathipillai Poopathy was a 56-year-old grandmother, a civic citizen, who fasted for 30 days before dying on 19 April 1988. It is believed amongst Tamil nationals that she was the first woman to have died for a political cause by fasting unto death. She conducted her fast at Mahmangam Pillayar Temple (Balasingham 1988).

5 Death and the Suicide Bomber

On 21 May 1991, at Sriperumbudur Stadium in Tamil Nadu (southern India) an LTTE combatant woman, Dhanu (real name Thenmuli Rajaratnam), placed a garland of flowers around former Indian Prime Minister, Rajiv Gandhi's neck and bent down to touch his feet as a cultural mark of respect. As she bent down, she pressed a button on her vest, which was packed with explosives carefully concealed under her dress. The subsequent explosion killed 16 people who were nearby, along with Dhanu and Rajiv Gandhi.

Whilst the precise circumstances were not known, culpability for the act was directed at the LTTE movement. Knowing the inevitable political backlash, the LTTE swiftly issued a statement denying any involvement in the attack[1] and claimed that Dhanu was, in fact, a victim of rape committed by the IPKF,[2] who were based in Jaffna from 1987 to1990. Whilst many ambiguities remain over Dhanu's motives, the LTTE stated that she carried out this act to avenge her loss of sexual purity (de Mel 2001; Schalk 1992; Narayan-Swamy 2003 and Knight 2005).

An analysis of Dhanu's act reveals a number of politicised issues ranging from body politics to the nationalist nation state. In the eyes of most combatant women, Dhanu's act had elevated her to an equal status with male combatants. Her actions crossed over gender polarisation into the realms of significant political activism by targeting the key player in the ill-fated Indo–Lanka Peace Accord. This can be seen as redressing the violation of her own and other women's bodies, and of her country. The symbolic nature of Dhanu taking her socio-culturally viewed, polluted body and engulfing it in fire feeds into her cultural upbringing, which views immolation as purifying. Dhanu's subsequent suicide mission can be interpreted as an act of redemption for the trauma and the culturally perceived shame she suffered (de Mel 2001: 220; Maunaguru 1995: 171 and Herath 2006b).

> **The woman killing her oppressor using her polluted body as a weapon symbolically performs the above two functions [taking revenge against the perpetrator and self purification]. In other words, by killing Rajiv Gandhi, she not only takes revenge against the enemy, but also performs an ancient purification ritual—the *agnipravesam* (immolation by fire). (Maunaguru 1995: 171)**

Other combatant women viewed Dhanu's suicide as a brave act of revenge, and regarded her as a goddess who will protect the living. Whilst I do not glorify Dhanu's actions, she can be recognised for being successful in assassinating the perpetrator (albeit not the individual directly responsible). She attained purification by fire and pushed the cause of Tamil *Eelam* to the forefront of the world's media. In so doing, she challenged the fundamental social construction of gender in relation to Tamil women. If her action was indeed revenge for the violation of sexual purity, it can be questioned whether this was an emancipatory act of the way in which the female gender role was constructed in Tamil society, as discussed in Chapter 1.

In this chapter, I put forward the argument that suicide bombing by the LTTE combatant women has to be understood as part of a rational strategy on the part of the LTTE and, in the case of the individual woman suicide bomber, an example of what Durkheim (1952) calls 'obligatory altruistic suicide'. I also suggest that suicide bombing contributes to the development of gender equality within the LTTE. In developing this argument, I start with an overview of women's suicide bombing in the LTTE. I explore the gendered dimensions influencing combatant women's social roles, and the possible motivational forces behind their participation in suicide bombings, including the impact of loss of sexual purity.

The last section focuses on the way the LTTE has constructed death as a form of reverence and presented this to both the civic society and to those within the movement, excluding religious variations and existing social perceptions. It further analyses the involvement of women as suicide bombers from the LTTE's perspective. It addresses issues that arise from women's participation in suicide bombings, including the changing perceptions of gender polarisation in the civic society and the way that suicide bombing was used by the LTTE as an argument for the existence of gender equality. I also discuss the creation of the elite Black Tiger squad, which recruited both men and women, and propose that this was seen as a further example of gender equality within the movement.

An Overview of Women as Suicide Bombers

A modern historical perspective reveals that the first woman suicide bomber was a 16-year-old Lebanese woman from the Syrian Socialist Nationalist Party (SSNP) in Lebanon named Sana'a Youssef Mhayadaliin 1985.[3] Her involvement was seen as part of then President of Syria Hafez al-Assa's attempt to 'secularise' the act of suicide bombing and gather support from the non-religious sector in his community (Victor 2004: 17). Since then there have been a number of incidents involving women suicide bombers around the world. Many of the women suicide bombers were labelled in gendered terms. 'The Army of Roses' (Palestine) depicts the beauty of a flower; 'the Black Widows' (Chechnya), named after a deadly spider (so named due to their wearing black clothes and some being widows); and the 'Armed Virgins' (LTTE), who represent moral virtues based on an assumption of sexual purity.[4]

An essentialist understanding of women as nurturers allow women suicide bombers a certain freedom to be a successful phenomenon in terrorist groups, and in particular the LTTE. The combatant women of the LTTE have been at the forefront of change by their active involvement in suicide missions since the early 1990s. The analysis of suicide missions by their very nature reveals an act that was differentiated from other forms of violence, where the focus was changed from an act-based event to one of an actor-based event. Such acts also create some deeper psychological issues by having to witness the destruction and loss of life. It gives a sense of both fear and helplessness, creating a highly useful weapon of psychological warfare that can touch the populace as a whole (Bloom 2005: 3 and Sri Kantha 2004: 5).

Androcentric beliefs in society have granted the success of women as suicide bombers primarily due to the gendered nature of social perceptions of women. This view, combined with an essentialist view of women being incapable of violence, creates a new kind of dynamism that adds to women's participation in suicide bombings. The use of women as suicide bombers had led to a paradigm shift that moved combatant women beyond the biological realms of essentialism focused on gender identity (based on physical/emotional abilities) to an alternative identity that challenged the androcentric nature of the patriarchal culture and its perceptions.[5]

The gendered perception that discriminates against women's abilities, as stated above, allowed a suicide bomber disguised as a pregnant woman to gain access to a military hospital within the army headquarters in Sri Lanka in April 2006. She carried out a suicide mission that killed her and many civilian bystanders, seriously injuring the target, a senior military commander of the Sri Lankan army. At the time of the attack there were conflicting reports as to the authenticity of the pregnancy.[6] The subsequent claim that the woman was in fact not pregnant has nonetheless challenged the cultural view of motherhood as a role created by nature to protect one's own child/children. That this has been viewed by the Sri Lankan society as a violation of the social reverence for motherhood; it must also be acknowledged that in global terrorism, this is a tried and tested method of gaining access to hard-to-reach targets. The Baader Meinhoff group in Germany was known to have used this method very successfully in the 1970s.[7] Therefore, the use of pregnancy and motherhood as disguise and subterfuge was neither new nor innovative, though the fact that such acts shatter the idealism of society makes them harder to accept.

Another issue pertaining to suicide bombers was their ability to leave the boundaries established by war zones where citizens actively take up arms and enter those areas where civic citizens have little or no involvement in the political violence. The fact that some citizens lived away from war zones was not accepted by many combatants to mean that they were innocent bystanders. I have been informed in conversation by both combatant and civic women that often those who do not condone political violence, living in cities away from war and destruction may inadvertently support the stance taken by the State simply due to their passive acquiescence.[8]

The LTTE is the first terrorist group to use large numbers of women as suicide bombers, and the only group so far to have carried out suicide missions away from its home soil by engaging a woman as a suicide bomber. Women suicide bombers were involved in a number of high profile assassinations such as the death of Rajiv Gandhi, several cabinet ministers, some high-ranking armed force officials and the failed attempt on President Kumaratunga's life.[9]

The single act committed by Dhanu invariably raised the awareness of the LTTE on a global scale, and the usage of a woman as a suicide bomber attracted and retained much of the world's attention. However, the extent of the literature that concentrates on women as suicide bombers is considerably less than that which focuses on male suicide bombers. The gender-blindness in literature relating to combatant women becomes noticeably narrow when considering the combatant women of the LTTE.

It must be understood that within the confines of the act there was a belief held by the suicide bombers that they were saving the Tamil nation through suicide bombing. Therefore, the violence committed in this extreme form was viewed by some civic citizens as well as combatants as an act of heroism. This emerged through the informal discussions with some of the participants—civic women, the Gatekeeper and combatant women themselves. However, a cautionary note highlighting that not all in civic society support or condone the violence associated with suicide bombings must be made.

Sexual Purity as a Motivation

Mirroring other ethno-national violent conflicts globally, the rapes committed on women in Jaffna carry a dimension of ethnic violation because women's bodies and their virtue are used to symbolise the Tamil nation's honour. Sexual violation provides a high level of motivation in gendered societies where female sexual purity forms part of the individual's as well as the family's honour.

> **The rape of Tamil women should not be considered as an expression of mere racism or sexual frustration. The basic aim of this is to humiliate in the most shameful manner the moral code of Tamil culture. The Tamil culture considers values such as purity and chastity as sacred. Hence, these rapes are planned assaults on the Tamil cultural values and moral codes.[10] (Balasingham 1984: 34)**

The highly gendered Sri Lankan public has accepted that women who commit acts of suicide bombings are often victims of rape and other forms of sexual violence. This public view gives rise to a false reality based on cultural perceptions of women that precludes them from committing such extreme forms of violence without having first endured personal violence.[11]

In Jaffna's patriarchal society, women's sexuality and reproductivity is held in high esteem. Virginity is linked to chastity, which defines a woman's virtue and morality, and is seen though a spectrum of nation's honour.[12] The loss of a woman's virginity due to violent sexual acts committed during conflict is emotionally and physiologically damaging, and becomes part of the gendered discourse. Such civic women become socially stigmatised as polluted beings that do not deserve care and respect. The future life options these civic women become limited to either living in the community as outcasts with little or no civic status, or joining the revolutionary movement, where women's gender construction is based on sexual purity in particular did not form part of their contribution to the armed struggle, or importantly, to women's perceived worth.[13]

Women's groups who challenged society's gender polarisation and androcentrism during the 1980s in Jaffna had to confront the discourse of rape, arguing that it did not reflect the way in which rape was perceived in the Tamil community. They discussed the cultural concept of female purity and chastity linked to virginity, the socio-patriarchal interest that underlies female sexual behaviour, and the social stigma (based on a patriarchal view of women) that apportions blame and encompasses the rejection of rape victims. The women's groups discarded the Tamil word *katpalippu*, meaning 'the abolition of chastity', which feeds into the notion of female purity, and introduced words such as *paladkaram*, meaning an act committed by force, and *paliyalvanmurai*, meaning sexual violence. The introduction of these words did not conform to the traditional view of purity and forced society to contextualise rape as a forceful and violent act committed against an individual's wishes (Maunaguru 1995).[14]

Interestingly the LTTE held an ambivalent position on the issue of rape victims. The cultural roots of the LTTE, as with civic society, were embedded in patriarchy and advocated sexual purity for its combatant women, who were known as Armed Virgins. However, they actively distanced themselves from the social perceptions of measuring a woman's worth by her sexual purity. Those in the LTTE movement recognised that those who were sexually violated received little or no support in the community, and they stepped into this void left by the community. The LTTE's advocacy of virginity and sexual purity was ostensibly contradicted by the acceptance of civic rape victims, thus disregarding the view that such women were polluted or social outcasts. These civilian women were accepted into the fold without any stigma being attached to them.[15]

This organisational non-judgemental view, along with the support and consideration of the LTTE, created a strong loyalty in the combatant women. The women who joined the terrorist organisations due to a loss of sexual purity developed a newly created sense of strength, both emotionally and physically. Part of their reconstructed identity within the movement was the ambivalent compartmentalisation of women as combatants who care for their community and sought to avenge their bodily violation. 'Acting as human bombs is an understood and accepted offering for a woman who will never be a mother' (Cutter 1998 cited in Beyler 2003: 16). The revenge aspect was nurtured separately by encouraging combatant women to feel hatred towards their aggressor with a heightened need for self-purification (Ramachandran 2005: 169).

As sexually violated women, they can achieve purification of a kind by first and foremost being strong in mind and body, and by dispelling any weaknesses associated with the socially constructed female roles by performing what was seen in traditional Tamil culture as self-immolation, *agnipravesam*.[16] By engaging in the cultural belief of purification by fire, the combatant women were treading a fine line between the traditional role, which requires purification by self-immolation, and modernity, where a shift in paradigm illustrates combatant women achieving a different kind of equality through being suicide bombers, as well as the recognition that comes with carrying out a successful mission.

The collective silence of the LTTE preserves a woman's honour and virginity. However, there was an instrumentalised manipulation of the very same silence when the revolutionary group was forced to justify individual actions of suicide bombing by claiming it as revenge for sexual violation. This manipulation of sexual violence was presented to the world as an individual avenging their own and collective violation, adding to the ambiguous roles of women within the revolutionary organisation. It is incorrect to assume that all women who were raped ended up as combatants or that all suicide bombers were victims of rape. A substantial number of young women have committed suicide, and there are an unknown number of women who do not discuss their ordeals due to social stigma. Instead, many internalise their anxiety and build a wall of silence in the name of honour and purity. Living combatants are granted a silence, whereas those that die become iconic images of avengers of sexual violence (de Mel 2001: 221).

Brainwashing and/or Religion

From a religious point of view, suicide is not a sin amongst those who practise religions with a belief in reincarnation, such as Hinduism and Buddhism. However, the linking of the LTTE motivations to a form of religious fundamentalism is a misnomer as religious differences are not a central component of the LTTE suicide bombings, but nationalism is. Nationalism is also central to the ethno-nationalist debate; thus, it becomes the core of the LTTE struggle. The LTTE used religious terminology to unite the main religions practised amongst Tamil nationals (Christianity and Hinduism) in its construction of martyrdom and death. Schalk describes the use of words such as *punita ilactiyam* (meaning 'holy aim') to describe the fight for an independent state (1997b: 27). He urges not to confuse the LTTE's usage of religious-based words with its secularist acts as they represent a more secularist terminology rather than a religious terminology.

The combatants' attachment to Prabhakaran may be seen as a form of cultism, as claimed by some authors,[17] but I would distance myself from such an analysis as it risks overlooking all other aspects that contribute to the greater discourse. However, the need to succeed that was profoundly engrained in all suicide bombers had a direct link back to Prabhakaran. An example of the fear of failure (based on total dedication and admiration) or of 'letting him down' or 'of disappointing him on a personal level', was referred to in Pratap's (2001: 104) interview conducted with two male suicide bombers of the LTTE.[18]

This is further reflected amongst the combatant women I interviewed who viewed the acts as recognition of themselves as individuals and as a collective reflecting Prabhakaran's faith in combatant women. Pratap (2005), Bandara (2002) and Gunaratna (1998) all argue that Prabhakaran was very aware of the power he held over the combatants and their desire to fulfil his wishes. It can therefore be argued that a subtle manipulation that was considerably more complex and significantly different to that of religious promises or cultism was used to motivate combatants. One notable factor in cultism is the group's isolation from any other social contact making them reliant only on each other.[19] Such isolation did not happen with the LTTE as they were actively engaged with the civic society as part of their ideological struggle for the greater good of all Tamil nationals.

When the motivational factors are unclear, authors tend to hypothesise that combatants were brainwashed into acting as suicide bombers.[20] It is true that the LTTE combatant training did include a substantial amount of visual imagery, such as that of schools and hospitals that were bombed by the State's armed forces; they also sang uplifting heroic songs of liberation that had a positive ending (Gunaratna 2003 and Bandara 2002). However, it would arguably be insufficient to count this alone as a formal way of brainwashing suicide bombers when considering that such training was given to all combatants in the movement.

The LTTE suicide bombers carried the term of endearment 'suicide warriors', which was given to distance them from terrorism and so avoid negative connotations and move towards a warrior image that conjures up images of those who were engaged in a path of righteous action. Thus they were regularly compared to *sanyasis*, meaning ascetic, for their willingness to give their lives up for the cause (Sri Kantha 2004).[21]

Altruistic Suicide

The LTTE suicide bombers are often described by academic scholars such as Schalk (1992, 1994, 1997a and 1997b), Pape (2005) and Sri Kantha (2006) as following the Durkheim model of 'altruistic suicide'. A closer reading of Durkheim (1952) reveals that the LTTE suicide bombers followed not merely an altruistic, but a closely defined category of *obligatory* altruistic suicide.

> **Having given the name of *egoism* to the state of the ego living its own life and obeying itself alone, that of *altruism* adequately expresses the opposite state, where the ego is not is own property, where it is blended with something not itself, where the goal of conduct is exterior to itself, that is, in one of the groups in which it participates. So we call the suicide caused by intense altruism *altruistic suicide*. But since it is also characteristically performed as a duty, the terminology adopted should express this fact. So we will call such a type *obligatory altruistic suicide*. (Durkheim 1952: 221)**

I would argue that the obligatory aspects of the altruistic model would explain to a greater extent the nationalistic commitment felt by the LTTE's suicide bombers. Such obligatory commitments were also reflected in the discourse of combatant women, as discussed later in this chapter. The motivations often appeared to be multi-layered, with their own set of dynamics which were deeply embedded in the nationalist commitment to the cause of a free state of Tamil *Eelam* and a need to succeed. It is also important to note that those who were involved in the LTTE's suicide squad were focused on death rather than life as part of their commitment to the cause. This was the main difference in comparison with the combatants of non-suicide squads, who were focused on life and living, where death in battle was counted only as a possibility, not an inevitability.

The LTTE and Suicide Bombers

The complex and secretive nature of suicide operations has inevitably made data gathering rather problematic.[22] Within the LTTE it was almost impossible to gather data from failed suicide bombers due to the cyanide poison they carried. In the rare circumstances where authors had the opportunity to interview combatant suicide bombers, the androcentric nature of the organisation becomes visible, as it has always been men who were participants of interviews.[23] It must also be recognised that there was no prior knowledge of the 'would be' suicide bomber until after the event. Rajasingham-Senanayake conducted the interview with Dhanu without having the faintest notion that she was talking to the future suicide bomber of Rajiv Gandhi.[24] During the interview Dhanu conveyed the same ideology as all other combatant women of the LTTE who supported the achievement of a separate state of Tamil *Eelam* above the promotion of emancipation of women, and no indication was given of her views on suicide bombings. Interestingly, the views expressed by Dhanu were no different from those of the women I interviewed over a decade later.

As stated before, the information and data about the LTTE's suicide bombers squad was virtually impossible to come by, except on a piecemeal basis, and with difficulty in verifying. However, it is noticeable that gender equality was less in need of negotiation within the suicide squad as the acceptance into the squad itself was recognition of equality. It can be argued that the equality was a necessity, but it needs to be acknowledged as a recognition that narrowed the gender polarisation which questioned women's abilities to carry out the same tasks as men.[25]

Kuppi: The Cyanide Vial

Prabhakaran first became aware of cyanide poisoning in 1974 through the death of Sivakumaran, a man he admired who committed suicide to avoid being captured by the police for his involvement in the militant Tamil student movement (Narayan-Swamy 2002).[26] As stated previously, part of the LTTE's graduation ceremony for combatants included the allocation of a necklace with a cyanide capsule in the form of a small glass vial known as *kuppi*, attached to it.

The glass vial was filled with cyanide and hung as a pendant on a string worn around the neck. Allegedly, the glass vials were manufactured in Germany; the cyanide (the effective form of cyanide is recognised as being sodium cyanide, not potassium cyanide) was purchased from India and assembled by the LTTE. The glass containers were bitten at the point of suicide to release the poison, which enters the blood stream and prevents oxygen entering into the body, causing pain, trauma and convulsions mixed with confusion, ending with a painful death. The duration of death will take no more than a couple of minutes, but taking an insufficient quantity will cause permanent brain damage. The vials needed to be replaced after every three months due to discoloration of the poison when exposed to sun and moisture. The new vials used since the final wave of violence started were believed to be easier to bite into than previous models. The vial contained sufficient poison to kill an adult; however, some combatants carried two vials to ensure death as a certainty.[27]

The combatant women were particularly in favour of the cyanide necklaces. They had been educated by the movement to understand that the State-armed forces would rape and torture them in search of answers before subjecting them to a brutal form of execution; thus, Roberts (1996) argues the cyanide vial to be both 'instrument and faith'.[28] This can be seen in context when analysing the epitaph written in the *Mavirarkurippetu* magazine (issue 1: 10) about the very first combatant who died by biting into the cyanide capsule: 'Having been surrounded in a hideout in Valvettiturai by Sri Lankan soldiers and having *enjoyed* cyanide, he died heroically' (translated by Schalk 1997a: 11; author's emphasis).

The wording that illustrates taking a cyanide capsule as a form of enjoyment needs to be seen in a situation-specific context of the combatants finding themselves confronted with impending torture, extreme violence and a slow death. Therefore, a painful yet quick death offered by cyanide poisoning was a highly preferred alternative. The first woman combatant to be considered a martyr was Malathy, a non-suicide squad combatant who used her cyanide vial at the point of serious injury received in battle. By her actions, she became a venerated figure in the movement, and her death was commemorated in October every year until the Final War in 2009.

The vial that was worn around the neck was fully exposed for all to see, including those from the civic society. By this action, those who saw it became de-sensitised and accepted it as part of the LTTE combatant's role and their commitment to the cause. Such openness removed the shock element from the civic society and indirectly removed any form of stigma or negativity that was associated with carrying a vial of poison.

Black Tigers

In 1987 Prabhakaran stated that 'the method of war may change. But the aim of our war will not change' (Schalk 1997b: 25). Part of the changing strategy of war brought the Black Tiger suicide squad into existence with their first reported action on 5 July 1987: the kamikaze-style suicide attack performed by Captain Miller.[29] The creation of the Black Tigers has been attributed to Prabhakaran's admiration for the Indian National Army (INA), the nationalist army of Subash Chandra Bose. This group was operational against the British rulers in India during the 1940s. The INA had an organised suicide squad and was the first to use suicide-belts that were tied around the waist. This particular method was further developed into a new invention of a suicide-vest by the LTTE, which was introduced to the world by Dhanu in 1991 in the assassination of Rajiv Gandhi (Schalk 1997: 174 and Narayan-Swamy 2006) .

The Black Tiger suicide operations were 'never spontaneous or arbitrary' (Schalk 1997a: 12), and were generally conducted in two ways: those who took part in the battlefield and those who were individual operators set up as lone bombers, penetrating heavy security to attack a hard-to-reach target. 'The Black Tiger constitutes the armour of self-defence for our ethnic group, and also serve to remove the barriers coming in the way of our struggle. They are the balls of fire smashing the military power of the enemy with sheer determination' (Prabhakaran's speech on *Mahaveera*, Martyrs Day, 5 July 1993, referred to in Narayan-Swamy 2006: 249).

The Black Tigers were a unique and deadly creation of the LTTE with the emblem of a dark silhouetted image of the head and shoulders of a soldier wearing a beret and holding a gun. The image itself was publicly displayed and believed to be the silhouette of Captain Miller. This specialised suicide squad had a reputation of being both fierce and elite, with loyalty given solely and unquestioningly to Prabhakaran and none other (Narayan-Swamy 2006 and Pratap 2001). The elitism was a direct result of special training that primarily focused the mind to distance itself from others and retain an unwavering focus on the assignment. The fierceness was a by-product of the strength of mind that has made the Black Tigers an enigma to all who study suicide bombers. They served a very useful purpose for the LTTE by being able to penetrate security and carry out successful missions.

The training programmes of the Black Tigers were a secretive affair but we can assume that women had negotiated gendered roles as combatants that were carried through to the next stage of training.

> **I think she wants to know how we join that group. There is not much difference, a normal Tiger only becomes a Black Tiger. Yes. If they want to become Black Tigers they need special training. They have to be trained in both, mentally and physically. (Arasi)**

Arasi's emphasis on mental and physical training resonated with the nature of pressure that a suicide bomber may face. Their specialised training was conducted separately from other combatants for a period of time. During this period they had minimum or no contact with consanguine and non-consanguine families, including those in the revolutionary family. The training they received was primarily focused on their mental status to ensure that when the time comes they would be fully prepared mentally and physically to carry out the act to the bitter end (Pratap 2001: 103).

The issue of an individual's autonomy and free choice in joining the Black Tigers was often at the forefront of discussions about suicide bombers. There was no evidence to suggest that individuals were either drugged or conscripted against their will into the elite squad.[30] Many of the combatants and civic women informed me that becoming a suicide bomber was a decision made by combatants, who then volunteered themselves. Pratap (2001: 102), however, claimed the best 200 combatant students were selected to join the Black Tiger squad, suggesting that being *chosen* meant the individual's choice of volunteering or putting one's self forward and retaining some autonomy was taken away. My informal discussions with the Gatekeeper and female combatants revealed that the individual's ability to make a choice was a widely held belief, and that those who became suicide bombers were allowed to make a *free* decision and were not forced into the role.

> **Say, I am a normal Tiger. I also can become a Black Tiger. The decision is mine. Yes, yes we have lot of choices. Even at the last moment, I can say I cannot do it. If one is not mentally strong enough or prepared then they cannot achieve what they set out to do. We believe in this very strongly. (Arasi)**

Arasi's description granted those who joined the Black Tiger suicide bombers a certain empowerment and control over their actions. However, Arasi's assurance that those who became suicide bombers were able to withdraw from a mission at the last minute was disputed in the writings of de Mel (2001). She referred to an instance when the decision to pull the cord of a suicide-jacket was taken away from the individual suicide bomber by it being remotely detonated.[31]

If we look beyond the accepted notion that it was a voluntary role to be a member of the elite force, then one tends to notice two strong influences involved in the decision-making process. Although this may not be coercion, the discrimination and suppression of one ethnic group and culture, together with the use of a combatant's emotional involvement with Prabhakaran, had an impact on the decision-making as discussed in previous sections. The following extract from Pratap's interview with male Black Tigers illustrates that the commitment to Prabhakaran outweighed all other factors.

> The only time they [Black Tigers] showed some emotion was when they talked about Pirabhakaran [Prabhakaran], their *Annai* [elder brother]. A Black Tiger named Sunil said with something close to awe, 'For us, he is mother, father and God all rolled into one. But I detected one fear in all of them: the fear that they might let Pirabhakaran [Prabhakaran] down. They would die happily; their only hope was their death would inflict the kind of damage on the enemy that would make Pirabhakaran [Prabhakaran] happy. Securing *Annai*'s happiness was all that mattered then; they would not have lived and died in vain. (Pratap 2001: 103–104; author's emphasis)

Suicide bombers who made the choice to put themselves forward believed it was their own conscientious decision. Through my interviews with combatant women it was clear that when an individual first volunteers to join the Black Tigers they were either chosen or rejected, based on the LTTE's assessment of an individual's capabilities. The potential women Black Tigers had to submit an application in writing, based on their skills, motivation and domestic situation (including care responsibilities); if successful, they became part of the elite squad. The transition from being a 'normal' Tiger to a 'Black' Tiger was seen as a procedural change, with a great deal of mental and physical training being given to toughen up the individual. The Black Tiger unit was differentiated from other units by a powerful song that expressed pride.[32] Those who joined the elite squad were the most dedicated and committed to the cause. As Arasi says, 'We never ever force anyone to fight [as a Black Tiger] if they don't want to. We explain to them why we have to fight [in this particular way] but the final decision to fight [in that way] is their decision....' Arasi's description revolved around choice being given to the individual to make the decision based on their own understanding. This, itself, may be asymmetric due to the nature of warfare and the explanation given to them by the organisation.

An enactment of their appreciation of Prabhakaran had become part of a created ritual of a suicide bomber's farewell, ceremoniously having their photograph taken with Prabhakaran. These photographs became a cherished possession of the dead suicide bomber's family. There is an unsubstantiated but popularly held belief that the photo session was followed by sharing a meal with him before the individual was sent out on their mission (Pratap 2001: 103; Narayan-Swamy 2006: 235 and 273 and de Mel 2004: 78). It must also be noted that those who were assigned a mission may or may not have know who the target was until the last minute. The chosen suicide bomber may have had to be a 'sleeper' for a period of time until she (or he) was given the go-ahead by the LTTE to carry out the attack.[33]

The freedom to decide needs to be seen within the context of the LTTE's teachings and its discipline, which merge in creating a hybrid (a special kind of) conscience that Prabhakaran described as:

> [t]hat commitment comes from discipline. From the beginning I felt that for a person to dedicate his life to a cause, he must be free from self-centred, egotistic existence. He has to renounce personal pleasures. I have instilled discipline in the (LTTE), and selected a group of persons capable of renouncing their lives. (Narayan-Swamy 2006: 233)

It can be argued that Prabhakaran's own statement was gendered by his referring to suicide bombers as 'he'. However, the message he conveyed was that those who were chosen to join the Black Tiger squad were of a higher calibre than the average combatant. It is a possibility that the unit was originally created for male combatants, with women added at a subsequent date.

Religious Aspects

My research confirmed that suicide bombings in the LTTE were a secular activity whose motivation was never based on religion or the gains of afterlife due to the fact that the LTTE was a secular movement and suicide missions were carried out by both Christians and Hindus (Schalk 1992, 1997a and 1997b and Sri Kantha 2004). Although in Jaffna the major religion is Hinduism, there were also a number of Christian and Brahmin faith combatants within the LTTE's terrorist family.[34] Once the combatants joined the LTTE, they often did not practise their religion or were unable to keep within the guidelines dictated by their religion. For instance, the Brahmin combatant women of the LTTE often found it difficult to follow religious directions on food preparation and consumption whilst being in active service.[35] Therefore, the values gained in the afterlife which were important for other groups of suicide bombers were neither relevant to the revolutionary culture nor their perceived symbolism of giving a gift of life.

Religious teachings and constraints were disregarded by many combatant women who prepared to sacrifice themselves for the cause, and especially for those within the LTTE, who had built relationships. Schalk (1992: 83) describes this as shown in one of their propaganda illustrations in the *Mavirarkurippetu* magazine depicting armed young men and women walking together with their heads held high. In the background there are Christian gravestones and a Hindu funeral pyre. The picture was titled 'Spirits of dead heroes and heroines from the tombs of Christian and pyres of Hindu unite'. Whilst the title was contradictory in 'uniting' Christians and Hindus after death, the emphasis here was on overcoming religious differences to attain a common aim. I would add that it further created an illustration of equality between male and female combatants which overrode the society's prejudicial views of gender construction by signposting masculinity and femininity side by side.

Although a majority of combatant women viewed the afterlife as being part of their religious upbringing, these traditional religious views underwent a change when a woman joined the movement, as illustrated by Kavitha:

> We must do good in this life so that in our next birth we will be blessed more. When we were growing up we believed in re-birth. But now we don't think like that. We feel we have to use this time given here properly by doing good. We don't think about re-birth and so on. Our main thinking is how we are living now. (Kavitha)

Kavitha's discourse showed that a change in belief occurred when continuously exposed to extreme forms of existence whilst living under the restrictions imposed by the State. The choice of words used in her narrative (such as 'now' and 'properly'), conveys a duality of determination (to carry out the tasks designated by the LTTE) and the temporality of life. The change of belief was a complex transition from 'what used to be' to 'what is currently happening'. This change of thought process also illustrates a move away from the consanguine family and its cultural upbringing. New thought processes directed by the 'new' LTTE family remoulded the individual's thinking to fit in with the movement's idealisation of martyrdom as a selfless act that must be venerated.

A selfless act given to others in this life emphasises betterment in the next, as the women have been brought up to believe. The pragmatic view of living 'here and now' comes from the understanding of the fragility of life, which also extended into the combatant women's formation of relationships with one another and the concept of a Tamil nation state. The combatant women believed they had a responsibility for the safety and welfare of civic citizens, with whom they had an extended kin identity as discussed previously.

Rationalities of Suicide Bombing

> You must explain to her this properly. Because this is very important. We are a minority. But the war that was imposed on us was a major one. Many international countries helped those who imposed the war on us. Our strength to oppose this war was weak. So to fight this big enemy only we invented this Black Tigers. Instead of losing many of our combatants in the war we were able to attack big targets but lost only one person. Yes, yes they are also a group. (Arasi)

Arasi's explanation affirms a strong justification for both the creation and use of the Black Tigers as the ultimate weapon born out of necessity. The explanation also carries a definitive pragmatism based on the cost/benefit of losing one combatant rather than a whole battalion. The death of a suicide bomber must be viewed logistically and pragmatically, as it only required one combatant to be trained and lost from the movement rather than risking a combat unit with no guarantee of success. Those who applied to be selected for a suicide mission also viewed it as a career pinnacle. Such selection elevated their status and affirmed their commitment to the cause (de Mel 2001: 225).

Overall, life was valued regardless of its male or female identity, and more importantly, suicide bombings were a rational strategy; hence the trained suicide bomber was a strategic weapon and a valued resource. It appears that a significant importance was placed on individual combatants in the LTTE regardless of their gender identity. The gender identity itself created an agent who was tasked into carrying out the policy/mission, and the value of the agent as a highly trained entity remained until their death.

By analysing the available literature on the LTTE suicide missions, it does appear that though combatants were sent to perform suicide missions it does not necessarily mean they have to die in the process. Death was a by-product of the act, but the act itself did not necessarily require the death of the combatant in order for the mission to be successful. The suicide bombers of the LTTE did not appear to have the humiliation of failure attached to them.

It must also be noted that there was no evidence to show that any of the LTTE's elite suicide squad ever abandoned a mission, which in turn meant their exact views will never be known as they always end up dead, except on one occasion.[36] Those who have written specifically about the LTTE suicide activities, such as Hopgood (2005), admit the difficulty in obtaining data as the death of the subject was a fundamental problem for the research.[37] When conducting research amongst the LTTE, researchers never knew who amongst their research participants was a future suicide bomber. Therefore, it is impossible to predict how many of those I have interviewed became suicide bombers since then. This uncertainty is primarily based on the fact that they either have not been chosen to become members of the elite Black Tiger squad or they were already trained and awaiting an assignment.

Altruism in *Thatkodai*: The Gift of Sacrifice

The gift of sacrifice made by women suicide bombers was explained to me as:

> The suicide bombers are known to commit 'Thatkolai', which means suicide. But these people [the LTTE combatant women] are known as committing 'Thatkodai'. 'That' means self and 'Kolai' means killing and 'Kodai' means gift. So when you say 'Thatkodai' it means they are giving themselves [as a gift]. (Kavitha's Translator)

As Kavitha says, 'Some people say, Christians also say that there is no better love than giving your life for a friend. That is what "Thatkodai" means.' The single thread that runs through the combatant women's own justification for a suicide act was the concept of giving a gift. The actual act of giving can be argued as a 'materialistic gesture' where the human value of the gift surpasses the materiality and places it in a superior category of a selfless act. Within this category women were often seen as selfless givers.

The words ending *Kolai* and *Kodai* convey a powerful message within the suicide discourse. The very act of taking one's own life in suicide, *Thatkolai* is separated from that of committing an act of suicide bombing, which was a selfless act of giving a gift, *Thatkodai*. The participants took a great deal of time to explain this difference to me, which was significant as it appears that my understanding of the difference was important to them. The significance between the words was not recorded in any of the literature by the academics who generally regard the combatant women as being 'used' by the LTTE (de Mel 2001 and Coomaraswamy 1996).

As Durkheim (1952) recognises, 'we actually see the individual in all these cases seek to strip him[her]self of his[her] personal being in order to be engulfed in something which [s]he regards as [her]his true essence.' (translated by Spaulding and Simpson 2000: 225). The altruistic suicide discussed by Durkheim is strongly reflected in Kavitha's discourse above, showing that she was aware that the social perception of self-sacrifice through bombings and other means was a negative one. Suicide, however, is not culturally frowned upon or stigmatised, but is seen as shortening the lengthy period of suffering endured during an individual's lifetime.[38] This view is very much based on the cause and effect in life's never-ending cycle of birth, death and re-birth. Such a cultural perspective remains very different from that of Christian Western societies, and contextualising the perceptions of suicide along with the movement's ethos of death attained during the cause of fighting was viewed as a 'gift' that was given to one's friends, family and the nation state of Tamil *Eelam*.

It must be recognised that neither the wider community nor the LTTE revolutionary group saw human life as cheap or worthless. Though the LTTE's use of human life to further the cause as battlefield combatants or suicide combatants can be viewed as contradictory to those who value life, it needs to be seen in a context of 'war' conditions, whereby the giving or sacrificing of human life was required to achieve their aims and objectives. The sentiment of being unable to put a value on life made it a priceless commodity. Hence the combatant women of the LTTE saw the sacrifice of life as giving the ultimate gift.

As Kavitha says, 'People refer to them as suicide bombers, but they are not committing suicide, they are gifting their life.' Kávitha's own insistence that this was a gift signifies an understanding of sacrifice similar to that described by Bauman (1992), who claims that the willingness to die for another is the 'only truly individual of human acts'. He further states that '[t]he greatest gift one human being can offer another is the gift of one's life. To die for another' is the ultimate ethical act; one by which all morality is measured' (Bauman 1992: 200).

Many in civic society felt a great obligation to the combatants for the sacrifices they made on behalf of the community.

> When you hear the news that many of the fighters have died fighting for us you feel bad. It is just like if one of my relatives have died. I have the same feelings. At times we help them in other ways by giving money. Yes, we do that a lot [helped out with food or money or medicines and bandages]. This is something everybody does and it is normal. We cannot repay them for the sacrifice. You cannot put a value on a life. (GV)

In the above discourse, GV harbours a strong sense of personal indebtedness toward the combatants, who were perceived by her as 'fighting for us'. The collective usage of the word 'us' in this instance focused on a transitional relatedness in kinship that was due to the act being committed on behalf of another; the 'us' in this instance referring to the Tamil community at large. Whilst the relatedness linked the combatant women to the civic society, it invariably created a complex situation by sharing both its achievements (the success in the attack carried out) and losses (of life), thus, invoking simultaneous senses of gratitude, admiration and guilt. The relatedness that linked the combatants and the civic community further carried a sense of familial identity when GV refers to the deaths as: 'It is just like if one of my relatives have died. I have the same feelings.'

These sentiments were also echoed in Sri Kantha's (2004: 3) writing in relation to suicide bombers, where he states that, 'all were superheroes of a higher order for Tamils like me. They belong to my extended family, and they are the real thing'. The sentiments expressed by both GV and Sri Kantha correspond directly with Durkheim, who argues: 'Because altruistic suicide, though showing the familiar suicidal traits, resembles especially in its most vivid manifestations some categories of action which we are used to honouring with our respect and even admiration, people have often refused to consider it as self-destruction.' (Durkheim 1952, translated by Spaulding and Simpson 2000: 239).

The identification of the suicide combatants as both heroes and kin placed the suicide bombers in an elevated position where they were not only removed from the society but also venerated. The kin identity formed a lifeline to the perceived heroic act, which then (indirectly) allowed the civic State to embrace the altruistic glory of the suicide martyrdom.

Gendered Dimensions

The suicide bomber's performance of *Thatkodai*, and not *Thatkolai*, gives credence to the paradoxical dualism of the destruction of life in order to give (the gift of life) to the nation. As Yalini says, 'Yes. Sacrifice is the most important thing. Living for other people and doing good for them and not thinking about ourselves.' Yalini's discourse illustrates a gendered dimension that was implicit in the female roles of Tamil culture, which suggested that sacrifice and selflessness were a part of a socially constructed womanhood. Even though combatant women have left the domestic sphere and entered into a more public sphere, the values of their upbringing permeated into the new roles as suicide bombers. This gendered aspect was also recognised by civic women, who stated: 'They [Tamil women] don't concentrate on how fair it is or what they want. Sacrificing is a main character of the [Tamil] women. There is no surprise in sacrificing. Anyway, she [Tamil woman] is sacrificing wherever she is, no?' (HA).

Based on these definitions, the self-sacrifice involved in suicide bombing was not an added 'extra' to the culturally accepted social roles of combatant women, and there is a noticeable difference between the language used by male and female combatants to describe what suicide bombing meant to them as gendered individuals. It must also be noted that the Oxford Dictionary (1980) definition of martyrdom significantly includes 'death or suffering for *any* great cause' (author's emphasis).

By analysing my own primary data and the existing secondary data, the gendered dimension of the act of suicide bombing was highlighted through the language used. The interviews conducted by the BBC with male 'would be' suicide bombers revealed that they viewed suicide bombing as an act of sacrifice, meaning to forgo, forfeit or surrendeı their life.[39] There is a similar argument of gendered manipulation that can be applied to the male combatants, as reflected in one male who stated, 'I feel honoured that my death will take our struggle one step closer to Eelam' (Pratap 2001: 103). The male combatants in this instance saw the act of suicide more as an internalised honour gained than an externalised sacrifice made.

Whilst acknowledging that it is often difficult to separate biology from culture (Eichler 1980 referred to in Mackie 1987: 3), it is none the less noticeable that the discourse between male and female suicide bombers reveals a gendered division. Interestingly, men do not use the same words, suggesting that sacrifice could be seen with a specifically gendered inflection. This was in stark contrast to my own research into the combatant women, who viewed suicide bombing to be a gift, a present, an offering or a contribution. Women suicide bombers called it 'an act of giving'. This may be tied to essentialist views of women's socio-biological roles as nurturers, defining them as 'givers'. The theoretical justification of *Thatkodai* (self-giving /gift) as a present to the nation to alleviate the nation's problematic state can be debated as a gendered facet of women that is deeply embedded in the culture of sacrifice. This was opposed to male suicide bombers, who call it 'an act of sacrifice', tied to the masculine role of a 'non-giver' or a 'receiver', which their socio-cultural roles have dictated. Therefore, I would emphasise the importance of understanding the multi-layered thinking that was contained within the LTTE's ideology of martyrdom and its gendered dynamics.

Friendship, Kinship and Death

Combatant women viewed dying for a kin relationship—or for the nation at large—as an extension of being physically responsible for the well-being of the LTTE kin family. Though social scientists such as Bauman (1992: 207) may argue this is a 'moral awakening from the egoistic somnolence in which life is for most people', the reality of life lived amongst friends in kinship carries far greater attachments of care and personal sacrifice.[40]

The selfless act of *Thatkodai* ('gift of self') which is steeped in altruistic suicide is much more significant on a personal level and works on several levels that are overlooked by many. A major theme amongst combatant women that appeared in Balasingham's (1993, writing as Adele Ann) writing was the use of a fictive kin identity (as in Kavitha's discourse referred to earlier) that indicated emotions towards 'a friend' were stronger than those for the consanguine kin family.[41] However, the sacrifices of this nature send ripples through the civic community, which positions itself within the fictive kin structure of the LTTE in relation to death. It also forms a part of a transitional consanguinity, as discussed earlier in Chapter 4.

It must be recognised that the sacrifice of life as a gift to the nation created a value-added commodity within the revolutionary movement. 'Values [are] often gained when people die.…In the end it is death, rather than lives it claimed to preserve, which turns into the supreme value. Death itself becomes the cause for the hero of a cause' (Bauman 1992: 209). Therefore, combatant women such as Dhanu and Malathy have become examples of heroes created in death. They were both young combatant women who sacrificed their lives for the cause of the LTTE and over the years have become highly revered legends.

Arasi discussed two deaths that mean a great deal to her emotionally: that of her sister and that of her close female friend, Sambathy. In Arasi's discourse, the death of a friend appeared to be discussed with a greater tenderness than the death of a family member.

In relation to the sister, Arasi states:

> My sister next to me was in the movement she was martyred. She was next to me so we both went through the same experiences. She was martyred in 1998. She was born in 1975 ... [after some calculation] ... she was 23. We were both together but then I had to go to do something else and it [death] happened then. [In] Killinochi. Not on any of those 3 operations [Never Ceasing Waves operations].[42] This was when the army moved forward there was a battle. (Arasi)

Whereas, in relation to her friend Sambathy, she states:

> In 1993 during the Poonahari Battle I lost a friend Sambathy. That was very shocking. She and I were very close friends. I was with her and saw her dying. When I went near her there were shells and rounds all around her. Before that we used to talk a lot about the people and about the status of women in the society. After my friend's death, I wanted to fulfil her desires and ambitions. (Arasi)

There was a strong sense of reflexitivity in Arasi's discourse regarding the two deaths that were of significance to her. A closer analysis revealed a difference between the two personal losses. Sambathy's death invoked emotionally revealing statements of the shock encountered in seeing her friend die, which then directly related to a close affinity before death: 'we used to talk a lot'. This type of bond between Sambathy and Arasi was missing in her discussion of her sister's death, which seemed more distant by comparison with the death of her friend. This may be due to reasons such as the friend being with Arasi during times of hardships and extreme physical endurance. Furthermore, witnessing Sambathy's death added further emotional turmoil in a way that her sister's death did not, thus removing her from the immediacy of her sister's death. It was the death of Sambathy that had inspired and created a yearning. As she said: 'I wanted to fulfil her [Sambathy's] desires and ambitions.' This also refers to the emotional ties that have been built with the non-consanguine family of the LTTE which overrode consanguinal ties, as discussed in the previous chapter. Firth (1999: xv) describes this as a key theme of friendship that relies on an assumption of 'benevolence and loyalty', which extends to combatant women preparing to sacrifice their own self for a friend and the greater civic community.

Celebration of Martyrdom

Roberts (1996) argued that the LTTE seized an opportunity to build martyrdom on a cultural value that is embedded in sacrifice. Death in the LTTE was justified as a form of martyrdom. Suicide deaths, in particular, followed the Tamil linguistic definition of *tiyakam*, meaning 'abandonment' rather than 'destruction' of life, and those who were engaged in such activities were considered to be ascetics who had given up the pleasures of life such as intimate relationships.[43]

Schalk has written seminal texts on the subject of LTTE martyrdom. Through his research in c.1990, he reveals ways in which the LTTE had constructed its suicide martyrdom ethos by usage of language and means of the revivalist literature used in India during its struggle for independence. The LTTE actively moved away from the Indian linguistic roots of martyrdom to the Tamil language's own hybrid version. Even though the Indian independence did not rely on the concept of martyrdom as popularised by the LTTE, Schalk (1997a) identifies a common link in the use of the concept *tyagi* from ancient Sanskrit. Whilst the Sanskrit language referred to *tyagi* as 'one who abandons life', this was changed to *tiyaki*, 'the one who loses one's own life in the act of assisting another'. In addition, the word *tiyakam*, translated as 'abandonment', was also used as part of martyrdom discourse and was given specifically to suicide combatants. He further identifies the separation of death in the battlefield from death as a suicide bomber through usage of the word *caatci.* The literal meaning of the word was 'one who endures submissively', but this was changed by the LTTE to 'one who fights furiously', which was only granted to combatants who died in the battlefield.[44] It was also understood that the LTTE needed to translate words such as *tiyaki* (meaning 'martyr') and *tiyaakam* (meaning 'martyrdom') into English and other languages for both the diaspora community and non-Tamil audience.

The LTTE's concept of martyrdom was developed in the 1980s and actively promoted later in that decade. It bore a level of constructed self-esteem that was actively reinforced by the organisation's glorification of self-sacrifice.[45] Martyrdom was a calculated and rationalised promotion linked not only to the violent armed conflict but also to the suffering of those in the civic society. Whilst the civic society had no control over the LTTE's ideology or its rationale, the LTTE had incorporated them into its thought process as a way of gaining an endorsement for its activities. The significance of this inclusion is seen in the way martyrdom was celebrated in society.

With the activation of suicide bombings, the LTTE made its first public proclamation on martyrdom in 1989 at the Great Hero celebrations, *Marvirar Nal,* stating that all who had sacrificed their lives for the cause is a martyr.[46] The martyrdom aspect of death was publicly celebrated in a number of ways. Firstly, there were set dates for celebrations such as 27 November (dating back to the first event in 1989), *Marvirar Nal,* honouring all the LTTE combatants who had died in battle. On 10 October, the death of Malathy (who died by taking a cyanide capsule in 1987 as the first woman combatant to die in battle), was celebrated. On 5 July, the death of Captain Miller (the first suicide bomber in 1987), was celebrated and the day was further identified as Black Tiger Day. All these days consisted of a ritualistic ceremony which included lighting candles at the shrine made for the dead, raising flags and parades combined with cultural entertainment such as music, dance and plays.

My research period coincided with the anniversary of Malathy's death, which gave me an opportunity to experience at first hand the kind of atmosphere that was generated by such occasions. Apart from the large paintings and posters that decorated the roads and junctions, it was very interesting to note the very prominent shrine for Malathy that was built in the stadium where the festivities were conducted. Every person present (approximately over a hundred people) attended the shrine to offer flowers, incense and prayers. The schoolchildren in their clean and smart white school uniforms appeared to be 'on duty', distributing picture cards, posters and pocket calendars with Malathy's image or were engaged in general assistance, and a number of school bands played at the celebrations. The atmosphere for the day was very much that of a family event, with free food and drink. However, it was not difficult to realise that such veneration and engagement of children in the process paves the way for the next generation of combatants, and maybe even suicide bombers.

The celebration of martyrs includes those who died in the battlefield whilst fighting, those who had to resort to cyanide poisoning, and those who were engaged in suicide missions. The collective memory of them is kept alive by pillars known as *Ninaivuccinnam* or Tokens of Commemoration erected by the LTTE that can be seen from the road and have the role of actively reminding civic society of the sacrifices made by the combatants of the LTTE. The tokens that I witnessed in Velvettiturai (the home town of Prabhakaran) were for the 12 members of the LTTE who were arrested by the IPKF and were on the verge of being handed over to the armed forces when they resolved to commit suicide by cyanide poisoning in 1987.[47] There were 12 pillars rising from the ground (some 12 feet or more) with widening columns that reached towards the sky. Each of the pillars contained a photograph of one of the people being commemorated, along with the dates of their birth and death. Although these structures were not gravestones and did not contain bodies or ashes, they were painted in the same sky blue colour as the LTTE gravestones. The deaths that had occurred in order for the movement to be built were strongly etched on the memories of all present through the impressive nature of these structures. Whilst the pillars commemorate the death of combatants who had community and family kin ties, both the construction and maintenance of the pillars were carried out by the LTTE with no involvement from the consanguine family members.

The distancing of dead combatants from their biological families was an interesting aspect of the LTTE which I suggest feeds into the creation of the non-consanguine LTTE family. Prior to 1991, the dead bodies of the combatants were handed back to the family for disposal, with the LTTE attending the funeral service and making speeches and salutations to the dead. This position changed after 1991, when the LTTE started to bury them in the LTTE's own cemeteries known as *Tuyilum Illam*, meaning Sleeping House. The official ceremony typically consisted of a farewell speech made by a leader from the LTTE followed by a gun salute. This is further followed by a ritual reading of a text comparing the dead person to a seed returning back to soil from which a new plant will emerge (Schalk 1997b: 45). Whilst this type of funeral ritual replaced the traditional religious funerals, highlighting the secularism within the LTTE, it none the less was interesting to note the link it had with the context of reincarnation and the perpetual cycle of life and death.

The cemeteries I visited had neatly arranged rows of headstones with mounds painted in sky blue. After the initial shock of realising a majority of the dead were in their late teens and early twenties, I noticed how extremely well maintained the grave yard was. There were no weeds growing anywhere, nor any paint chippings; in fact, it all looked immaculate. At both the cemeteries I visited, I was informed that not all mounds actually contained bodies, and that sometimes there were no whole bodies to bury. One of the cemeteries I visited located in Mulathir district, Pudukudiirupu, had an unusual layout with identical neatly arranged mounds all starting from a central podium and spreading outwards, reminiscent of the rays of the sun. The reason for identical mounds was explained to me as an intention to give each dead person a space as an equally valued combatant within the LTTE. The creation of a separate cemetery for the LTTE combatants who died contributed to them being recognised as different from civic society. Furthermore, by separating the dead combatants from their consanguine family burial grounds (many use part of their family land as a collective family cemetery), the LTTE had, in effect, created their own family cemetery, with all the care and maintenance being the responsibility of the movement.

It is notable how devoid of religious imagery the LTTE cemeteries were. None of the graves had any form of religious symbols attached to them. This gave me a sense of an active propagation of the LTTE's secularist ideologies. All religions have their varying practices, especially for death; for instance, burial of the dead is usually conducted in the Christian faith, whereas Hindus normally carry out a cremation. However, the LTTE bury all their dead rather than follow the dead person's original religious background.[48]

The LTTE's veneration of the dead had been addressed by the State armed forces by bulldozing/flattening a number of the LTTE cemeteries. At one of the cemeteries I visited they had collected some of the rubble and had showcased it with an epitaph to the destruction.[49]

During his reign, Prabhakaran raised the profile of dead combatants by actively recognising their contributions at public celebrations with speeches that were directed at dead combatant's parents: 'Your children love the independence of the motherland more than their life. You must feel great and proud of being the parent of those who have given these extraordinary beings for a *holy aim*. Your children have not died; they have become history' (Prabhakaran, cited in Schalk 1997a: 15; author's emphasis)

The above speech by Prabhakaran instils a sense of pride into parents, as the life of their child was not wasted; the child was fulfilling holy aims and was granted a place in history. Prabhakaran's use of the term 'holy aim' was not aligned to any religion, as discussed previously. However by using this term he was attempting to give the fight for a free Tamil nation State some moral justification.

The families of martyrs were honoured and looked after financially from a welfare aspect, which is not dissimilar to Palestinian suicide bombers. A notable difference amongst the Palestine women suicide bombers is in the monetary remuneration received by the families, where noticeably the financial remuneration paid to a female suicide bomber's family is only half that of a male suicide bomber.[50] The justification of a lesser payment for a woman suicide bomber has been that had he lived, the male would have been able to earn a higher amount of money than a woman would. Information concerning any payments from the LTTE was unobtainable as it operated on a closed book basis. Families of martyrs did not discuss financial remunerations and were often kept in a highly visible social position, especially during the time of festivals. During the celebrations of *Mahaveerar Nal* (Martyrs Day), the parents of dead martyrs are paraded in front of cameras and are honoured for their loyalty shown to the cause and for the sacrifice their children had made.[51] The photographs taken on such occasions were posted on the terrorist group's various web pages for the world to view. Further, there were commemoration cards that can be purchased though the websites to celebrate the LTTE's martyrdom from any part of the world. The LTTE had granted its female suicide bombers the same martyrdom recognition as male suicide bombers.

Summary

Female suicide bombers had become a *cause celebre* in the world of revolutionary warfare, raising issues about feminist body politics, individual agency and autonomy along with gender identity within terrorist movements. Social perceptions have made the existing male-focused analysis of the gender discourse sensationalised in the media reporting of women who commit such acts. The essentialist views in society may have added to the refusal to accept the reality of the rising phenomenon of women as suicide bombers, and it appears that analysts are less willing to address this phenomenon. It is a mistake to overlook the rising phenomenon of women suicide bombers as it clearly suggests a change in the negotiated traditional roles of women as combatants in both revolutionary groups and civic society.

The reasons for women becoming suicide bombers were both complex and multi-layered. An analysis of suicide bombings committed by the LTTE combatant women reveals that it was an empowering act that reinstated an individual's lost agency, and can be seen as the ultimate gift given to those they care for and the nation at large. Some had seen the role of women suicide bombers as a clear manipulation of women by patriarchy. However, the women revolutionaries saw this as a career pinnacle, where their complex gender negotiation granted them the same 'high' status awarded to the men who became suicide bombers.

The reality of the socio-cultural situation dictated limited options for a sexually violated young woman in a highly patriarchal society where women's sexuality is linked to the moral virtue of the nation state. In such circumstances, the terrorist groups provide a valuable social service that the community may be unable or unwilling to provide. Some sexually violated civic women who feel vulnerable do end up as strong-willed combatants who received no discouragement to paying with their lives. Such women may harbour deep-rooted feelings of impurity from a violated body that turns into the victim's right to avenge.

It can be argued that Dhanu became an avenging angel of death rather than a mere suicide bomber on a mission, and her act was emancipatory by targeting the head of the nation state that violated her sexual purity. However, it can also be seen as purely instrumental in feeding into the cultural construction of women's roles, whereby they were in need of purification for the sexual violations committed by others on their bodies. Therefore, I would say that until society changes its attitudes whereby the worth of a woman is no longer measured by her sexual purity, and sexual violence against women is recognised as not being a fault of the victim, there will continue to be a risk of those who are marginalised being directed into carrying out extreme acts of violence.

Whilst the actions of women suicide bombers are highly visible, their motivational factors are often overlooked by focusing on religious fundamentalism (Middle East-based perspective). This narrow view reduces the impact of other culturally dictated motivational factors, especially those felt by women (such as the hatred and hopelessness created by the many kinds of personal losses and violations, and the loss of sexual purity in particular). It must also be noted that there were no religious motivational factors within the LTTE linking female combatants to suicide bombings; it was seen as an entirely secular act that was part of a rational strategy of altruistic suicide.

An analysis of the way in which the LTTE dealt with their dead highlights a number of key points. First, the dead were kept alive in the collective social memory by building monuments in public spaces. Second, the dead were separated from the greater society and placed in an elevated position by being buried in a cemetery of their own. Third, the religious, caste and class segregation as practised in the society was replaced by the LTTE's own set of rituals. Fourth, the dead combatant was no longer part of their consanguine family but a substantial part of the LTTE family. Hence s/he is buried in the LTTE's 'own' cemetery, which can also be seen as the LTTE family cemetery, by the side of their non-consanguine kin members. Also, the act of combatant women being buried next to male combatants illustrates a sexual equality in death through the act of burial.

The gender equality argument must be seen in the context of violent political conflict. Whilst women took an equally active role in becoming suicide bombers, it was questionable whether they were able to maintain this form of equality gained through an extreme form of self-sacrifice during a post-war era. This in turn questions the sustainability of this particular form of negotiated equality achieved by combatant women of the LTTE.

Notes

1 The LTTE as a practice deny any responsibilities for political violence, especially high profile assassinations.

2 There is a lone claim made by Bloom (2005a) that it was Dhanu's mother who was raped rather than Dhanu.

3 Bloom refers to her age as 27. Both Pape (2005) and Cronin (2003) state she was aged 16. The age 16 needs to be viewed in relation to the culture of the country. In this case, Sana'a was seen as an adult woman (as discussed in Chapter 4) as the definition of a child varies greatly according to the State. The name is also spelt as 'San Mheidleh' in Cronin (2003), who describes the event as 'Mheidleh] … drove a car packed with 450 pounds of dynamite into an Israeli check point, killing herself and two Israeli soldiers' (2003: 86).

4 I use the word *assumed* in order to include victims of rape as part of the Armed Virgin group.

5 The views of women as passive caregivers made it easier for women to penetrate high security areas. Leila Khaled (1973) of the Palestinian Liberation Organisation (PLO), perhaps one of the world's most renowned female terrorist, has stated, 'Strategically women are able to gain access to areas where men had greater difficulty because the other side assumed that the women were second class citizens in their own society—dumb, illiterate perhaps, and incapable of planning an operation' (Bloom 2005a: 3).

6 The earlier belief that the woman suicide bomber was pregnant gave way to various rumours questioning the moral legitimacy of the pregnancy. For instance, was it created by an act of rape by Sri Lanka armed forces? On the other hand, was it the result of a woman avenging death of a husband by the hands of Sri Lanka armed forces?

7 Also see Das Spiegel, Kampfmittel Baby-Bombe Tarnung, Klasse, einfach besser aals Manner (date not known).

8 This view is not limited to those of Jaffna, but has a resonance amongst Chechen revolutionaries who consider the Russian civic citizens as silent supporters of the State armed forces committing violent act in Chechnya (Bloom 2005: 99).

9 The December 1999 attack on President Chandrika Kumaratunga caused the death of some 23 bystanders and her to lose the sight of her right eye.

10 This statement of Balasingham was cited in Ramachandran (2005: 168).

11 The violence suffered by the person can also be non-sexual physical violence, but it is the sexual violence that is considered far more damaging, especially to a woman.

12 de Mel (2001: 214) sates, 'The chastity of a woman, like the so-called purity of a language, becomes a code for the nation's honour in nationalist discourse.'

13 Also see Cutter in Beyler (2003: 16).

14 For a detailed explanation, see Maunaguru's (1995) essay 'Gendering Tamil Nationalism: the construction of woman in projects of protest and control' in Jeganathan, P. & Ismail, Q. (Eds) *Unmaking the Nation: Politics of Identity and History in Modern Sri Lanka.* During my research in Jaffna, I was informed by a number of older women participants about the feminist nature of the women's groups and their political activisms. Some times these activisms were conducted via 'Study Groups'—when a group of women get together to discuss the political situation in Jaffna and how it was affecting them and other women in their community. They would then devise a plan of action to try and change the situation.

15 Schalk (1992). It must also be noted that the social rejection of rape victims is reminiscent of Vietnam's traditional society where rape is viewed with shame. However, the Vietnamese revolutionary movement have been active in dispelling and discouraging the continuation of prejudices against women who have been raped (Eisen-Bergman 1974: 75).

16 Whilst Maunaguru (1995: 171) discuses *agnipravesam* at length, it is also worth noting the writings of Thiruchandran (1997b) and Cutter (1998) in Beyler (2003).

17 Reuter (2004) claims Prabhakaran had a cult status due to the care and attention he received from the combatants.

18 Pratap (2001) conducted her interviews with permission from Prabhakaran. The combatants she interviewed only showed some form of emotion when discussing Prabhakaran. 'For us, he is mother, father and God all rolled into one' (p. 103).

19 Pape (2005:179) describes these to be the qualities of cultism.

20 Reuter (2004) claims that 'Brainwashing methods have played a significant role in the Tamil Tiger organisation' (2004: 160). He suggests that combatants are brainwashed into acting as suicide bombers, which is not an accurate representation as confirmed by Hopgood (2005).

21 Also see Wilson (1988) *The Break-up of Sri Lanka: The Sinhalese-Tamil Conflict* as referred to in Roberts (2004:101). In this book, A.J.V. Chandrakanthan, a former lecturer at the University of Jaffna and a Catholic clergyman provides an 'insider view' of Tamil nationalism.

22 The data on combatant deaths published by the LTTE on their official web page, 'Eelam web', gives an indication of the gender blindness by not separating the number of male and female Black Tiger deaths, but giving the total sum as 241 killed between 27 November 1982 and 30 September 2002. However, there is a gendered breakdown of combatants (non-Black Tigers) killed which indicates that 3,766 female and 13,882 males combatants were killed during the same period. De Mel's (2004) data obtained from the army media spokesman's office in Colombo claims that 64 of the suicide attacks were carried out by women, a figure that also ties in with Sri Kantha's (2004) data. None of the data recognises Dhanu as a suicide bomber, which is not surprising considering that the LTTE only admitted responsibility for the assassination of Rajiv Gandhi in 2006. It is also interesting to note that Sri Kantha also recorded a further 26 separate incidents (both male and female) of combatants who had died whilst training. Black Tiger training requires a higher level that can and does cause accidental deaths during training and rehearsal runs for specific missions. Furthermore, his data reveals that the first officially recognised Black Tiger woman was Captain Angaiyarkanni of the Sea Tiger squad that specialised in suicide sea attacks, in 1994. In addition, a majority of women Black Tigers are of at least 21 years of age at the time of their mission. Further, the majority of Black Tiger combatant women deaths occurred in 1998, totalling 13 deaths. My own data gathered from the Mulathir district Tamil *Eelam* Heroes Office Political Wing (the office is situated in the cemetery), Pudukudiirupu, Northern Jaffna, indicates that there were 18 Black Tiger and 46 Sea Tiger Sea Tigers deaths, giving a total of 64 deaths from 27 November 1982 to 31 October 2002. This latter figure ties in with the data de Mel obtained from the Sri Lankan armed forces. Within this period the information board also stated that 64 deaths were attributed to women suicide bombers, and the total number of male and female suicide deaths were 241 (indicating that 177 were male suicide bombers). My research reveals that there were 3,768 female combatant deaths (2 more than cited on the LTTE web page). It must also be noted that

my research data extends one month beyond the LTTE web page information. Overall, my findings support the information stated on the *Eelam* web page. The total numbers that were given on the board were not broken down to show details of the deaths, which are not uncommon when dealing with the LTTE as their mode of gathering data is never explained, nor are the LTTE willing to let into public domain information that could be used against them. It must also be noted that since the ceasefire unofficially ended in 2005, the number of women suicide bombings had increased with no current accurate data to reflect the true numbers involved.

23 As discussed in Pratap (2001) and in BBC 'Inside Story' Programme (2004).

24 Rajasingham-Senanayake (2001) interviewed Dhanu some time before the Gandhi assassination, when she was a commander of an LTTE women's wing.

25 The equality to die for one's own country is a demand that the women of Hamas have been asking for many years, and which was finally granted to one woman in 2005. As a good Muslim woman she was chaperoned by a male relative to the venue. Of course, this could also be to ensure she carried out the act (it appears that Hamas has finally come to realise how effective the women are as suicide bombers).

26 The fact of Sivakumaran's case stands as police raided the World Tamil Research Conference held in Jaffna in 1974, causing deaths of a number of delegates. This action angered Sivakumaran who planned a retaliatory attack on the police, but the information reached the police before the attack, leaving him no option but to commit suicide to avoid a painful death in police custody Narayan-Swamy (2002: 55). Also see 'Martyr Sivakumaran Remembered to Day', June 2005, at www.ltteps.org.

27 The occasions when the vial should be used is described in the LTTE's *Mavirarkurippetu* magazine as, 'in a frontal attack by the enemy where there is [a] threat of possible extermination or capture; when surrounded or in a prison; after the infliction of a mortal wound when the LTTE fighter realises that there is no chance of survival and that [s] he is an obstacle to his or her comrades; and after capture, facing torture and death' (Schalk 1997a: 11).

28 Schalk (1997a). Hopgood (2005: 74) expands the point further by stating, 'excruciating torture would almost likely be followed by execution in any event'. In addition to Roberts' (1996) article referred to in this chapter, also see his (1994) article 'LTTE suicides and the Cankam World of Devotion', 15 July 1994, Sri Lanka Guardian news paper. In this article, he traces LTTE cyanide culture to the *purananooru* poems.

29 Captain Miller filled a truck with explosives and drove into the Neeladi school grounds, which was occupied by the Sri Lankan army (Narayan-Swamy 2006).

30 Hopgood (2005: 67). Also note Roberts' (1996) argument that unless there is an existing cultural bedrock of filial piety and devotion to god, it is not possible to have such total commitment to an ultimate goal of death.

31 de Mel (2001: 225), referring to *Tamil Times* (15 March 2000), argues that the freewill to decide may not be as clearly defined once a combatant becomes a member of the elite squad. However, it must also be noted that there is no published material

to illustrate a change of mind being an issue for combatants in the elite squad to withdraw their services. The change of mind argument seems to appear in fiction and cinema, as discussed later on in this chapter.

32 Sri Kantha (2004) has translated many such songs, including the one at the start of this chapter.

33 A good example of a 'sleeper' was Babu, the 23-year-old male suicide bomber who assassinated President Premadasa on 1 May 1993. He was also believed to have been part of the community for a long period of time. Also see Narayan-Swamy (2006: 239–240).

34 It is believed that there have been Muslim nationals amongst the LTTE at the earlier stages of its formation based on an ideology of a minority Tamil language speakers. Over the years, the Muslims have disappeared from the fold. Lately there have been a number of bitter incidents between the Muslim and Tamil groups based on the LTTE wanting to have Tamil only ethnic groups in Jaffna and certain parts of the N.E. province of Sri Lanka.

35 BBC 'Inside Story' programme, shown on UK History Channel (17 July 2004).

36 The single occasion where a member of the Black Tiger squad did not die was due to his ability to leave the vehicle full of explosives that was about to explode and escape to safety.

37 The women-focused research that is currently available is gathered primarily from failed women suicide bombers held in various Israeli gaols (Victor 2004, Channel 4 programme 'The Cult of the Suicide Bomber', 11 September 2006).

38 Sri Lanka has the highest rate of suicides amongst its female population, according to statistics produced by the World Health Organisation in 1991. Also referred to in Hopgood (2005: 76).

39 BBC 'Inside Story' programme, shown on UK History Channel, 17 July 2004.

40 Bauman (1992: 209) argues that in death and morality there are two kinds of individuals present: the hero who acts to promote the cause and the moral person who sees the cause as life/well-being of another person. Both these individuals are called upon to sacrifice themselves for the cause that is far nobler than the value of their lives.

41 Women combatant who have fought in the Elephant Pass battle said, 'our friends and colleagues have voluntarily given their lives to a cause which they firmly believed in and held precious to their hearts…they died expecting us to carry on the struggle after their death. So when we see them fighting with all their strength, when we see them dying, when we are side by side with them as they die, our determination to fight the enemy does not diminish, it grows even more stronger' (Balasingham writing as Adele Ann 1993: 84).

42 LTTE conducted a series of attacks against the State armed forces code named Never Ceasing Waves. A great number of human losses were incurred on both sides.

43 Schalk (1997a and 1997b). It is of uttermost importance to understand the concept of *tiya[a]kam* as a reaction of encountering death. *Tiya[a]kam* is a specific type of

aggressive mourning behaviour in the martial culture of the LTTE. (Schalk 1992: 51). 'Aggressive mourning', as referred to by Schalk (1992) above, defines instances where a sense of loss is felt when a comrade who has been a close friend in a kin relationship dies. This sense of loss and bereavement can act as a trigger for avenging the death through self-sacrifice, and often of volunteering to be a suicide bomber. Though my research did not reveal the range of meanings that are discussed by Schalk (1992), I was informed of the ethos and the sentimentality behind the self-sacrifice of undertaking suicide missions.

44 Schalk's linguistic linking of the LTTE's Hinduism and Jaffna's Christianity has resulted in him arguing that the word *caatci*, literally meaning to 'submissively endure all suffering to the end without using violence' (Schalk 1992: 53), was, in effect created by Tamil Christian (Catholic, to be precise) priests when describing the LTTE combatants who have been killed in combat. At the earlier part of the struggle there was some notable support for the LTTE by the Church, giving credence to the Church's willingness to make the combatants both martyrs and heroes. Arguably there is a fundamental difference between the literal meaning of the word and the adoption made by the LTTE, which Schalk claims is an anomaly, whereby the LTTE in fact uses the word to describe aggressive and extreme form of combat committed prior to own death in battlefield. The word *caacti* has some of its roots in colonial period when a person was willing to sacrifice own self to uphold a personal conviction (ibid.: 53–54). *Tiyaakam* in reference to an armed struggle is to be found in Bhagavad Gita, the sacred scriptures from ancient India that is believed to have been the spoken word of Lord Krishna. This notion of the armed struggle was revived in India during the period of conflict against the British. A further development of terminology extends to *Cattiyaccaaski*, meaning 'truth-witness', or *Irrattacaaksi*, meaning 'blood-witness'. Blood-witness was a title handed over by Christian missionaries upon translating the Greek word Martyr from the New Testament. An example of this can be seen in Matthew 18, 16 and many other places in the translated version of the Tamil language New Testament (Schalk 1992: 52).

45 de Mel (2004: 77). This is a view based on the work of Hage (2003). Writing about Palestinian suicide bombers, Hage states that self-esteem and the glorification of martyrdom are primary motivational factors for suicide bombers. The martyrdom aspect, which is mostly discussed amongst the literature relating to Middle Eastern suicide bombings, is seen as an extreme form of religious belief which is manipulated to create an end with immediacy of reward.

46 *Mavirar* is plural and *maviran* is singular. *Mavirar* means 'Great Heroes' (*nal* means day). Therefore, all combatants who sacrifice their life for the cause are 'Great Heroes'. Schalk (1997a: 4).

47 A visiting LTTE leader handed the cyanide capsules to the 12 members.

48 Though Schalk (1997b: 45) does not engage in the religious difference debate, he does say that the LTTE found it hard to convince families of Hindu combatants that

their family member should be buried rather than cremated. He further states that, 'Since July 1991 all martyrs have been buried and not burned in the tuyilum illam [Sleeping House]. The official reason for this was that the martyr should feel close to the soil which [s]he defended. The non-official reason is that Yalppanam [Jaffna] suffering from a lack of firewood.'

49 I was informed by the Gatekeeper that the idea to prepare a showcase was given to the LTTE by one of the civic women who was part of my interview group, whose specific identity (as well as the name of the second cemetery) I wish to withhold for safety reasons. Also, see Narayan-Swamy (2006: 259).

50 A lifetime stipend of four hundred dollars is paid by whichever organisation claims responsibility for the attack (eg. Hamas, POL or Islamic Jihad) for male suicide bombers, and two hundred dollars per month was paid for women suicide bombers (Victor 2004: 35).

51 BBC 'Inside Story' programme, shown on UK History Channel (17 July 2004). Also see de Mel (2001).

6 *Ah-lu-mai*: Equality and Empowerment of the New Woman, *Puthumai Pen*

The term 'empowerment' is used widely within the feminist discourse to imply the possession of some form of power. A working definition that I will use here to represent this term defines empowerment as a 'multi-dimensional social process' that enables individuals to gain some kind of control or authority over some aspects of their lives in society. It suggests some change in the existing power relations, and relates specifically to individuals and their relationships with others in their communities.[1] The definition of *Ah-lu-mai* given below represents similar sentiments, and as such should be treated as same.

There is no definition of empowerment in Tamil language that relates specifically to women in recognising the control or authority they have over their own lives. Therefore, when women combatants came to be recognised for their abilities and resilience, there was a need to define this development. The LTTE created the word *Ah-lu-mai,* which was reflective of the new woman that was seen amongst their combatant women, who regularly used the word *Ah-lu-mai* to mean empowerment. The word *Ah-lu-mai* encompasses 'governance, authority, or leadership roles', and 'authorise, give power, make able', to provide a new word that was used by the LTTE women to represent their new identity. The lack of a direct translation caused a problem during the interviews; this was resolved by the women combatants and their translator coming to an agreed decision as to what it could mean, even though the meaning was imprecise. It must be noted that the word *Ah-lu-mai* was often used by combatant women, but never by civilian women.

The war had challenged gender identity in civic society, which in turn had opened up possibilities that were unknown and certainly unavailable to women in the pre-war era. In this chapter, I discuss the prolonged war and the LTTE's intervention in civic life in Jaffna as the catalyst for a notable number of women leaving their traditional roles and embracing a completely new way of life: a life that offered a new purpose, a new aim and a new ambition, one that retained traditional views about female modesty, chastity and other forms of normative femininity as practised in Tamil society. This created a paradoxical position for women who entered the revolutionary movement and granted a certain degree of freedom for civic women in Jaffna.

In this chapter, I will explore how gender was (re)constructed within the revolutionary movement and how such (re)constructions of gender had reverberated through civic society to challenge the existing social construction of female roles in Tamil society. The chapter will further analyse *Ah-lu-mai* in relation to the traditional and changing roles of women in Tamil society and the creation of a new woman—*Puthumai Pen*. I will also critically examine the role played by Prabhakaran in the formation of the new gender discourse to asses the extent to which he had assisted in developing women's roles both within the LTTE and in civic society.

Changing Views of Traditional Roles

As discussed earlier, Tamil women in Jaffna have a long history tied to the cultural values and practices of southern India. These form the basis of Tamil women's social roles within the confines of the home in Jaffna, where women have begun to negotiate a new kind of identity. The negotiated identities are the result of a situation where women were engaging in new roles by physically fighting for an independent state of Tamil *Eelam* while still maintaining most of the traditional social values.

Sakti, the power held by women effectively formed the basis of Tamil women's overall social position that posits women in an inner and an outer realm in society. The inner realm, known as *akam*, is the domestic sphere, where women were powerful as their voices were heard and their views were aired. In the outer realm, known as *puram*, they were visibly controlled by the men in their families.[2]

Akam, or the inward power of Tamil women in general (both combatant and civic), must not be disregarded as it forms a strong foundation for our understanding of combatant women. Reynolds (1978: 69) refers to a Tamil proverb that states, 'Through woman is being; and through woman is downfall',[3] which means that within Tamil society, a woman is believed to have the power to control and alter significant events effecting life such as health, wealth, happiness and death. Wadley (1980: 153) argues the power held is so great that 'in order to control and direct powers, the dominant ideology states that the Tamil woman should be constrained and controlled by her male kin'.

Tradition demands a form of self-control that is embedded deep in patriarchal culture, giving Tamil women a degree of social power that is recognised as being confined to the domestic sphere but is nonetheless controlled by the male relations in the family. The creation of the domestic sphere and its boundaries is an act of patriarchal control. There is an ambiguous acceptance by society of a woman's recognised social powers within the confines of domesticity based on sexual purity (virginity) and morality linked to motherhood, which in turn places women on a pedestal and likens them to goddesses. At the same time, her sexuality causes a great deal of concern to the four male family entities (father, brother, husband and son) that are in charge of controlling it through a guise of stringent female behavioural expectations.[4]

The socially contradictory position that a Tamil woman finds herself in is of particular interest as she is overtly dominated by men, but covertly recognised as having an exceptional power as a woman. However, the public image is predominantly ruled by a social position assumed of women. A closer inspection reveals that women primarily interact with kin and non-kin folk, but not necessarily with strangers. This asymmetrical social relationship positioning has brought observations from David, who notes that:

> The public image of Jaffna women, putting it bleakly, is that women are selectively ignorant and incapable of learning crucial kinds of social knowledge, that they are dominated and

> **subordinates to men, and that these states of affairs are ideologically represented as the state of nature. (David 1980: 106)**

Though this notion is not applicable to all women, it is often perpetuated by women who actively distance themselves from any open debate about politics. David (1980) acknowledges that the men in society confirm this view by claiming that women's unwillingness to participate in such conversation is due to their lack of knowledge. However, I did see exceptions to David's observations amongst many of the combatant and civic women I met in Jaffna (including those I interviewed) who were an educated, socially conscientious minority. Their social conscience can be attributed not only to education, but also to the changing political climate that emphasises women as active participants in society.

Reynolds (1980) argues that women's acceptance of a subservient social position derives from Tamil women's need to be secondary to men in order to maintain a powerful position as an auspicious being who holds the responsibility for the well-being and maintenance of the family's lineage through selfless acts of suffering. She argues that beliefs such as self-denial and self-sacrifice are seen in religion and that this ideological social position then translates as 'a salvific condition' (Reynolds 1980: 57), whereby the women act in a covert manner to perpetuate their subordinate state and maintain the power it yields.

Social Change: Rationale and Impact

Through my own research I noticed that, though women (combatant and civic) agreed unanimously that women's status in Jaffna's Tamil society is certainly secondary to men, none of the civic female supporters and advocates of equality practised an alternative social role within their own confined domestic sphere. Women were able to exert some autonomy within the confines of the patriarchal-defined private space, but it is within the public place that social change was more visible. Thus, with the controlling mechanism set in the domestic sphere, civic women have embarked on social changes in the public domain where even the simple act of women riding bicycles through the streets of Jaffna is seen as a symbolic reference to the independence of civic women.[5]

Women riding bicycles was an act born out of necessity rather than an evocative emancipatory action. During prolonged periods of warfare, public transport was no longer available, and the petrol embargo resulted in private vehicles being garaged.

> Here we are affected by the war. Because of the war there were no buses, no electricity, no such as thing!!!. So every working woman in Jaffna was forced to ride [a] bicycle. Otherwise, they can't get to work. Because work place is more than two miles from their home. So they have to walk otherwise no other transport....Nobody is there to take them to office. Who's here? So working women suffered. I first started walking to my school. One week I went walking. It took one hour ... two miles ... yeah. Very difficult. So I was forced to learn to ride a bicycle. Second week I started going by bike. This thing 'I am a woman I mustn't go on my own or, I can't expect others to chaperone me....I didn't think like that, but *the need* forced me to change....This [social change] was induced by war. Luckily, we are now happy. I saw lot of women older than me riding bicycles and we were very happy....So many women. Very grass root memory... We are so happy because we are not obliged to younger brothers or sons. We don't have to ask 'Son can you take me to the temple, can you take me to the hospital', that thing is out now. Before that we were dependent on others. (BP)

This view was shared by GV:

> Tell her this. A woman had to always live depending on her father first, then the husband and then son. But now she is going abroad or going to another place leaving young children to work. Not that she has no love for her husband or children, but she is more capable of doing these things now. She is able to ride the bicycle and go about doing what she wants to do. She can now live alone and send her family away to educate or work. (GV)

Women's experiences of social change were emancipatory. The independence and freedom discussed by them was reflective of their own changing attitudes as well as that of civic society as a whole. Added to this, many young men were not available to assist women with daily tasks or act as chaperones. Some had willingly joined the movement for protection from the State or were forcefully recruited by the terrorist group in its need for fighters; others have fled the country in fear of being shot as suspected rebels by the State-run army. The result of this shortage of able-bodied young men in families meant women had to mobilise themselves by any means available in order to attend to their daily needs.[6] Undoubtedly, this resulted in definitive social changes that took place in women's lives after the war started.

> **So everything happens, there was a change in the society, and in women also. So we can survive. So the concept of the family is changing. Before war and displacement, we had to balance everything. We had to adjust to the men. All because of this cultural concept. Since the war and the displacement, the women said ok you go, I will live alone. I can manage well on my own. There was courage to do it. (HA)**

The word 'courage' as used by HA encompasses both admittance and reflection of major social changes that had occurred in women's lives. A loosening of the patriarchal grip of male control meant that in a post-displacement period, Tamil women became aware of their own potential, and this released a body of women to become combatants and assume the role of the male fighter. This particular role was so alien to the traditionally passive social roles of Tamil women that it became a significant addition to the already changing roles of women in civic society.

Impact of the LTTE on Society

The transition made by women from a dependent to a relatively independent role was often seen in Jaffna as a radical aspect of empowerment. Some women, such as BP, ES and DK, were also of the view that women change their social behaviour in order to survive, and that it was a necessity induced by the war rather than a part of a social revolution.[7]

The direct influence of the LTTE on the lives of civic women can be seen in the key areas of marriage and widowhood, although the levels of achievement of the LTTE over such ingrained social practices were limited. Through self-confidence, the women combatants were able to influence some of the social restrictions imposed on women's lives, such as choices of marital partners and the social views of widows.

Marriages of personal choice, colloquially known as 'love marriages' which are generally frowned upon and discouraged in society at large, were accepted by the LTTE along with traditional arranged marriages. However, the LTTE thoroughly disapproved of the dowry system practised in Jaffna, which they saw as being an insult to a woman for her worth was being measured in moveable and immovable property. The LTTE issued laws disallowing this time-honoured practice, which was undoubtedly an economic relief for many of the poor in Jaffna, but failed to eradicate it as the dowry system changed its name to 'donations' and was thus resurfaced. The metamorphosed dowry as a donation was given to the groom's family by the bride's family. The difference was that a dowry was agreed prior to the marriage, then written down and formalised; but the donation was a verbal agreement with no documentation.

The only change on this issue was seen when women combatants retire from the revolutionary organisation and marry a man in the civic society. Many women (such as AK) have not exchanged any 'donations', staying true to the LTTE ideologies. The women combatants who entered into matrimony found it harder to conform to the expectations of in-laws and those of the greater civic society. These expectations were often simple practices such as wearing jewellery or flowers in their hair, or any such female-centred beautification. In traditional society, when such customs were not followed, it conveys a message of widowhood.

Traditionally, widows are shunned from public life and excluded from auspicious occasions such as weddings. They are often condemned to wearing white saris and seen as bearers of bad tidings, and are not accepted as a part of the functioning society. Within the Jaffna peninsula, widows were not stigmatised to the same extent as before, and were an accepted part of society. Though the overall status of a widow in Tamil society has improved greatly, it is a mistake to believe that the status has totally changed. However, many women, including BP, DK, ES, GV and HA, have said that they will not allow their widowed mothers to wear white saris and live in the shadows anymore.

The LTTE was very successful in repatriating widows back into civic society. Whilst the removal of the socio-historical stigma of widowhood was perfectly admirable, it must also be noted that since the war there had been a rise in the number of female-headed households. Many of these were widowed women struggling to bring up young families with the added burden of care responsibilities for the elderly. The women of the LTTE had been active in promoting the ideology of a non-stigmatised social status for widowed civic women and had started to address it formally as an issue. The women combatants gave confidence to the widowed women in civic society and educated them in trades that were never opened to them before, including roles that were traditionally perceived as masculine employment, such as motor mechanism.

The LTTE discouraged the traditional reverence bestowed upon the fertility of married women, whereby infertile wives held a lesser social role than that of fertile women. The LTTE did not regard women as the keepers of purity of race and caste,[8] nor did it consider them subservient to men in all aspects of life. Neither the traditional nor the revivalist attitude reveals the fundamental problem that the LTTE had in creating a combatant woman and linking her to history.

Women's Initiation and Perceived Feminism in the LTTE

The rationalisation of women carrying arms had been a difficult concept in comparison with the notion of a militant mother that was steeped in history.[9] As with the militant mother, there needed to be a moralistic justification for creating an image for women that could be acceptable to all. In a culture where sexual purity for women was valued highly, it was important to show the combatant women in a favourable light. Therefore, the LTTE created an image of a beautiful soul that was sexually pure and would rise in times of need as a true warrior to fight a just cause. The notion of an avenging virgin was an appealing concept that the LTTE knew would be agreeable to both the patriarchal civic community and the combatant women. Thus the LTTE actively promoted the image of the Armed Virgin who combined the beautiful soul and the just warrior.[10] The constructed image of an Armed Virgin was also highly appealing to the mass media and its depiction of the LTTE's combatant women as seen in many newspaper articles of the time.

The emergence of combatant women in the *Vituthalai Pulikal Munani Pen* (Women's Front of the LTTE) was undoubtedly a new phenomenon, though a historical recording of women's involvement in political struggles reveals that Tamil women were involved in Gandhian-style peaceful protests. A number of women (including AK) from varying socio-political backgrounds did contribute to the LTTE's armed struggle from the outset, albeit as non-combatants. Their roles at the time (early 1980s) were limited to socially defined 'women's work': providing safe housing and caring for the sick and injured.

The combatants that joined in the mid-1980s (such as Arasi, AK and Kavitha) had to continuously prove themselves in order to claim their place beside male fighters as competent combatants. 'Women can do everything as good as the men, but we did have to work harder' (Arasi). By the time Yalini and others joined the revolutionary movement, women combatants were seen as a normal part of the revolutionary family. Those who joined later, around 1990, did not feel that they had to work to gain respect from the male combatants and were able to reap the same benefits as established female combatants because their roles had already been defined within this gendered sphere.

> **They [combatant men] also came from the same society. At the beginning they also had their doubts. When they saw how we performed and saw our *ah-lu-mai their* views changed, from looking down on us now they have changed to treating us as their equals and respect us more. (Arasi)**

In order to gain equality and respect, the women combatants often undertook tasks that were arduous and, above all, dangerous. For AK, the ability of women combatants to perform acts that historically have been in the male domain, such as digging deep wells for water (and the socially recognised female act of carrying away of the sand being completed by male combatants), was a sign of a reversal of roles. AK reveals, 'When I was in the Mulatheevu jungle, we had to dig a 60 feet deep well. We did the drilling and put explosives, went down and if we did the digging at the bottom they [male combatants] will take the soil away.' The reversal of traditional roles within the LTTE movement had created a perception of equality that had empowered women to believe in themselves.

Mallika says, 'I don't think there is any difference between men and women in the movement. We are all treated equally. Whatever a man is doing in the battle we are also doing the same thing.' So who was responsible for getting women involved in combatant roles? When I questioned any combatant or civic individual, they always claimed that the originator of the idea to engage women in combat was Prabhakaran. This was also reflected in Balasingham's (1993, written as Adele Ann) writings.

> Mr Prabhakaran, who views the successful induction of women into the armed struggle as one of his major achievements, will, without reserve, promote the holistic development of the women fighters, as part of his vision of women's path to liberation. For him the independence of women is crucial to their liberation and the assertion of courage and self-confidence is a prerequisite to the realisation of such independence. (Balasingham 1993: 110–111, written as Adele Ann)

Schalk (1992: 84) claims the originator was the Western-educated academic Nirmala Nithyanathan (an English language lecturer attached to the University of Jaffna known as a feminist sociologist and a political scientist), who was (with her sister Rajani Thiranagama)[11] actively involved in the LTTE during the early days of its formation. According to Schalk, Nithyanathan's role included translating key feminist texts relating to women's involvement in the armed struggles of other regions, such as Latin America. Balasingham (2003) claims that the Western 'second wave feminism' as learnt by Nithyanathan during her period of education in the West was neither understood nor appreciated by Prabhakaran, and was viewed as being too 'radical' for the female recruits from villages to understand.[12]

Jayawardena (1992: 1) argues, 'Those who want to continue to keep the women of our countries in a position of subordination find it convenient to dismiss feminism as a foreign ideology.' Therefore, Prabhakaran's dismissal of Nithyanathan confirmed Jayawardena's argument that feminism was viewed as a diversion that distracts women from familial responsibilities or, worse still, the 'revolutionary struggle for national liberations' (Jayawardena 1992: 2).

Jayawardena (1992) sees feminism as a tool to understand women's oppression in the public place and private space, but Prabhakaran viewed feminism as Western and therefore an alien concept for Tamil women in the LTTE and for himself. His views were very much in line with traditionalist Tamil society, which understands feminism to be 'a product of "decadent" Western capitalism; that is based on a foreign culture of no relevance to women in the Third World' (Jayawardena 1992: 2). This was a particularly problematic position for the LTTE. On the one hand, feminism is Western and problematic, and on the other, the movement needs to challenge traditional roles in order to allow women to fight. Therefore, when an ideology of militancy was developed for the women of the LTTE, it was promoted within the patriarchal values of Armed Virgins. Thus the LTTE was able to resolve a problematic situation without overtly challenging the existing traditional view. The kind of radicalism that was seen in Nithyanathan and her teachings was not an agreeable quality for the women of the LTTE to develop in contrast with the qualities of aggression they were expected to develop by becoming combatants.

Balasingham (2003) states that Prabhakaran has the ability to relate to women combatants far better than Nithyanathan, as his own background was more in line with the lower-middle and working classes from which the majority of the women combatants came. Interestingly, participants of this research strongly believed that it was truly a long-sighted view by Prabhakaran to allow women to join the LTTE and become an equal part of the struggle for Tamil *Eelam*. They felt as women combatants they were accepted as an integral part of the revolutionary group.

The LTTE perceived the struggle for independence as common to both men and women, and that power relation in a post-conflict period would affect both parties equally. They held the view that 'the struggle for independence is the frame, base, or the background for the struggle for rights of women' (Schalk 1992: 78). Hence, they argued that priority must be given to the cause of an independent State, and added to this were the specific demands of women. The liberation of women was directly linked to the liberation of the Tamil State. Enloe (2000: 62) claims that asking women to wait until the nationalist goal is achieved is 'weighted with implications'. She argues that 'it is advice predicted on the belief that the most dire problems facing the nascent national community are problems which can be explained and resolved without reference to power relations between men and women'. Women combatants of the LTTE viewed this equality linked to their liberation as primarily a political freedom which would be followed by an economic and social freedom from the Sinhalese government. However, it was difficult not to notice that the women in the organisation were not sufficiently independent to state an alternative view.

One theme common to both civic and the LTTE women was their belief that a nation state needed to be created before women's true emancipation could be addressed. It was difficult to ascertain if normative femininities were the cause of women combatants saying that they would want a free State before total emancipation or whether they truly believed it.

> **The movement was started to free us from being oppressed. The main aim of the war was to free people who were oppressed and for the people to enjoy freedom. For this reason they are ready to sacrifice. Which is something we have to appreciate. For our society to move forward first the political barrier has to be broken and people have to be free. Then only the cultural barriers can be broken. Barriers with regard to cast and widows etc can be removed only if the political situation is resolved and people are free. Yes. And the main objective of the war is to break the internal barriers and be politically free. The internal barrier is male dominated society has to break up and also cast and cultural changes has to break up. (GV)**

Why the LTTE could not have achieved both simultaneously was never mentioned in their discourse, but it may be because all their learning in relation to women combatants had been from revolutions that fought first to create an independent State before attempting to liberate women from society's constraints. The LTTE claimed that it was imperative for women to take part in the revolutionary struggle for the ultimate aim of emancipation and truly be a part of the achievements within the organisation.

> **Women's participation in the struggle is an important thing. Because our policy, LTTE's policy is emancipating our society is part of our liberating our homeland. So here, in the north and east women's participation is equal to men's participation. If we have to free our society and if we have to make the women's awareness, first we have to free our homeland. Then we can deal with women's awareness. So the women's participation in the struggle is very very important. (Yalini)**

The claim that the homeland must be freed before dealing with the issue of equality in society resonates deeply with other global revolutionary groups in which women have participated.[13] There was an unquestioning acceptance of women's equality taking a secondary position, but there was also a conviction that it needed to be dealt with in that order, and not simultaneously.

Glass Ceiling: Women in Leadership

A general perception existed amongst the LTTE combatant women that leadership of a combat unit was a natural progression for women combatants with battle experience. There were examples of fighting units led by women, and though these were fewer in number than the male-led units, women combatants viewed this as an opportunity that could be achieved regardless of the social perception that relegates women to the role of being led. It is pertinent to note that women were in a minority as leaders within the LTTE despite a large proportion of its combatants being females. According to Arasi, the Central Committee of the LTTE claimed that there was one woman in every three members (at the time of interviews), indicating that at least one-third of the LTTE combatants were female.[14]

Balasingham (1993: 15, written as Adele Ann) says, 'The emergence of Liberation Tigers on the Tamil national political scene has provided

Tamil women with opportunities and horizons that would never have entered the minds of Tamil women a decade ago.' Balasingham (1993, written as Adele Ann) claims that being a part of the LTTE had granted women an opportunity to learn alternative skills. However, the extent to which women were involved in both decision-making and high-level leadership appeared to have been limited.[15] This also suggests that the combatant women did not achieve full socio-political empowerment. This may illuminate a certain defect in the LTTE leadership, which only develops women up to a certain point and not beyond, arguing that the women were only accepted because of a militaristic need for foot soldiers rather than a need to develop or improve their role in society (Thiranagama et al. 1990: 19). Further, women would fit easily into the trained roles with a belief that they were at par with the men in Tamil society, which of course would increase their self-confidence. The change that took place within the women's own social perception of themselves did not appear to be reflected at the strategic level of the LTTE. Although a limited number of women held key positions, these were not necessarily positions where the decisions made affected the whole movement.

Although there was a lack of transparency regarding the LTTE leadership that prevented the emergence of a complete picture illustrating women's involvement at the highest levels, the evidence from my interviews indicated that the combatant women believed there was an attempt to show an equal representation between men and women at higher levels.

> **In the LTTE Central Committee there are two men cadres and two women cadres. The director is Mr ... Deputy Directors there are two one is a lady and other one is a man...and another lady secretary. We will be very friendly. We will talk friendly. We will do our work ... even help each other. The Central Committee of the LTTE has a two male and two female participatory units. The director of the committee is a male. (Yalini)**

The women combatants appeared not to be concerned by the fact that the Director of the Committee had always been a man and was likely to remain so. The acceptance of a male leader did not completely determine the position of women combatants within the organisation, but it did reach far into the Tamil cultural mindset, where women were seen in the *akam* (inner) and *puram* (outer) social locations, as discussed earlier.

The issue of women as leaders needs to be looked through cultural norms where an individual's own upbringing plays a part in the desire to lead men and women to war. For many years, the cultural norms and patterns of behaviour have prepared women to take orders and directions. Once they joined the LTTE organisation, their confidence was built up to regard themselves as an equal amongst other men and women, but within a hierarchical militarised structure. Promotion of women within the organisation helped women combatants strive for more (male-centric) leadership roles.

Women-only committees dealt with the decisions that focused on women's welfare. Men primarily dealt with the decisions that affected the whole organisation, but with some input from women. As Kavitha says, 'There are men working under women … and in the women's section the women leaders made decisions and there was no need to ask the men for any decisions regarding the women. Whatever decisions we make we will let them [male combatants] know.' On closer examination, this contradiction changed to include separate decision-making trajectories. The harmonious picture created to illustrate the neutrality of the power relation between male and female combatants was that women were the decision-makers, and men were only kept informed of the decisions made. Although the Women's Section and the Women's Committees were able to make decisions, none of the women combatants interviewed said that they had the authority to direct men in any strategic or policy-led matters. This raises the question as to what levels can women rise within the movement.

An analysis of the power to make one's own decisions revealed that there were complex negotiations of gender relations in transition. The power described by Arasi was very much a delegated authority with some room to manoeuvre within a given structure created by men to achieve the nation state. The roles to which women were directed and have gained some empowerment from were primarily in the female domain. The combatant women's decision-making power was limited to making decisions that only concerned women within the movement. These 'women's issues' reminded me of Tickner's (1992: 2) argument that women in politics are channelled into policy areas centring on issues relating to women, thus giving them a limited amount of controllable power. Such power, I would argue, was controlled by the leadership (which is male); hence such allocated or transferred 'controllable power' bore a strong resemblance to the masculine leadership roles of the LTTE.

On rare occasions when the LTTE leaders ventured out of the country to meet other terrorist groups, there was usually a woman combatant to complete the picture. A closer look will reveal the participatory role of the woman combatant in attendance to be merely symbolic, as she did not contribute to political discussions. It is therefore a tokenistic inclusion, and evidence that the LTTE leadership knew that they needed to offer a vision of equality to gain favour and widen their appeal.[16]

The lack of female involvement at the higher levels of the LTTE politics was an important point in an ethno-national liberation group that promoted female equality, and women were believed to form one-third to half of its fighting combatants.[17] Highly eloquent female leaders such as Arasi were visible within the LTTE but had a relatively obscure international profile. The only woman seen in political discussion groups was Adele Balasingham, the Australian wife of the LTTE's political theoretician. However, since the death of her husband in 2006, Adele Balasingham has taken a back seat in the politics relating to the Tamil *Eelam*.

Upon questioning the Gatekeeper on the visible lack of female participation in actual discussions, the reply was that women combatants of the LTTE were still not ready for such political roles. Whilst this view was not from a combatant woman, it must nonetheless be seen within a context of a patriarchal construction, which forms the strong social foundation that harbours an accepted perception of the limited abilities of women as political representatives. The women's levels of power do not reach to the top, but stop at a Glass Ceiling with the Head of the women's Political Wing—the highest female rank in the LTTE.[18] Whilst the lack of female combatants in the uppermost positions of the LTTE was identified, one must not make the mistake of undermining the leadership roles held by women combatants, as they were powerful within a complex negotiation both inside the organisation and in the greater civic community.

Is Prabhakaran a Feminist?

Prabhakaran did not indicate any affinity with women's social roles or a need to challenge the restrictions imposed on them by society. However, he became the champion of major social change that (re)constructed the female identity for women combatants and impacted on civic women. It is highly probable that Prabhakaran may not have been overtly aware that his actions in engaging women in combatant roles would create a feminist challenge and change many Tamil women's lives. During my visit to the Women's Political Office in Vanni, I noted that every room carried portrait photographs of him, and women combatants were almost sentimental in their references to him. The women combatants I interviewed saw him as unlike any other man in Tamil society, for he had bravely gone against the cultural normative practices to transpose his faith in women (combatants). He had instilled into them the confidence to succeed as the equals of men. This progressive view of gender equality was in complete contrast with the society's general view of women and their capabilities.[19] In the speech below Prabhakaran identifies the contributions women can make as equals to men:

> **The Liberation Tigers is one of the greatest accomplishments accomplished by our movement. This marks a revolutionary turning point in the history of liberation struggle of the women of Tamililam. Women can succeed on the ideal path towards their (own) liberation, only through joining forces with a liberation movement. (Women) [of civic state] can change into revolutionary women who have heroism, abandonment (of life), courage and self-confidence. Only when women join forces with our revolutionary movement that has formulated (a path) to liberation of our women, our struggle also shall reach perfection. (Prabhakaran cited in Schalk 1992: 50)**

The speech remained a call for more women to join the LTTE (especially if they were concerned with self-liberation from the patriarchal chains of Tamil society) and was reflective of the faith he had in women combatants. He regularly vocalised this faith in public speeches to encourage women combatants to be more active and civic women to join an organisation that appeared to practice equality regardless of gender differences.

> **In our movement, opportunities are equal to every one. In the name of women we are not oppressed there. Our leader is the reason for this. It is important that we rise up to these expectations. Our leader has a very high regard towards the women. He has lot of confidence in the women's *Ah-lu-mai* ...we didn't have many obstacles just because we were women. You must understand this properly and explain to her. We all get equal opportunities. (Arasi)**

The recognisable admiration for Prabhakaran in Arasi's discourse was very much repeated by all the women combatants I spoke to. The veneration of Prabhakaran extends to the moment of dying, when the women of the LTTE are often known to call out '*annnay*' (elder brother).[20] Whilst this can be argued as a form of patriarchal reverence, I would say this has a much deeper kinship identity that extends beyond a consanguine family tie to the very special kind of loyal veneration held by a dying individual. This unwavering loyalty was encapsulated in the personal oath taken by each combatant to support Prabhakaran. It was also reflected in AK's narrative when she refers to Prabhakaran: 'We [women combatants] didn't have any problems as our leader has very clear ideas about women cadres. He always gave us the opportunity to be in the front and get involved in the fights and this was an example to others.'

Prabhakaran actively encouraged women combatants to take part in battles and be seen as an example to others. One can argue this was the callous trickery of a male leadership to direct the women to the frontline, or that it was a form of recognition of women's capabilities to be brave and active in the frontlines (as viewed by the combatant women). It could also be seen as a challenge to the patriarchal society that undermines women's abilities. The women in Tamil society were seen as being incapable of taking on the tough, masculine-orientated roles of protectors of the nation. However, the combatant women have shown that they too were capable of meeting the demands of such activities.

Although it can be argued that women combatant's trust and loyalty to Prabhakaran had been exploited by the overt encouragement of the leadership, it nonetheless appeared to have made the women combatants feel that they were treated equally within the revolutionary movement. This contrasted with the women in civic society who were marginalised for being women. Reflecting on Prabhakaran's recognition of combatant women, Arasi states: 'Our capabilities, our dedication and our goal were only important to us and we didn't have any obstacles to go up because our leader has lot of confidence in the *Ah-lu-mai* of the women.'

Women combatants viewed *Ah-lu-mai* as a direct result of Prabhakaran's active encouragement and forceful advocacy of equal rights for women. However, closer inspection of Prabhakaran's own family reveals a lack of that same promotion of equality in his private life: he has kept his wife, Mathy, away from the movement completely, even though she was an activist during her undergraduate days (as discussed in Chapter 4). Pratap (2001: 176) observes, 'Prabhakaran married the prettiest of the fasting girls....As she sat by his side during the interview, Prabhakaran's wife did not speak even once out of turn. She wore a printed wrinkle-free sari and a modest blouse. She seems gentle and domesticated.'

Pratap's observations of Mathy presented a picture of a traditional Tamil woman who was the 'beautiful auspicious mother'. Mathy continued to wear traditional clothing and stayed within cultural expectations with a lack of sophistication befitting her modesty and respectability until her death in 2010. Mathy's behaviour of sitting quietly by her husband's side without intervening 'in male businesses' projected the traditional image of the non-interfering 'good' Tamil wife. Her demeanour in the public arena presented her as 'gentle and domesticated', and her appearance and mannerisms were a complete contrast to the combatant women. The fact that the social changes for Tamil women were led by her husband appeared to have made little difference to her own continuation with tradition, where normative feminine practices were considered the 'only' acceptable form of behaviour for women.[21]

It can be argued that Mathy's appearance and behaviour was a clever strategy to show herself as a conventional Tamil woman merely to be a part of the civic society, which became tenuous for many of the women combatants after they joined the LTTE, as discussed later in this chapter. This image of Mathy may be reminiscent of Elshtain's *Beautiful Soul* (1987: 9), a woman who can lay claim simultaneously to family and society; Mathy's appearance of unselfish devotion was needed in order for the country and the family to survive.

Mathy's position does question whether the LTTE's approach really challenged existing attitudes, and whether Prabhakaran was committed to truly challenging traditional views or was keen to uphold part of its traditions to gain support from the civic society. That said, Mathy's normative femininity contrasted with the LTTE's martial feminism and seems to uphold the traditional values of civic society, stopping the struggle from being isolated from the much-needed support of civic society.

Puthumai Pen: The New Woman

Maunaguru (1995: 166–167) describes the new phenomenon of *Puthumai Pen* as a concept that was transferred from twentieth-century Indian nationalism to the Tamil national discourse of the 1980s in Sri Lanka. Under the creation and construction of a *Puthumai Pen,* the four virtues that all Tamil women were tied to (modesty, charm, shyness and respectful fear) were challenged.[22] Although Tamil women (both combatant and civic) have taken on new roles and (re)constructed an alternative gender identity, the greatest change (from the traditional view to the newly re-created alternative) was seen in the combatant women.

Balasingham (1993: 5, written as Adele Ann) claims that the deepening genocidal oppression resulting from the race riots of 1983 propelled young women into a revolutionary world. Balasingham (1993: 6, written as Adele Ann) says, 'Young women broke the shackles of social constraints; they ripped open the straight jacket of conservative images of women. The militant patriotism of Tamil women finally blossomed as they entered into a new life of revolutionary armed struggle.'

In the new life of armed struggle, the main qualities that were valued of women were the ability to self-sacrifice and the ability to be courageous in the face of death, clearly demonstrating the rise of a new kind of Tamil woman, *Puthumai Pen*,[23] who had self-assurance and assertiveness. Thus the combatant woman in Tamil society was taking over the traditional image under the guise of 'militant nationalism' (Maunaguru 1995: 167) and changing it to suit the times.

The Tamil women who become combatants also become new women. The fearless reputation, tough external appearance and the widely discussed (and publicised) sexual purity of women combatants have all fed into the public imagination to create and harness the image (Schalk 1997a). Their lack of dependency on men in society stood in direct contrast with the historical relationship between the sexes, whereby women depended totally on men for their needs and welfare. The combatant women not only boast about their ability to look after themselves, but also those around them, including men.

The women of the LTTE were aware that the change in traditional roles of femininity in society is a challenge to the patriarchy and viewed this as a positive and progressive way forward. The ability to maintain the change that had occurred in society and in women's lives was a challenge for combatant women in a post-war era.

Identity Politics

The normative femininity that was practised in society distanced the combatant women from those of the civic society, but also brought forth a slow process of nuanced change in their relationship with one another. In addition to holding the necessary social appearances required of combatant women as part of society's collective identity as Tamil women, they also needed to fulfil the collective identity of the revolutionary movement as combatants. It is the second of these that differentiates the women combatants from civic women and sets them apart in their unique position. This separation between the two groups of women also removed the combatant women from becoming a direct part of the cultural practices that prescribed female roles and governed their behaviour.

It is important to recognise women combatants for their achievements as women in warfare rather than an appendage to the masculine separatist struggle.[24] Whilst there were issues of feminine modesty that came through in interviews, it was also clear that a need for non-gender-based recognition was required, especially when Arasi claimed, 'We [women combatants] don't want importance. We want to be simple'. Her discourse was strong in rejecting gender-orientated achievements. The simplicity that Arasi claimed was humbleness and humility that were accepted behavioural traits of modest Tamil women who does not crave glory or draw attention to themselves. Within the same modesty, certain strength identified her as a woman who was capable of dealing with complex and difficult issues. Arasi further says, 'Another thing is we don't want importance just because we are women. We don't believe in that culture [*of giving importance to women*]. It is important they recognise her "Ah-lu-mai" and her capabilities.'

Arasi's insistence on being recognised for her own ability, rather than an identity based on her gender, contradicted the traditional female identity that had been created within the culture. It was important to show the community as well as the world that these achievements were due to the individual's effort and commitment to the revolutionary cause rather than to a gender-based positive discrimination. This, however, must not be viewed in isolation, as the achievements were both tied to, and gained through, the movement.

The confidence gained by combatant women was often visible, and they were happy to discuss their achievements. They were also vehement in denying that any aspect of their lives was controlled by men in the organisation. Arasi explains, 'Under any circumstance we do not get dragged behind the men. We have our own individuality. We have authority to make decisions about anything. We will join and do things. But we are separate. But nobody can impose their views on us.'

Arasi took a strong view in defending her role as a woman combatant in a male combatant's environment. She rejected the notion that as women combatants they were hindered in the progressive path of female liberation. Arasi's apparent refusal to acknowledge male dominance may be a way of rationalising gender in ways that permitted her to continue to believe in equality despite debates over the apparent lack of it.

The extent of the male influence over women combatant's lives, which could be seen through the intricacies of male–female relationships, was often disclosed in a careful manner. When Arasi was questioned about working with men within the revolutionary organisation she paused for a long time before answering, suggesting that she was guarded in her reply, which might indicate a fear of misinterpretation. The deliberate caution I detected could also have been an attempt to disclose cultural confinements that prevented 'talking together' or any social interaction between men and women generally, as male and female roles were divided in society. It may also be that Arasi was formulating a line to appease what she assumed I wished to hear. Upon reflection, it appeared the caution was highly likely to stem from the male hierarchy that was operating within the LTTE and the potential repercussions that discussing a socially sensitive subject such as male–female interaction could cause. Arasi clarifies, '....They [men] are looking at us in a positive way. How can I say it....We are very helpful to each other. We talk to each other about our day-to-day problems. Whatever we decide we all talk together and come to a decision. We share our work.'

This painted a picture of modernity, where male and female relationships were in a comfortable zone of familiarity. The expected feminine behaviour of modesty was seen again in Arasi's diffident take on being recognised as a woman. Of course, the crux of her argument was that women must be recognised for their individuality rather than a collective gender identity.

> **Women cannot be separated from the society. They are very important part of the society. So it was inevitable that women also took part in the fight for freedom. When the enemy came to war against us he didn't differentiate between man and woman. War is common to everyone. So we also look at it the same way. (Arasi)**

This view was an acknowledgement of her being a woman and still managing to obtain recognition for her achievements. By the same token, she refused that acknowledgement in favour of an individual identity that was based on acts of achievement alone, not gender.

Image

The image presented by the LTTE women—wearing combat fatigues or male shirts and trousers, and carrying a gun—directly challenges the social conventions of the symbolically bejewelled and sari-clad women as the ideal of normative femininity in Tamil society. The deeply ingrained views of what women 'ought' to be is defined by a series of symbols such as appearance, conduct and behaviour, and by fitting into a culturally mapped out social role in Tamil society. In contrast with this, the combatant women's unyielding refusal to be conformist in their appearance openly challenged this social convention, causing some to argue that their appearance was androgynous and part of the LTTE's agenda to distance women from femininity in favour of 'self sacrifice, [and] austerity' (Coomaraswamy 1996: 10).[25]

Such arguments were viewed by many in Jaffna's Tamil society as an unfair claim against women combatants. It can be said that, by definition, women who move away from civic society to become combatants challenge normative feminine behaviour and the society's symbolism. The wearing of traditionally symbolised feminine clothing, such as long skirts and saris or having long hair, was impractical for carrying out the tasks necessary for surviving under extreme circumstances. The swapping of feminine clothes for masculine ones and carrying out masculine-oriented tasks inevitably made some in society to refer to it as maleness. However, my research participants in civic society explained that the clothing was not worn to appear as men, but for convenience of fighting. BP explained that when the women combatants first started to wear trousers and shirts, those in society did object, but with time they had gained an understanding of the practicality of such clothing.

> I think their clothes are very necessary for them for their work. When they first wore shirts and trousers, civilian people didn't like. Why these girls are wearing trousers and shirts and they are not very good. Later on there were discussions among

> women some are said it is needed for the work they do. They are driving tractors and vehicles in battle. (BP)

A similar view was also shared by ES:

> They are in the field no? They went to the field and fight with the army. So with this dress [men's shirts, men's trousers] they can do that. Yes it is convenient for them. So it is like the police it is their uniform no? No I don't think that it makes them look masculine. For us no ... there is a reason. And wearing a trouser like that won't be bad. It is not a bad thing. So it's ok. They won't show anything of their body. Not like short blouses. It is ok. (ES)

ES's acceptance of women combatants' clothing contained a particularly interesting point of modesty. According to her, the masculine dress worn by women combatants in fact doubles up as a garment of modesty that does not reveal any part of the female body, thus conforming to the social expectations. Whilst this particular aspect of modesty was overlooked in the account of combatant women, the civic women agreed that the reason this attire was adopted was the practicality that such clothing provided, rather than a transformation of gender identity. Roja, who claimed that shirts and trousers or combat fatigues were, in fact, less restrictive in comparison to traditional women's clothing, confirmed this view:

> Also with these clothes we can run and do our training; in fact we can do anything with these type of clothes. Our stripes [combat fatigues] is not only for fighting. That is our considered normal clothing. And we use it for fighting as well. Now we are wearing these clothes [shirts and trousers] because the army won't let us come out in the stripes.[26] (Roja)

Arasi contributes to the explanation of ease and comfort in wearing masculine clothing specific to the roles they were playing in Tamil society. She said, 'In our society nobody wears jeans and shirt. The main reason we started to wear was for our convenience.' However, the masculine clothing offered a dual purpose, which appears to have been overlooked in the mainstream discourse. The combatant women and the civic women both stated that by wearing masculine clothing women tended to be far safer than when they wore feminine clothing. As BP says, '... some girls, their face telling [feminine] but their clothes and other things don't tell', while Mallika claims, 'Men have a habit of trying to be funny with women [take advantage]. The clothes that we are wearing now protect us from that and we feel safer.'

It is also worth noting that there is a school of thought developing amongst the women of Jaffna that challenges the wearing of traditional clothing such as saris. 'Yes, everybody says that it is a cultural dress, but I don't think that we have to wear a sari to keep our culture' (AK). The challenge to the traditional wearing of a sari was viewed by some civic women in this research as contributing to female sexualisation and objectification by the way it accentuated the feminine body.

> **Sometimes this sexual view comes with the sari .... If a girl goes in a sari they [men] can *see* and they [men] can *feel* that there is a girl. When you are beautiful, they treat you as a doll [objectified]. So I don't want to be treated as a doll every time. (DK)**

Such recognition of femininity as a beautiful doll is also representative of women's objectification combined with a perception of weakness and supposed inability to be independent. They further argued that the clothing restricted their physical movements to such an extent it made them dependent on men.

Both civic and combatant women shared these views, as confirmed by both BP and Roja's discourse. However, some civic women such as DK claimed that by wearing masculine clothing the combatant women contributed to their gaining some form of equal status with men, both in the civic society as well as in the movement. Therefore, the theory of secondary gender equality that emerges here was an effect, rather than an aim, of wearing practical masculine clothing.

How Combatant Women View Civic Women

Women combatants, having to negotiate their multiple femininities in a highly gendered society, have claimed that civic women were passive victims of society.

> Women [of civic society] are soft [passive]. They need to wear lot of jewellery, they need more money for marriage and dowry. They also have safety problem....Men from young age are used to hard work but women are not like that. They [women] are very soft, and they [are] unable to make decisions on their own. (Arasi)

The combatant women often used non-complimentary words such as 'soft' to describe civic women, meaning the civilian women were 'passive' and 'dependent'; qualities which were seen as weaknesses by the combatant women. The strength of combatant women's self-belief was directly born out of being fighters and contributing to the attempt of creating a new nation state. They saw this as an achievement that had elevated them beyond civic women, and far beyond the gender boundaries that constrained women in civic society.

> The changes have come about very quickly. Because a woman could not go out alone in the night before the war. The society did not accept that. Also the woman didn't have the courage to go out on her own. Both prevailed. Because we got involved in the war the society began to understand that a woman could go out alone and the woman got the confidence that she can go out on her own. The society which did not accept a woman going to the seaside, saw the women being in charge of boats and fighting from the boats and lead a life in the sea, [the society] accepted it all very easily. (Arasi)

They also viewed this social position as a responsibility that required them to educate the civic women to be similarly independent and self-reliant.

As Arasi says, 'The first job is to teach the women to make decisions on their own. Only we can teach the women to stand for themselves.' On the other hand, Mallika claims, 'I don't think that women [in civic society] are fully aware of their status. From the beginning women have been dominated, now some women coming out of this tradition, and we [LTTE] are also slowly trying to assist this [change].' Both Arasi and Mallika's views on civic women can be described as a personal challenge to ensure that civic women who are incapable and passive are changed to take control of their own destiny by being pushed into building a strong mind that would form the base of overall empowerment. Nevertheless, the women combatants saw the change that needed to take place as a task that could only be fulfilled by the LTTE women. The women combatants blamed the normative femininities in Jaffna as the original source for female subjugation and servitude to men. This made women combatants view masculine dominance in Tamil society as making their task harder to perform.

How Civic Women See the Combatant Women

The civic women I met were not 'for' the war, nor were they 'against' the war. This mindset needs to be understood in a time, place and space context whereby a long and hard 30 years had changed their views about the war. That is not to say that they condoned it, but rather that they had become somewhat war weary.

Age plays an interesting part in the women's discourse that reflected on their achievements both in the civic State as well as in the revolutionary group. The differences cut across life choices, education and social upbringing.

Unlike the young interviewees, the older combatant group (age 30 and above) were far more reflective about their experiences. This was also noted amongst older civic women who were cautious in saying anything overtly negative about the LTTE's claims of their pioneering contribution to the empowerment of women in civic society. The cautious approach may well be due to an awareness of safety of self as well as family members, for they were very aware of the early demise of those who criticise the LTTE.[27] The younger women (both civic and combatant) had an approach to life that was neither cautious nor reflective, and their abrupt style may be a result of only ever-knowing war and the instability it brought.

Delving further into the differences between the women revealed that the older group of civic women felt much more indebted to the women combatants than did the younger women in civic community. The respect shown to combatant women by civic women appeared to be due to social changes that had taken place since the beginning of the war, as the older civic women understood the gender development that had ensued since women joined the LTTE. The younger civic (and combatant) women grew up knowing that the LTTE had women combatants; hence, they did not see it as a phenomenon that ought to be recognised in any special way.

There were highly visible levels of confidence that had been built up amongst the young women of Jaffna even though some of them claimed that the effect on society was not as great as that claimed by older civic women. The newly gained confidences also made some of the young civic women much more self-assured in their dealing with men, creating a considerable concern amongst the older generation of women who feared that the young women were 'asking for trouble'. This may be due to a change in the code of conduct from the pre-war era governing women's social behaviour with men in the public places. Despite these criticisms, the older women did not openly confront the younger women about their behaviour. The women aged 30 years and above held directly opposing views on equality in comparison with those who were younger than 30 years of age, and this was reflected across both the civic and combatant women's groups.

The older educated civic women saw the word 'feminism' flaunted around as an achievement of modern Jaffna society but questioned the levels of understanding of the term. There were still uncertainties as to what equality or emancipation they had achieved, or needed to achieve in order to gain equality with men. Some older civic women felt that the lack of a formal understanding of equality between men and women marked the current view of equality a self-centred act. This was illustrated by HA, who believed that young women joined the revolutionary movement to avoid traditional responsibilities as a result of the media and cinema presenting it as a phenomenon that claims 'women are free to do anything'. HA was particularly aggrieved by the lack of a theoretical knowledge of feminism as she said, 'Here we don't learn feminism theoretically in this soil. In this soil there is no political concept regarding feminism.'

It was interesting to note that the younger women (both civic and combatant) were more critical about their current roles. The older civic women were more comfortable in discussing times before the war and were not at ease when discussing the modern social roles of women and the empowerment that had taken place. My research showed two opposing views on the contributions of combatant women to civic women's social empowerment. GV was in awe of the combatant women for all their achievements in a highly patriarchal society where women's social roles were very much defined from the time of their birth. The older civic women appeared to appreciate the level of self-confidence that the women combatants exerted, and they viewed this achievement as being due to their engagement in the LTTE. In contrast with this, other civic women, especially the younger women such as ES and DK, did not view the achievements of women combatants with any special dispensation, but were of the view that global change itself would have altered the roles of women in Jaffna regardless of women joining the LTTE.

The actual cause of women's empowerment was argued by women of civic society to be the result of a prolonged war; others gave credit to the combatant women of the LTTE, stating that their radical lifestyle has been the significant driving force for women's social change.

The non-conformity of combatant women to the social practices in Jaffna challenged the hegemonic masculinities that were implemented in society and often viewed as being nurtured and perpetuated by the women in civic society. The civic women did not always approve of women who radically broke with traditions. Since Balasingham joined the LTTE, she has noted: '[p]ublic opinion as a mode of social control of women was an issue that surfaced again and again in various degrees and forms through out my life in India and Sri Lanka....[it] is an issue hugely perpetrated by women themselves' (Balasingham 2003: 85).

The view of civic women condoning or colluding with dominant power relations to continue traditional cultural values and practices needs to be viewed within the context of the complex nature of social interactions which women (both civic and combatant) have in society. A closer analysis of the difference between the combatant and civic women revealed that combatant women were more critical about the other group (civic women). When questioned whether being a combatant woman had affected their status in civic society, Arasi responded that:

> we [combatant women] are not affected in any way. We are well respected in the society. Whatever we ask they [those of civic society] are doing. They have faith in us that we will do everything well. We are not just fighters only. We do fight but at the same time we take part in all other aspects of the society. Our ideology is a very wide one. (Arasi)

The description by Arasi was representative of how the combatant women believed that they were viewed by civic society. However, within the civic society women were identified firstly as combatants, and secondly as women. Being identified in a masculine role of a combatant meant that they were placed outside the traditional feminine roles of the patriarchal society where boundaries were clearly defined. Whilst the LTTE maintained some of the patriarchal views of femininity, it also placed combatant women in a complex social location that was an ambivalent position culturally and socially. The women combatants failed to notice that they were seen differently to male combatants by the civic society. Whilst the combatant women had earned respect from the civic society, it had come at a price, which they appeared to be unaware of.

> And in each and every place they have to fight and they are not getting anything very easily. And you know in the society also they praise them and treat them as very high-level people. But they don't move with them closely. With the men [in civic society] LTTE cadres move freely but with the girls[combatant women] still they have difficulty. What I am saying is there is a problem in interaction between the society and these cadres. Because they are very much apart from the society. The society feels something like that. Because in this society girls can't achieve that level very easily. Very much separated from the society. [They are] so different. The difference, from my point of view the difference is very good. Their achievements are very good. That is a need for this society. These people [civic society] will take sometime to realise it. Yeah! ... sure ... admire them

> **for what they are doing. Even so many girls in the society admired them....Because they are restricted no? (DK)**

There was much recognition by the civic women of combatant women's achievements. As stated in DK's narrative, much of the admiration was based on an understanding that combatant women were breaking restrictions in society to fulfil a role. Her narrative revealed that the male combatants were able to move freely with men in civic society, in the external social spaces (as opposed to internal domestic spaces). Whilst the women combatants appeared to have been accepted on a certain level to be in the male social space, they were not fully embraced as equals by male society. The very same achievement that earned the combatant women admiration from civic women of being in the male space had distanced them from the civic women too.

Whilst it is generally accepted among civic women that women combatants have contributed to a substantially elevated social position for women as a whole, civic women did not acknowledge the hierarchy assumed by the women combatants. They, however, did not necessarily criticise the women combatants either. The role played by the combatant women was still seen by women in civic society as a major sacrifice, following the traditional path of women as 'givers' rather than 'takers'. HA claims, 'They [women combatants] don't concentrate on how fair it is or what they want. Sacrificing is a main character of the women. There is no surprise in sacrificing. Anyway she, the woman, is sacrificing wherever she is no?'

As previously stated in HA's discourse, to become a woman combatant was, in effect, to become a selfless woman: one who will not debate about unfairness or personal needs but raise to the role of the combatant who sacrifices her own needs for the benefit of others. The self-sacrifice by the women combatants embraces a role that is similar to the traditional role dictated by society.

The civic women insisted that, although the combatant women were attending to what was essentially a male activity as a protector, they were by no means masculinised by this action or experience: 'We don't see them [women combatants] as men. We see them like brave ladies who are fighters' (ES). This view was also shared by other civic women such as BP, who explained:

> **I don't think women combatants are masculine. Masculine means rough type what you see. I don't think they combatant women are rough. Some places they should have dealt with rough things. In a war they should be very rough, otherwise they will get killed. But normally we are talking with them they are not so rough. (BP)**

While the civic women acknowledged the work conducted by combatant women to be masculine, they have also retained the combatant women in a feminine role. This was reflective of the complexity of women combatant's gender identities, which were constantly negotiated. The civic women's views on combatant women were particularly pertinent for the women combatants who negotiated new identities and shifted paradigms in order to remain as a part of the civic society. The shifting of paradigms effectively created 'the new women' who was able to fit into the circumstances she found herself in.

Summary

Tamil women in civic society have the dual roles of being an all-powerful woman in the inner realms of the domestic sphere of *Akam*, and a powerless dependent in the public sphere of *Puram*. Whilst the power of *Akam* was recognisably within the home, it was still subject to masculine authority. Within the past three decades, women's social roles have changed. Some civic women credited the visible changes in women's social roles to the LTTE, and others to the war itself. The women combatants claimed that it was the LTTE that paved the way for social change by actively enforcing initiatives in society such as the discouragement of the dowry system and the repatriation of widows into society.

The engagement of Tamil women as combatants dates back to the mid-1980s when they were continuously being compared to male combatants. This created a need for them to prove themselves as competent individuals. The women were trained to the same standard, and fought alongside of, their male counterparts. The role of gender equality amongst combatants was referred to in Arasi's, AK's and Kavitha's narratives; they had to work hard and undertake arduous tasks in order to prove themselves worthy in a masculine organisation. This need to prove their worth was not seen amongst the younger women combatants such as Roja and Mallika, who entered an organisation that already accepted women as equals.

However, this perceived equality needs to be seen in the context of women who attained leadership positions. It was estimated that one-third of the LTTE organisation was made up of women combatants. However, proportionally the number of women reaching the senior ranks was extremely low, which brought into question the true level of equality in the movement. It must none the less be recognised that gender relations in the LTTE was a series of complex negotiations in transition.

The women of civic society, as well as the combatant women, have recognised Prabhakaran to be a champion of women's social progress. A close analysis of Prabhakaran's relationship with his wife, Mathy, presented a different picture, whereby the traditional role of the supportive wife and auspicious mother was publicly practised. However, the women combatants viewed their *Ah-lu-mai* (empowerment) as a direct result of Prabhakaran's faith in women, which in turn had created *Puthumai Pen*, the new woman. *Puthumai Pen*, who had emerged from the war period, was both tough and fearless and, above, all sexually pure. These qualities had contributed to the public imagination and assisted in the creation of the 'Armed Virgin'.

Undoubtedly, the role played by combatant women within the LTTE revolutionary organisation challenges the existing patriarchy and existing gender norms in Tamil society. The gender (re)construction within the revolutionary movement had a great social impact, the result of which was seen amongst the confidences and empowerment gained by women in civic society. Whilst this chapter discusses the achievements of combatant women, it also notes the limited numbers of women who were in senior positions of the LTTE and their lack of contribution to high-level decision-making. This, however, was negated by the major social impact women combatants of the LTTE have had upon civic women and Tamil society in Jaffna as a whole.

Notes

1 Page and Czuba (1999). Also see Rapport (1984), Zimmerman (1984), Afshar and Alikhan (2002), Wray (2004) and Rowlands (1998).

2 'Jaffna Tamil culture views women as outwardly enslaved and inwardly powerful' (David 1980: 103–104).

3 In Wadley (1980: 153).

4 See Wadley (1980) and David (1980).

5 In a culture where female modesty is a key part of the gendered behaviour for women, riding a bicycle was seen as a masculine activity or an activity which could only be practised by pre-pubescent girls.

6 At times when there was no electricity, bicycles were used to power radios through their dynamos in order to hear news both nationally and internationally.

7 I have separated the act of war and aggression from social revolution in order to define that social revolution in this instance is viewed as part of women's social evolvement, which is not necessarily tied to war and its aggression.

8 Some Sri Lankan academics have claimed otherwise.

9 The directional link had to be from either the leader as the 'creator' of the combatant women or from borrowing an image from contemporary violent political struggles of other nations. According to Schalk, this link can be further developed with the introduction from Tamil cultural values of a 'virgin' linked to arms; hence, the concept of an 'Armed Virgin' was born (1999: 135).

10 See Elshtain (1987) for description of Beautiful Soul and Just Warrior.

11 Doctor Rajani Thranagama was a lecturer attached to the Medical Faculty, University of Jaffna, who was allegedly killed by the LTTE due to her criticism of the movement.

12 'In Mr Pirabakaran's [Prabhakaran's] ideological perspective, Nirmala's idea of women's liberation represented more the stereo-typed conception of western women's liberation than any emancipation which the masses of Tamil women could identify with and embrace as their own. Not only he [Prabhakaran], but also the girls who were with us, had difficulty in relating to and comprehending Nirmala's "radicalism". She was a world apart from the village girls who had come to join the struggle and fight for their homeland and had no real idea of women's liberation, nor necessarily aspired for it' (Balasingham 2003: 87).

13 See Wilson (1991), Hale (2001a and 2001b), Muller (2006), Helie-Lucas (1988), Knauss (1987), Gordon (1968), Afshar (1985), Eisen-Bergman (1975), Turner and Hao (1998), Young (2001), Young (1998), Rovira (2000) and Kampwirth (2001 and 2002).

14 Information gathered at the interview held by me with Arasi, Head of Women's Political Wing of Jaffna, October 2003.

15 This is addressed by Coomaraswamy (1996: 9), who states that 'despite the celebration of armed cadre by LTTE ideologues, there is still no evidence that women are part

of the elite decision-making process. They are not initiators of ideas, they are only implementers of policy made by someone else, by men'.

16 An example of this was seen a few years ago. The LTTE sent an envoy including a number of men and one woman, leaders of various fighting units to Ireland in October 2003 to conduct a series of discussions with the IRA and Sinn Fein on how the LTTE should progress their struggle.

17 As stated previously, there is no formal record of the exact number of women combatants in the LTTE, except for Balasingham's statement of 1994, which said that one-third of the LTTE were women (Schalk 1997). This figure was taken as a basis by many academics, and the numbers, if not the proportion, are presumed to have increased since then. Also see c.f. 169.

18 Also see Samuel (2000) and Alison (2003).

19 'Pirapakaran [Prabhakaran] is very much appreciated by LTTE women, who praise him as King of Tigers' (Schalk 1997a: 7).

20 Whilst Prabhakaran has been elevated to a level of a national leader, he still carries strong kinship ties with women combatants, thus they refer to him as the elder brother *Annay*.

21 Also see Banerjee (2006).

22 Maunaguru (1995: 166) discusses that part of the challenge was creating new words for the usage in language to describe female sexual purity, an important part of the Tamil women gender identity within the community, where words for violent sexual acts did not exist prior to this time. With the creation of the New Woman, words such as *Paliyalvanmurai* (meaning sexual violence) entered into Tamil linguistic discourse. This is also discussed in detail in Chapter 5.

23 *Puthumai Pen* is also written as *Putiyappen* by Schalk 1997a.

24 To conform to a notion that women's liberation struggles were and are simply by-products of patriarchal nationalist struggles would potentially erase women's histories and women's experiences, and displace women from any history of every day organised resistance to patriarchal authority. (Sangarasivam 2003: 63).

25 '...wearing of rich saris, brilliant jewellery, flowers in flowing hair, silver anklets, a silver toe ring and red pottu on the forehead. Today the views presented are women in combat fatigues, in boots, with no-make up, jewellery or ostentation, often with their hair cut in short male styles, wearing a cyanide capsule round their neck' (Coomaraswamy 1996: 9).

26 During the period of ceasefire, women combatants were not allowed to wear camouflage clothing away from Vanni area.

27 Thiranagama's colleagues have gone underground due to fear of reprisal, as discussed in Chapter 1. It must also be noted that at an earlier stage of fieldwork, I became quite aware that Thiranagama and the University Teachers on Human Rights in Jaffna (UTHRJ) are not a line of inquiry I should pursue.

7 Ending a Journey

Final Reflections

The overall aim of this book was to analyse how gender was (re)constructed within the LTTE movement, and how such a construction impacted upon the civic society as a whole and in particular for the Tamil women of Jaffna. As the movement was founded upon a society that is steeped in a masculine culture with a historically defined socially marginalised position for women, it was important to identify how women become a part of the LTTE. I have argued that the engagement of women in the LTTE challenged the existing social formation in Jaffna's Tamil society, and I have supported this argument with empirical evidence. This knowledge was further developed as a tool to assess the ways in which the conflict-affected women as a social group in Jaffna, and in particular those women who later become combatants.

Ah-lu-mai or empowerment, as described by women combatants, had become the foundation of *Puthumai Pen*, a (re)constructed gender identity that was created through a series of events that challenged the gendered attitudes of Tamil society. In the LTTE movement, the women combatants had opportunities for equality and empowerment which was rarely available in the civic society. The conflict enabled Tamil women to embrace a new identity that was needed to survive in the extreme conditions of a civil war, and which was far removed from traditional roles and the traditional female identity based on subordination. With the (re) constructed gender roles within the LTTE terrorist movement, the combatant women gained a form of equality for themselves and an indirect recognition for other women in Tamil society.

As new women, the combatant women challenged the patriarchal cosmology by performing many activities that were traditionally in the masculine domain. I argue that these acts and deeds must be seen within the context of a culturally restrained female social position and a prolonged ethnic war. The women combatants saw the opportunity to be in the frontline of battles or to participate in suicide missions as recognition of their ability, their agency and, above all, their *Ah-lu-mai*, their empowerment. Whilst it may be argued that the LTTE had manipulated the situation of female fear and anxiety to gain the much-needed human resources, it can also be seen as a form of emancipation where women felt empowered and valued in a highly gendered society.

The wide range of views about combatant women arose because of their new identity. Some of these views debate whether women's involvement in the conflict leads to emancipation, while others suggest that women play only supporting roles that will not make a substantial impact. However, if these new roles are viewed free from any preconceived notions, it is clear that combatant women moved from historical 'support' roles to modern 'active' roles.

The achievements of combatant women have earned them the name of Armed Virgins that was both reflective of their new identity as women warriors and symbolic of the sexual purity that is valued in patriarchal society. However, the fact that it was a 'symbolic' virgin that was created within the confines of the armed struggle, and that there was a continued reliance on traditional metaphors of women as protectors of the nation and homeland (future mothers of the free), raises a question as to the extent of emancipation that the combatant women have achieved.

Within this book I have identified several catalysts that influenced women in their decision-making process by pushing and pulling them towards the LTTE. Through kinship the LTTE was successful in creating a non-consanguine kin family that overrode familial ties and facilitated tight bonds to form between combatant women. The empirical evidence in this book suggests that the attachments made by combatant women through non-consanguine kinships in fact extended into embracing the greater civic society with a sense of nurturing responsibility.

Gift of Death

The key objective amongst most who study the rising global phenomenon of suicide attacks is to find the rationality and motivational factors behind such missions (Hassan 2004; Gambetta 2005; Hage 2003; Reuter 2004; Pape 2005; Hoffman 2003; Zedalis 2004 and Skaine 2006). Through empirical evidence, I have illustrated in this book that the LTTE combatant women believed the act of suicide bombing as giving a gift of self to the greater good of the Tamil nation and for the cause of a separate state of Tamil *Eelam*. The reasoning behind the act, however, remains complex and cannot be explained with a single reason for it encompasses multiple reasons that are often at an intimate level, as discussed in this book.

Within the global discourse of women's involvement in suicide bombings, the Palestinian, Chechen and Sri Lankan conflicts are grouped together with an occasional comparative study. Such assemblage runs the risk of a Western bias being imposed on non-Western cultural pattern and overlooking the unique ways in which women negotiated their gender roles within the context of their own cultural confinements. Research conducted in the field of violent conflict tends to distinguish the combatant women of the LTTE and other terrorist organisations by labelling them as the Other. Ryan-Flood (2009: 182) has argued that identification of Otherness instantaneously invokes an epistemological marker distinguishing boundaries as relational opposites to those who make hegemonic categories meaningful. This action also creates a marginalised identity that is far removed from the social normative, making it difficult to comprehend.

The combatant women of the LTTE have actively negotiated a kind of gender role that was different to their socio-historical roles. A Western bias overlooks this negotiation and fails to understand the complexities and dynamics that were involved in the new social roles. This contribution caused the type of literature to change from an essentialist feminism, which argued that women should not be involved in violent activities, to an alternative liberal form of feminism that began to question the actual achievements of such participations. It is too early for this view to have made any significant impact on literary discourse, but nonetheless it is more representative of the current reality where women's involvement is assessed within the cultural context of what was essentially a masculine act of self-sacrifice for the greater good of the nation.[1]

With that in mind, it must be also noted that the majority of literature written on suicide bombers is androcentric, which I would argue is a result of war being perceived as a masculine act in the male domain, limiting the advancement of knowledge gained in relation to suicide bombers to nothing other than a masculine bias. This highly gendered aspect was highlighted by Vinogradova (2003) in the article 'Deadly Secret of the Black Widow' regarding Chechen women suicide bombers. Here, she questions a Moscow resident Chechen professor who did not wish to disclose his identity.

> **Question:** So is human life of no value in Chechnya today?
>
> **Answer:** No, you have misunderstood ... the human life is, it's a woman's life that isn't.

This suggests that Chechen men are valued far greater than Chechen women; thus, women were expendable to the terrorist group and the greater society. Not only do women have a lesser social value than men, they also continue to carry the burden of care into the afterlife, as seen in Palestine. In Victor's (2004) book *Army of Roses,* she discusses the popular belief amongst Palestinian women suicide bombers of afterlife providing them with many riches and comforts that they lacked in present life. The single requirement needed to ensure receiving such riches was to commit the act in the name of holy war, *jihad*. Sheik Yassin claims that women suicide bombers will be 'even more beautiful than the seventy two virgins ... if they are not married they are guaranteed a pure husband in Paradise, and of course they are entitled to bring seventy of their relatives to join them there without suffering the anguish of the grave'(Victor 2004: 113).

It is assumed that marriage was still every woman's goal, as was physical beauty and allegiance to blood ties; thus, women are gendered even in the afterlife. These hyper-masculine versions of female needs were notably missing amongst the women suicide bombers of the LTTE. Their afterlife has no promise of a paradise to gain but focuses on the damage and destruction created in their wake.

There is a paradoxical argument of biological essentialism here and a claim that the combatant women have no agency of their own and act against the nurturing and preserving instincts of women. Through my empirical research, it became evident that the LTTE combatant women saw the act of suicide bombing as an obligatory act of altruism. This was an interesting development as in the beginning their views appeared to contradict the traditional view of women's roles as life-givers by being life-takers. However through the narrative interviews it became clear that in fact the combatant women saw the act of suicide bombing transpose nurturing and giving into a familial nurturing instinct of protecting the nation as a whole. The argument of giving was described by the combatant women as *Thatkodai*–giving oneself as a gift, as opposed to *Thatkolai*—which is suicide. The dynamism of the role of carer was thus extended into caring for the whole of Tamil nation in Jaffna.

You and I Across the Ethnic Divide

The book further contributes to the discussion of feminist methodology in representing the Other across an ethnic divide. It analyses the complexities and challenges involved in issues that arise from conducting research with multiple identities that required constant negotiation throughout the time spent in the field. These negotiations formed a strong basis in the book on reflexivity that linked me as the researcher to the women combatants through our shared Sri Lankan identity but also separated us through our ethnicity and language.

Language brought a stimulating dynamic to the research project. Although many in Jaffna understood English language, the ability to communicate in English was mainly restricted to the educated middle classes, many of whom had a bilingual upbringing. This was evident in the interviews where a majority of civic women were able to communicate in English, whereas a majority of combatant women spoke in the Tamil medium only. This may be reflective of a class dimension for those who are from the lower-middle and working classes, where choices and options were limited. These limitations inevitably impacted upon the decision-making process to join the LTTE and become combatants.

The women I interviewed or had social interaction with within the confines of an interview scenario were not familiar with the word 'feminism', but they were familiar with the term 'women's liberation' or 'women's lib' as they called it. The word 'women's lib' was a highly publicised word in Sri Lanka in the 1970s, around the time of the creation of many Tamil armed resistance groups in Jaffna. Therefore, one of the challenges in this research was not to use words that were not readily understood, such as 'feminism', but to find terms that might be more familiar, such as 'women's lib'.

It was interesting to note that the combatant women in a group, away from their rank hierarchy, would giggle and laugh when discussing certain topics raised with English words such as 'boyfriends'. Amongst most women combatants there was an initial shyness in the beginning of an interview. They soon lost this shyness and became eager to participate. This was particularly visible in the group interview of Arulvili, Aruna and Yalini. This could be due to the fact that they were of the same age and knew each other well, making it possible for them to tease one another and laugh freely. In contrast, the two younger combatants who were interviewed together maintained their shyness throughout the interview, but they were still fully engaged in answering the questions asked. I noticed this was due to BP, an older and much respected civic woman who acted as the interpreter, thus bringing in an element of respect the younger women needed to pay the older woman.

The atmosphere at civic women's interviews was different from the beginning; they were much more relaxed as many were able to express themselves in English. Often the interviews allowed a space for them to open up and talk about themselves, a rarity in their conflict-filled lives where the self often became secondary to collective daily existence. An example of this single time and space allocated solely to one person was seen when I interviewed one of the civic women who was keen to tell me about events that affected her, in particular the issues of displacement that had forced her to re-evaluate her life in a completely new way, in complete contrast with her conservative upbringing. After the interview, she sighed deeply, held my hand and said, 'thank you for listening to me'.

Negotiated Identities and Binary Positions

Women combatants raised issues of negotiated identities and questioned their binary position within the normative femininity practised in civic society. This challenge to tradition became a catalyst for the separation between the two groups of women. The new identity seen in combatant women appeared to create a complex social interaction between the combatant and civic women. The combatant women viewed civic women to be overtly dependent on men, whereas the civic women did not always approve of women who so radically broke with traditions, which caused civic women to distance themselves from the combatant women. Paradoxically, the combatant women had achieved a more elevated social position than women in civic society. However, they were also excluded from masculine social inclusions that formed the socio-cultural foundation in Jaffna. The combatant women appeared not to be aware of the exclusion and were contented in a strongly held belief that their social acceptance was on par with male combatants and the hegemonic masculinity in Jaffna.

There was also a level of Otherness from both Tamil epistemological and hegemonic perspectives. The combatant women's non-normative choice did create a substantive distance between themselves and women in civic society. This marginalised social position, however, did not affect the sisterhood that was created between the two groups of women. The civic women often rose to support and show allegiance to combatant women whenever they were criticised. Civic women were notably united in preserving combatant women's feminine identity disregarding their non-feminine external appearance. Their abandonment of culturally feminine symbols, such as jewellery and saris, being replaced by a masculinised image of shirts and trousers, was stemming from a need to engage in active combat duty. Civic women often stated that taking part in a nationalist conflict, wearing perceived masculine clothing and becoming willing combatants to share the burden of war did not change women into men by masculinising femininity. Nor do they become men or masculine by developing a conscience that is contrary to the traditional female social positioning of *Kula Makal*, the good woman, who stays within the confines of *akam*, the inner realm. It was the women's decision to become combatants, and by doing so they have determined their own agency.

Where are the Women in Nation Building?

A significant part of gender theory in the LTTE's discourse (and terrorist/revolutionary groups in general) requires women's engagement in the building of a nation state. As Prabhakaran was aware of this requirement, a critical look needs to be taken at his motives. During this research project, two key objectives were revealed: a short-term objective highlighting the grave need for trained combatants to continue the armed conflict against the Sri Lankan State army, and a long-term objective requiring the engagement of women in the process of nation building. Some view the short-term objective, which formed the foundation for the long-term aim, as 'using' Tamil women. This was a view that was not supported by combatant women who were adamant in claiming that Prabhakaran had enabled them to challenge the patriarchy that kept them subordinated in the first instance to the men in their households (father, brother, husband and son), and in the second instance to men at large in the civic society. Prabhakaran, who had one foot firmly placed in patriarchal civic society, continuously stated his support for combatant women and their *Ah-lu-mai*, empowerment that enabled them to achieve many things within a Tamil patriarchal cosmology. However, his view of building a nation state superseded his support and recognition for female emancipation in civic society, thus, pushing Tamil women's emancipation as an agenda item for the future: *a future he thought was his.*

The question of whether the women combatants have achieved equality by their active participation in the war needs to be seen within the context of how female emancipation was constructed and, more importantly, understood by combatant and civic women. The feminist teaching that Nithyanathan tried to introduce to the LTTE was dismissed as being too Westernised for both combatant women and Prabhakaran to accept. In dismissing a developed argument of female emancipation, Prabhakaran successfully presented *his version* of feminism and female emancipation, which was acceptable to combatant women, and had adopted and adapted them. To claim that Prabhakaran's version of female empowerment is not emancipatory would be to disregard all that has been achieved by women as combatants. Therefore, it is important to recognise that women combatants have made achievements and sacrifices in changing the face of Tamil women in Jaffna. However, the ability to sustain or maintain such changes was not clearly identifiable. The global history of women's involvement in revolutions highlights the risk that much promised equality eventually gets lost in the pursuits of hegemonic masculine nationalistic goals.

Mirror Cracked

Whilst the women combatants were convinced of their equal status to men both in the movement and in society, there was a noticeable lack of female representation in senior LTTE positions. It could be argued that culture and upbringing have resulted in an acceptance of being led, but these two issues did not in themselves prevent women combatants from leading men to war, albeit not in highest battle ranks. The next step would have been for women combatants to enter the political arena and use the skills and abilities of decision and debate. In order to avoid being overlooked in this arena, they would have needed substantial training to be able to engage in the greater nationalist debate on a global stage.

The reality of women's emancipation within the confinements of war, displacement and changing social roles as discussed in this research were complicated. Displacement invariably leads to the breakdown of familial structures paving the way for many other social orders to fail progressively. These included the parental inability to provide safety and security for the family, women being violated (or the continuous threat of sexual violence along with the social stigma associated with loss of purity and honour) and children being denied the normalcy offered by everyday activities such as schooling. All these culminate in a situation where the LTTE had stepped in as a protector to restore their lost agency. By joining the LTTE movement, the women gained a new identity and a new kinship, and they became a part of the LTTE family.

Displacement clearly acted as a catalyst in a notable number of combatant women's lives. It exposed female vulnerability in times of war and pushed and pulled them towards the revolutionary organisation as a form of protection. The LTTE movement was seen as the only protector able to provide a safe haven from the behemoth of the State and its violence. Through empirical evidence, I have illustrated a previously unrecognised link between displacement to the LTTE-controlled areas of Vanni and the voluntary enlistment of women. The importance of this link contrasted the sense of security with no comforts felt by the women in Vanni with that of other areas where they had comforts but no security. This finding is a key to understanding how displacement acted as a catalyst for those who later became willing combatants.

No Peace No War

On 19 May 2009, the Sri Lankan President declared that three decades of war had ended with the demise of Prabhakaran and the LTTE leadership. This announcement created shock and disbelief amongst many in Jaffna. In order to prove the death to be factual, the State published photographs of Prabhakaran's dead body with a head wound, and a statement saying that he was trying to escape when the armed forces opened fire and killed him. By this action, the Sri Lankan State was able to curtail what may otherwise have been a long drawn-out judicial outcome.[2]

The collective demise of Prabhakaran's family—wife, Mathivethani (Mathy); daughter, Duwaraka; and youngest son, Balachandran—has given a space for many conspiracy theorists to debate how they died. Some say they were shot in the head in execution style, whilst others say they died in an air raid. The only reliable fact is that their bodies were found at Nanthi Kadal lagoon and were sent for autopsy reports. These reports have not been published to date, and it is highly unlikely that they would in the future. In regards to Prabhakaran's oldest son, Charles Anthony, who many believed was in training to take over from Prabhakaran, died in battle on or before that same day at Karyamullavailkkav. All their deaths took place a few miles apart from each other in Mullathivu district.

The LTTE struggle had a beginning, middle and an end. In a similar vein to most nationalist struggles, their initial engagement was driven with a pure vision and ideologies of creating a nation state for those who have been marginalised. The end, however, contradicted that ideal. The long, drawn-out war exposed the LTTE struggle to be neither perfect nor complete. In fact, they slipped from the role of being the protector of its own people to the abusers of its own people, the Tamil nationals.

The violence that was committed in the northern and eastern areas of Sri Lanka is not limited to humans, but also extends to the land, to the forests, to the lagoons and to the wild life. The land mines that were installed by both the State and the LTTE are currently being cleared. Whilst the State is engaged in this slow and laborious work; many farmers and their cattle continue to get injured. Arguably, since the declaration of ending the war, Jaffna has turned a new and different chapter where many have started to distance themselves from the LTTE. Rightly so too, for there may be repercussions not only for the individual, but also to all with whom they associate too.

The infrastructure that is required to rebuild Jaffna sees no urgency. I will only refer to two key items as examples of this slowness: the rule of law and education. The LTTE, with all their faults, kept the rule of law operating in Jaffna, which under the State ruling appears to have failed. This is seen with a rise in abduction and ransom demands. With regard to education, schools have reopened, and the student numbers have risen, but there is an issue of coping with the demand after many years of damage done to the system.

Within this period there was a whole generation that grew up not knowing peace, never moving beyond certain geographical boundaries of the country, and harbouring many hand-me-down prejudices. A generation from both sides of the ethnic divide grew up distrusting the other. Once, I met a young Tamil postal worker in a London post office, who seeing the destination of my letter as Jaffna, said to me that he had never met any Sinhalese people when he was growing up in one of the islands off Jaffna peninsula. When he finally did meet Sinhalese people, he was very surprised to realise that the Sinhalese were no different from his own ethnic group with all their foibles.

Many Tamil nationals in Jaffna are aware that there are no short cuts to rebuilding their lives. The Tamil diaspora, who could provide a positive influence and truly assist the rebuilding of Jaffna, in effect are still in denial of the failed State of *Eelam*. The State, as the victor in the war, appears not to have any allocated space for nation building with modern Tamil thinking. The State, which has the power to introduce a culture of inclusivity that embraces diversity, is openly slow to engage. The State is in need of actively creating a new identity that is not embedded in a Tamil versus Sinhalese divide but in a united Sri Lankan identity, thus making the culture of inclusivity a true reality. On 15 May 2010, the ruling government created a Lessons Learnt and Reconciliation Commission (LLRC) to look at the civil war-related events from 21 February 2009 to 19 May 2009. The Reconciliation Commission created in the style of the South African Truth and Reconciliation, with a difference to suit Sri Lanka, is primarily ineffective. There are a number of reasons for this ineffectiveness. A key reason is the commission's State bias due to its members being hand-picked by the government to ensure its loyalty is met against allegations. Another is that the arrival of the committee rarely being published ahead of time gives civic citizens with concerns that need reconciliation little or no time to prepare before the hearing. It is also noted that no allegation can be brought against the armed forces; they are stamped on from the outset. Therefore, it is questionable whether the women and girls will get the support they need to seek redress for abuse and violations they suffered at the hands of the State's armed forces. Furthermore, the compensations due to Tamil nationals are either delayed or never paid, unlike their ethnic counterparts.

Are the Tamil women of post-war Jaffna able to carry the struggle for women's emancipation? Will there be a new generation of Arasis who are able and, more importantly, willing to fight oppressive measures brought in by the ruling Sinhalese government? The combatant and the civic women expected a change in their socio-political environment through the Final War but not necessarily an end—certainly not the kind of ending that occurred in May 2009. It is arguable whether the 30-year interminable struggle has left those living in Jaffna too exhausted to rebuild a new society. They have seen the State openly ignoring the world's admonitions regarding the way it conducted the Final War, violating many Tamil nationals' human rights. This is further compounded by the State's use of power to overlook humanitarian violations and the armed forces lack answerability heightening the mistrust felt by the Tamil population. Therefore, many in Jaffna carry a level of distrust about their future in Sri Lanka in the hands of the Sinhalese.

Final Thought...

This book is an outcome of a specialised piece of research around a small group of participants to gain an insight into the way the LTTE had constructed gender that was acceptable to those within the movement and those within the civic society. Its findings are not generalised across the whole terrorist organisation but contribute to the currently limited knowledge of the combatant women of the LTTE. The limitation of the research has in fact opened up possibilities for further research and development in a post-conflict environment.

One overarching question is whether women's involvement with the LTTE has accelerated the social process of raising both groups of women's awareness of their social position within a gendered society, or whether social change is a side effect of a prolonged war that sweeps women towards a new gender identity irrespective of their individual beliefs and values. It is apparent that the war and the LTTE's recruitment of women may each have changed social roles on their own, and I would say together they are a more powerful force for social change and have radically altered the perception of women in society. From the evidence gathered during my research it is clear that the rate of social change seen in today's Tamil society would not have been possible without women's involvement in the LTTE.

In post-conflict nation building, there is a genuine need for a female identity to be part of the historically patriarchal political system with its roots deeply embedded in masculine authority. Whilst responding to the needs of many war-weary in Jaffna, where the conflict had marked each day of their lives, the State must evolve strategies encouraging female civic citizens to participate in the democracy that Sri Lanka has always been proud of. It must also bear in mind the differing needs, vulnerabilities and coping strategies of those who have been displaced and have spent many months in camps. Whilst many have struggled to articulate these experiences as positively as possible, it does not remove the trauma and other forms of mental agony experienced. The State needs to encourage new political parties that have started to emerge in Jaffna to include women and assist them to articulate their views. The State must actively increase female participation in design, implementation and evaluation of all development projects in the reconstruction of Jaffna.

During the period of this research, the combatant women of the LTTE expressed a desire for *all* women to make a difference in society. They harboured strongly held beliefs that they, as combatant women, can and do make a difference. They held a keen sense of obligatory altruism and an awareness of being effective. They achieved a form of equality that was unique within the historical framework of Tamil women in Jaffna. The (re)constructed gender identity had in fact taken women from an identity of a 'Beautiful Soul' to that of a 'Just Warrior', as claimed by Elshtain (1987), or an 'Armed Virgin', as declared by Schalk (1997a). This new (re)constructed identity had combined both existing traditional normative femininities with newly created ones to form a new woman, *Puthumai Pen*. It is important to note that the women in Jaffna, both combatant and civic, were not victims of history but active participants, and they need to be recognised as that. They have long since anticipated that they will have to be equally proactive in the future to maintain the momentum of social change and the negotiated gender identity of *Puthumai Pen*—the new woman. The new destination of *Puthumai Pen* is yet to be defined in the context of a post-war Jaffna, Sri Lanka.

Notes

1 During the early period of the Sri Lankan struggle there was a notable absence of Western feminist writings that were willing to engage with the LTTE's violent political discourse on suicide bombings. Interestingly post 9/11, this position has changed dramatically with literature emanating from Western women academics with some focusing on women's involvement and participation in suicide bombings. Much of the literature regarding women's involvement in the LTTE and their active participation as suicide bombers was written primarily by Sri Lankan female academics from all ethnic groups in the island. They include de Alwis (1998b), de Mel (2001 and 2004), Thiranagama et al. (1990), Samuel (2000), Maunaguru (1995), Tambiah (2005) and Coomaraswamy (1996 and 2002). A number of books and articles published on women as suicide bombers by Western academics include authors such as Skaine (2006), Brunner (2005 and 2007), Zedalis (2004), Bloom (2005), Cutter (1998), Alison (2003), Beyler (2003), Cronin (2003) and Victor (2004). Their focus is primarily on women of Palestine and Chechnya. The women of the LTTE are mentioned, but I feel that the due recognition is not always given, even though the women of the LTTE have carried out considerably more suicide bombings, some which have been deeply challenging such as lone deep-sea attacks on armed navy vessels etc.

2 Prabhakaran's death is reminiscent of another Sri Lankan terrorist leader, a Sinhalese by the name of Rohan Wijeweera who led the violent Janatha Vimukthi Permuna (JVP) Party c.1980s. He too was killed whilst 'trying to escape'.

Bibliography

Adele, Ann. 1990. *Women and the Struggle for Tamil Eelam: Freedom Birds of Tamil Eelam*. Jaffna, Sri Lanka: Publication Section LTTE.

———. 1993. *Women Fighters of Liberation Tigers*. Jaffna, Sri Lanka: Publication Section LTTE.

Adler, P. 1985. *Wheeling and Dealing: An Ethnography of an Upper Level Drug Dealing and Smuggling Community*. New York: Colombia University Press.

Adler, P. A. and Adler, P. 1987. *Membership Roles in Field Research*. Qualitative Research Methods University Paper. California: SAGE Publications Inc.

———. 1993. *Ethical Issues in Self Censorship: Ethnographic Research on Sensitive Topics*. California: SAGE Publications Inc.

Afshar, H. (ed.). 1985. *Iran: A Revolution in Turmoil*. London: Macmillan Press Ltd.

———. 2004. 'Women and Wars: Some Trajectories towards a Feminist Peace', in H. Afshar and D. Eade (eds), *Development, Women and War: Feminist Perspectives*, pp. 178–188. UK: Oxfam.

Afshar, H. and F. Alikhan. 2002. 'Age and Empowerment amongst Slum Dwelling Women in Hyderabad', *Journal of International Development*, 14: 1153–1161.

Albert, I. A. 2005. 'Applying Social Work Practice to the Study of Ethnic Militias: The Oduduwa People's Congress in Nigeria', in E. Porter, G. Robinson, M. Smyth, A. Schnabel and E. Osaghae (eds), *Researching Conflict in Africa: Insights and Experiences*, pp. 64–89. New York: United Nations University Press.

Alison, M. 2003. 'Cogs in the Wheel? Women in the Liberation Tigers of Tamil Eelam', *Civil Wars*, 6(4): 37–54.

Allen, G. A. 1979. *A Sociology of Friendship and Kinship*. London: George Allen and Unwin Publishers Ltd.

Amnesty, I. 2003. Open letter to Liberation Tigers of Tamil Eelam (LTTE), Sri Lanka Monitoring Mission (SLMM) and Sri Lankan Police concerning recent politically motivated killings and abductions in Sri Lanka. 12 August 2003, in <http://web.amnesty.org> as accessed on 19 April 2007.

Ang-Lygate, M. 1996. 'Waking from a Dream of Chinese Shadows', in S. Wilkinson and C. Kitzinger (eds), *Representing Other: Feminism and Psychology Reader*. London/New York: SAGE Publications.

Anthias, F. 2002. 'Where Do I belong? Narrating Collective Identity and Translocational Positionality', *Ethnicities*, 2(4): 491–514.

Ariyaratne, N. 2001. 'Ethnic Crisis in Sri Lanka'. Published at Lankaweb. 18 December 2001, in <http://www.lankaweb.com> as accessed on 30 September 2003.

Atran, S. 2003. 'Genesis of Suicide Terrorism', *Science*, 299 (7 March): 1534–1539.

Auerbach, C. F. and Silverstein, L. B. 2003. *Qualitative Data: An Introduction to Coding and Analysis*. New York: New York University Press.

Bachelard, G. 1969. *The Poetics of Space*. Boston: Beacon Press.

Balasingham, A. 1984. *Penngalum Puratchiyum: Tamizheezha Desiya Viduthalai Pohratathil Penngalin Pangu (Women and Revolution: The Role of Women in National Liberation Struggle of Tamil Eelam)*. Jaffna, Political Wing LTTE.

Balasingham, A. 1988. 'Annai Poopathy's Fast for Freedom', in <www.tamilnation.org/indictemtn/indict051> as accessed on 15 January 2006.

———. 2003. *The Will to Freedom: An Inside View of Tamil Resistance*. England: Fairmax Publishing Ltd.

Bandara, S. M. 2002. *Lionsong: Sri Lanka's 'Ethic Conflict'*. Colombo: Sandatuwan Madduma Bandara.

Banerjee, S. 2006. 'Armed Masculinity, Hindu Nationalism and Female Political Participation in India: Heroic Mothers, Chaste Wives and Celibate Warriors', *International Feminist Journal of Politics*, 8(1), March 2006.

Barns, J. A. 1979. *Who Should Know What? Social Science, Privacy and Ethics*. Harmondsworth: Penguin.

Baron, J. 2001. 'Political Action vs. Voluntarism in Social Dilemmas and Aid for the Needy', University of Pennsylvania', in <http://www.sas.upenn.edu/~baron/paction.html> as accessed on 10 February 2008.

Basu, A. 2005. 'Women, Political Parties and Social Movements in South Asia', Paper No. 5. Geneva: United Nations Research Institute for Social Development.

Bauman, Z. 1992. *Morality, Immorality and Other Life Strategies*. UK: Polity Press.

———. 1987. *Legislators and Interpreters: On Modernity and Intellectuals*. Cambridge: Polity Press.

BBC News. 2003. 'Inside Chechen Bomber's Mind'. Television news shown on 4 September, BBC (UK).

———. 2005. 'Tamil Tigers Drafting Children'. *BBC News*. In <http://news.bbc.co.uk/2/hi/southg_asia/4171251.stm> as accessed on 12 June 2007.

Becker, H. S. 1964. 'Problems in the Publication of Field Studies', in Vidich, A., Bensman, J. and Stein, M. R. (eds), *Reflections on Community Studies*. New York: Wiley.

———. 1967. 'Whose Side Are We On?', *Social Problems*, 14: 239–247.

Bell, S. and S. Coleman. 1999. 'The Anthropology of Friendship: Enduring Themes and Future Possibilities', in S. Bell and S. Coleman (eds) *The Anthropology of Friendship*. New York: Berg Oxford International Publishers Ltd.

Bell, S. and S. Coleman. 1999. *The Anthropology of Friendship*. New York: Berg Oxford International Publishers Ltd.

Beyler, C. 2003. *Messengers of Death: Female Suicide Bombers*. In <www.ict.org.il> as accessed on 3 August 2005.

Blackwood, E. (ed.). 1996. *Falling in Love with an Other Lesbian: Reflections on Identity in Fieldwork*. London: Routledge.

Bloom, M. 2005. *Dying to Kill: The Allure of Suicide Terror*. New York: Columbia University Press.

———. 2005a. 'Mother, Daughter, Sister, Bomber', *The Bulletin of the Atomic Scientists, 61*(6) (November/December): 54–62. In <www.thebulletin.org> as accessed on 18 June 2006.

Bola, M. 1996. 'Questions of Legitimacy? The Fit between the Researcher and the Researched', in S. Wilkinson and C. Kitzinger (eds), *Representing Other: Feminism and Psychology Reader*, pp. 125–128. London/New York: SAGE Publications.

Bose, S. 1994. *States, Nations, Sovereignty: Sri Lanka, India and the Tamil Eelam Movement*. London: SAGE Publications.

Bourgoius, P. 1989. 'In Search of Horatio Alger: Culture and Ideology in the Crack Economy', *Contemporary Drug Problems*, 16: 619–649.

Bradburn, N. (ed.). 1983. *Response Effects*. New York: Academic Press.

Brannen, J. 1988. 'The Study of Sensitive Subjects', *Sociological Review*, 36: 552–563.

Brenner, M., Brown, J. and D. Canter. 1985. *The Research Interview: Uses and Approaches*. London: Academic Press.

Brewer, John D. 1991. *Inside the RUC: Routine Policing in a Divided Society*. Oxford: Oxford University Press.

Brownlees, L. 2004. 'Power and Empowerment in Refugee Camps: Armed Group Activities and the Laminality of Youth', in A. Bolesta (ed.), *Conflict and Displacement: International Politics in the Developing World*. Poland: Libra.

Brun, C. 2005. 'Women in Local/Global Field of War and Displacement in Sri Lanka', in *Gender, Technology and Development*. London: SAGE Publications.

Brunner, C. 2005. 'Female Suicide Bomber: Male Suicide Bombing? Looking for Gender in Reporting the Suicide Bombings of the Israeli–Palestinian Conflict', *Global Security*, 19 (1): 29–48.

———.2007. 'Occidentalism Meets the Female Suicide Bomber: A Critical Reflection in Recent Terrorism Debates—A Review Essay', *Signs: Journal of Women in Culture and Society*, 32(4) (Summer). In <http://www.journals.uchicago.edu/Signa/journal/issues> as accessed on 24 June 2007.

Burgess, R. 1991. 'Sponsors, Gatekeepers, Members and Friends: Access in Educational Settings', in W.B. Shaffir and R. A. Stebbins (eds), *Experiencing Fieldwork: An Inside View of Qualitative Research.* California/London: SAGE Publications.

Burns, T. 1953. 'Friends, Enemies and the Polite Fiction', *American Sociological Review,* 18: 654–662.

Butalia, U. 2001. 'Women and Communal Conflict: New Challenges for the Women's Movement in India', in C. Moser and F. Clark (eds), *Victims, Perpetrators or Actors? Gender, Armed Conflict and Political Violence*. London: Zed Books.

Caiazza, A. 2001. 'Why Gender Matters in Understanding September 11: Women, Militarism and Violence', *Institute for Women's Policy Research*, (November), in <www.iwpr.org> as accessed on 15 December 2003.

Cairns, E. 1996. *Children and Political Violence*. UK: Blackwell Publishers.

Carey, J. T. 1972. 'Problems of Access and Risk in Observing Drug Scenes', in Douglas, J.D. (ed.), *Research on Deviance*. New York: Random House.

Carreiras, H. 2006. *Gender and the Military: Women in the Armed Forces of Western Democracies*. New York: Routledge.

Carsten, J. 1997. *Heat of the Hearth: The Process of Kinship in a Malay Fishing Community*. Oxford: Calrendon Press.

———. 2000. *Cultures of Relatedness: New Approaches to the Study of Kinship*. New York: Cambridge University Press.

———. 2004. *After Kinship*. New York: Cambridge University Press.

Chandrasekaram, V. 2000. *Play, Forbidden Area*. Colombo: Rajah and Sundaram Publishers.

Coalition to Stop the Use of Child Soldiers. 2004. Child Soldier Use 2003: A Briefing for the 4th UN Security Council Open Debate on Children and Armed Conflict. In <http://www.child-soldiers.org.> as accessed on 9 May 2007.

Cockburn, C. 2001. *The Gendered Dynamics of Armed Conflict and Political Violence*. London: Zed Books.

Collective, S. W. 1990. 'Editorial', *Sinister Wisdom*, 42(94): 1–6.

Collier, J. F. and S. J. Yanagisako (ed.). 1992. *Gender and Kinship: Essays Towards a Unified Analysis*. California: Stanford University Press.

Collins, M. 1980. 'Interviewer Variability: A Review of the Problem', *Journal of the Market Research Society*. Issue no. 22, pp. 75–95.

Connell, R. W. 1987. *Gender and Power: Society, the Person and Sexual Politics*. Stanford: Stanford University Press.

Contarello, A. and C. Volpato. 1991. 'Images of Friendship: Literary Depictions through the Ages', *Journal of Social and Personal Relationships*, 8: 49–75.

Coomaraswamy, R. 1996. 'Tiger Women and the Question of Women's Emancipation', *Rajani Thiranagama Memorial Lecture*, Parvada, Colombo.

———. 2002. *Violence, Armed Conflict and the Community*. London: SAGE Publications.

Coomaraswamy, R. and N. Wickramasinghe. 1994. *Introduction to Social Theory*. Delhi: Konark Publishers Pvt Ltd.

Cooper, C. 1974. 'The House as Symbol of Self', in J. Lang, W. Burnette, C. Moleski and D. Vachon (eds), *Designing for Human Behaviour*, pp. 17–34. Philadelphia: Dowden, Hutchinson and Rose.

Cronin, A. K. 2003. 'Terrorist and Suicide Attacks', in Linden, E. V. (ed.), *Focus on Terrorism*. New York: Nova Science Publishers Inc.

Cutter, A. 1998. 'Tamil Tigress, Hindu Martyr', (Spring). In <www.colombia.edu> as accessed on 3 August 2005.

D'amico, F. 1998. 'Feminist Perspective on Women Warriors', in L. A. Lorentzen and J. Turpin (eds), *The Women and War Reader*. New York: New York University Press.

David, K. 1980. 'Hidden Powers: Cultural and Socio Economic Accounts of Jaffna Women', in S. S. Wadley (ed.), *The Powers of Tamil Women*. USA: Syracuse University.

Davis, P. 1985. *Echoes of War: A Child at Arms*. London: Hutchinson and Co.

de Alwis, M. 1994. 'Towards Feminist Historiography: Reading Gender in the Text of the Nation', in R. Coomaraswamy and N. Wickramsinghe (eds), *Introduction to Social Theory*. Sri Lanka: Konark Publisher.

———. 1998a. *Maternalist Politics in Sri Lanka: A Historical Anthropology of its Conditions of Possibility*. USA: University of Chicago.

———. 1998b. 'Moral Mothers and Stalwart Sons: Reading Binaries in a Time of War', in L.A. Lorentzen and J. Turpin (eds), *The Women and War Reader*. New York: New York University Press.

———. 2004. 'The "Purity" of Displacement and the Reterritorialization of Longing: Muslim IDPs in Northern Sri Lanka', in W. Giles and J. Hyndman (eds), *Sites of Violence: Gender and Conflict Zones*. Berkley: University of California Press.

de Alwis, M. and J. Hyndman. 2002. *Capacity-Building in Conflict Zones: A Feminist Analysis of Humanitarian Assistance in Sri Lanka*. Colombo: International Centre for Ethnic Studies.

de Alwis, M. and K. Jayawardena. 2001. *Casting Pearls: The Women's Franchise Movement in Sri Lanka*. Colombo: Social Scientist Association.

De Mel, N. 2001. *Women and the Nation's Narrative: Gender and Nationalism in Twentieth Century Sri Lanka*. Colombo: Social Scientist Association.

———. 2004. 'Body Politics: (Re)cognising the Female Suicide Bomber in Sri Lanka', *Indian Journal of Gender Studies,* 11(1): 75–93.

de Silva, A. 2004. *Socio-political Implications of Conflict Related Internal Displacement in Sri Lanka*. Sri Lanka: Peradeniya University.

de Silva, C. R. 1978. 'The Politics of University Admission: A review of Some Aspects of University Admissions Policy in Sri Lankan, 1971–1982', *Sri Lanka Journal of Social Science*, 1(2): 89–90.

de Silva, K. M. 1984. *A History of Sri Lanka*. Oxford: Oxford University Press.

———. 1986. *Managing Ethnic Tensions in Multi-ethnic Societies, Sri Lanka 1880–1985*. Lanham, New York: University Press of America.

———. 1997. 'Affirmative Action Policies: The Sri Lankan Experience', *Ethnic Studies Report*. *XV*(2) (July): 245–287, ICES (Kandy).

———. 1998. 'Introduction', in K. M. De Silva, P. Duke, E. S. Goldberg and N. Katz (eds), *Ethnic Conflict in Buddhist Societies: Sri Lanka, Thailand and Burma*. London: Pinters Publishers.

de Silva, M. 1994. 'Women in the LTTE: Liberation or Subjugation?', *Pravada* 3(7): 27–31.

Del Viso, N. 2005. Interview with Kumudini Samuel, Head of Women's and Media Collective and a Member of the Gender Subcommittee of the Sri Lanka Peace Process. *Peace Research Centre, Centro de Investigacion para la Paz CIP-FUHEM*. In <www.cipresearch.fuhem.es/pazseguridad> as accessed on 22 October 2007.

De Votta, N. 2007. *Sinhalese Buddhist Nationalist Ideologies: Implications for Politics and Conflict Resolution in Sri Lanka*. Washington: East–West Centre.

Dexter, L. N. 1970. *Elite and Specialized Interviewing*. Evanston: Northwestern University Press.

Durkheim, E. 1952. *Suicide: A Study in Sociology*. Translated by J. A. Spaulding and G. Simpson (2000). London: Routledge.

Edgerton, R. B. 2000. *Warrior Women: The Amazons of Dahomey and the Nature of War*. USA: Westview Press.

Eichler, M. 1980. *Double Standards: A Feminist Critique of Feminist Social Science*. New York: St. Martins Press.

Eisen-Bergman, A. E. 1975. *Women of Vietnam*. San Francisco: Peoples Press.

Elshtain, J. B. and S. Tobias. 1990. *Women, Militarism, and War: Essays in History, Politics and Social Theory*. USA: Rowman and Littlefield.

Enloe, C. 1993. *The Morning After: Sexual Politics at the End of Cold War*. Berkley: University of California Press.

———. 2000. *Bananas, Beaches and Bases: Making Feminist Sense of International Politics*. Berkley: University of California Press.

Enloe, J. B. 1988. *Does Khaki Becomes You? The Militarization of Women's Lives*. London: Pandora Press.

Fabricius, J. P. 1972. *Dictionary: T. P. Fabricius's Tamil and English Dictionary—Digital Dictionaries of South Asia*. USA: Evangelical Lutheran Mission Publishing House.

Farberrow, N. L. 1963. *Taboo Topics*. New York: Atherton Press.

Fiedler, J. 1978. *Field Research; A Manual for Logistic and Management of Scientific Studies in Natural Setting*. Washington: Josssey-Bass Publishers.

Firth, R. 1999. 'Preface', in S. Bell and S. Coleman (eds), *The Anthropology of Friendship*. New York: Berg Oxford International Publishers Ltd.

FMO. 2004. Two Decades of Civil War (Forced Migration Online: Causes and Consequences). In <http:// www.forcedmigration.org/guides/fmo032/fmo032-3htm> as accessed on 14 June 2007. Refugees Studies Centre, University of Oxford.

Francis, D. 2002/3. *Gender and the Process Towards Peace in Sri Lanka*. Colombo: Berghof Foundation for Conflict Studies.

Galser, B. G. and A. L. Strauss. 1967. *The Discovery of Grounded Theory*. Chicago: Aldine.

Gambetta, D. 2005. 'Foreword', in D. Gambetta (ed.), *Making Sense of Suicide Missions*. New York: Oxford University Press.

Gardner, J. and J. El Bushra. 2004. *Somalia—The Untold Story: The War through the Eyes of Somali Women*. London: Pluto Press.

Gelsthorpe, L. and A. Morris. 1998. 'Feminism and Criminology in Britain', *British Journal of Criminology*, 28(2) (Spring): 93–110.

Gilmore, D. D. 1991. 'Subjectivity and Subjugation: Fieldwork in the Stratified Community', *Human Organisation*, *50*(3) (Fall): 215–224.

Global IDP. 2002 (December). 'LTTE and Sri Lanka Government Agree to Negotiate within a Federal Structure Endure Rreturn of IDPs'. Published at Global IDP in <www.db.idpproject.org>, as accessed on 25 January 2004.

Goldstein, J. S. 2001. *War and Gender: How Gender Shapes the War System and Vice Versa*. Cambridge: The University Press.

Gomez, M. 2002. 'National Human Rights Commission and Internally Displaced Persons', Illustrated by the Sri Lankan Experience, July 2002, The Brookings – SAIS Project on Internal Displacement.

Goodwin–Gill, G. and I. Cohn. 1997. *Child Soldiers: The Role of Children in Armed Conflict*. USA: Oxford University Press.

Gordon, D. C. 1968. *Women of Algeria: An Essay on Change*. Massachusetts: Harvard University Press.

Graves S, R. 1981. *Goodbye to All That*. England: Penguin.

Green, L. 1995. 'Living in a State of Fear' in C. Nordstrom and A. C. G. M. Robben (eds), *Fieldwork under Fire: Contemporary Studies of Violence and Survival*. Berkeley: University of California Press.

Gunaratne, R. 1998. 'LTTE Child Combatants in Sri Lanka', *Jane's Intelligence Review*, in *http://www.janes.com/security/international_security/news/misc.*' as accessed on 4 March 2003.

———.1987. *War and Peace in Sri Lanka*. Colombo: Institute of Fundamental Studies.

Gunaratna, R. 2003. 'A Reprieve for LTTE's Child Soldiers', *South Asia Intelligence Review*, *1*(31) (17 February): 1–8, in www.satp.org/satporgtp/sair/archive1_31.htm

Hage, G. 2003. 'Comes a Time We Are All Enthusiasm: Understanding Palestinian Suicide Bombers in Times of Exighophobia'. *Public Culture*, *15*(1): 65–89.

Hale, S. 2001a. 'The Soldier and the State: Post Liberation Women—The Case of Eritrea', in Waller, M. and J. Rycenga, (eds), *Frontline Feminism: Women, War and Resistance*. New York: Routledge.

———. 2001b. 'Liberated But Not Free: Women on Post-War Eritrea, in the Aftermath—Women in Meintjes', in S. A. P. A. M. T. (ed.), *Post Conflict Transformation*. New York: Zed Books.

Hammersley, M. 2000. *Taking Sides in Social Research: Essays on Partisanship and Bias*. London: Routledge.

Harris, S. 2004. 'Gender, Participation, and Post-Conflict Planning in Northern Sri Lanka', *Gender and Development*, *12*(3) (November): 60–69.

Harrison, F. 2003. 'Analysis: Sri Lankan Child Soldiers'. *BBC News: The World*. In <http://news.bbc.co.uk/1/hi/world/south_asia/2713035.stm>, as accessed on 15 November 2007.

Hassan, R. 2004. 'Terrorists and Their Tools (Part I): Suicide Bombings Driven More by Politics Than Religious Zeal'. Published at Yale Global Online, in <http://yaleglobal.yale.edu>, as accessed on 19 September 2006.

Hatim, B. and I. Mason. 1994. *Discourse and the Translator*. London: Longman.

Hayes, H. R. 1972. *The Dangerous Sex: The Myth of Feminise Evil*. New York: Pocket Books.

Hellman-Rajanayagam, D. 1986. 'The Tamil Tigers of Northern Lanka: Origins, Factions, Programmes', *Internationale Asienforum*, 17(1–2): 63–85.

———. 1994. 'The Tamil Tigers: Armed Struggle for Identity', Stuttgart, F.Steiner -series Beitrage zur Sudasienforschung; Bd157.

Herath, T. 2006a. 'Black Widows, Army of Roses, and Armed Virgins: An Overview of Women's Involvement in Suicide Bombings', *Policing Futures*, 1(4): 35–46.

———. 2006b. 'In My Honour: Contextualising Rape in Suicide Bombing', in <http://wgc.womensglobalconnection.org/conf06proceedings/Herath,T.pdf.epublication> as accessed on 17 March 2007. San Antonio, Texas: University of Incarnate Word.

Herringshaw, V. 2000. *Education in Conflict Cannot Wait*. CS.org Publications.

Hillyar, A. and J. McDermot. 2000. *Revolutionary Women in Russia, 1870–1917: A Study in Collective Biography*. Manchester: Manchester University Press.

Hock-Smith, J. and A. Spring. 1978. 'Introduction', in J. Hock-Smith and A. Spring (eds), *Women in Ritual and Symbolic Roles*. New York: Plenum Press.

Hoffman, B. 2003. 'The Logic of Suicide Terrorism', *The Atlantic Monthly*, 291(5) (June): 1–10.

Hooker, E. 1963. 'Male Homosexuality', in N. L. Farberow (ed.), *Taboo Topics*. New York: Atherton Press.

Hopgood, S. 2005. 'Tamil Tigers, 1987–2002', in D. Gambetta (ed.), *Making Sense of Suicide Missions*. New York: Oxford University Press.

Human Rights Watch Report. 2003a. 'Sri Lanka: A Briefing for the 4th UN Security Council Open Debate'. In <http://hrw.org/reprots/2004/chidlsodliers0104/16.htm> as accessed on 18 April 2007.

———. 2003b. 'Sri Lanka: Karuna Group and LTTE Continue Abducting and Recruiting Children'. In <http://hrw.org/englsih/docs/2007/03/28/slanka15584> as accessed on 18 April 2007.

———. 2004. 'Living in Fear: Child Soldiers and the Tamil Tigers in Sri Lanka'. *Human Rights Watch Report*, *16*(13C), In <www.hrw.org/reports/2006/ltte0306> as accessed on 20 October 2007.

———. 2005. 'Sri Lanka: Child Tsunami Victims Recruited by Tamil Tigers: LTTE May Seek Children to Replace Lost Forces', 14 January. In <http://hrw.org/englsih/docs/2005/01/14/slanka10016.htm>, as accessed on 12 June 2007.

———. 2006. 'Funding the "Final War": LTTE Intimidation and Extortion in the Tamil Diaspora', *Human Rights Watch Report*, 8(1C) (March). In <www.hrw.org/reports/2006/ltte0306>, as accessed on 20 October 2007.

Hunt, J. 1984. *Psychoanalytic Aspects of Field Work*. Newbury Park California: SAGE Publications.

Hyndman, P. 1988. *Sri Lanka Serendipity under Siege*. London: Spokesman.

Ibanez, A. C. 2001. 'El-Salvador: War and Untold Stories—Women Guerrillas', in C. Moser and F. Clerk (eds), *Victims, Perpetrators or Actors? Gender, Armed Conflict and Political Violence*. London: Zed Books.

IDMC (Internal Displacement Monitoring Centre). 2006. 'Sri Lankan Escalation of Conflict Leaves Tens of Thousands of IDPs without Protection and Assistance: A Profile of the Internal Displacement Situation', 16 November. In <http://www.internal-dispalcment.org.> as accessed on 14 June 2007.

Jamieson, J. (ed.). 2000. *Negotiating Danger in Field Work on Crime: A Researcher's Tale*. London: Routledge.

Jayawardena, K. 1984. 'Class Formation and Communalism', *Race and Class*, 26(1) (Summer): 57–62.

———. 1986. *Feminism in Sri Lanka in the Decade 1975–1985: Third World Perspective in Women, Struggles and Strategies*. Colombo: ISIS International.

———. 1992. *Feminism and Nationalism in the Third World*. London: Zed Books.

Jayawardena, K. and G. Kelkar. 1989. 'The Left and Feminism', *Economic and Political Weekly*, 24(38): 2123–2126.

Jayawardena, K. and M. De Alwis. 2002. 'The Contingent Politics of the Women's Movement in Sri Lanka after Independence', in S. Jayaweera (ed.), *Women in Post-independence Sri Lanka*. London: SAGE Publications.

Jayaweera, S. 2002. *Women in Post-Independence Sri Lanka*, London: SAGE Publications.

Jenkins, R. 1984. 'Bringing it All Back Home: An Anthropologist in Belfast', in C. Bell and H. Roberts (eds), *Social Researching: Politics, Problems and Practice*. London: Routledge.

Johnson, J. 1975. *Doing Field Research*. New York: Free Press.

Kadirgamar, A. 1998. 'Women as Soldiers and Fighters', *The Island News Paper*. In <http://www.tamilcanadian.com/page>, as accessed on 12 December 2006.

Kalansooriya, R. 2001. *LTTE and IRA: Combating Terrorism and Discussing Peace Based on Reuter Foundation Research Paper*. Green College, Oxford University. Sri Lanka: Sanhinda Printers and Publishers.

Kaldor, M. 2001. *New and Old Wars: Organized Violence in a Global Area*. Cambridge: Polity Press.

Kalu Sudu Mal. 2005. Film directed by M. Niyaz. In Sinhalese with English subtitles. Distributed by Torana Video Movies, Sri Lanka.

Kampwirth, K. 2001. 'Women in the Armed Struggles in Nicaragua: Sandanistas and Contras Compared', in V. Gonzalez and K. Kampwirth (eds), *Radical Women in Latin America: Left and Right*, pp. 79–110. Pennsylvania: Pennsylvania State University Press.

———. 2002. *Women and Guerrilla Movements: Nicaragua, El Salvador, Chiapas, Cuba*. Pennsylvania: Pennsylvania State University Press.

Keairns, Y. E. 2003. 'The Voice of Girl Child Soldiers'. In <http.//www.quno.or/newyork/resources/girlsoldierssrilanka.pdf> as accessed on 21 April 2007.

Kearney, R. N. 1964. 'Sinhalese Nationalism and Social Conflict in Ceylon', *Pacific Affairs*, 37: 126–136.

———. 1973. *The Politics of Ceylon (Sri Lanka)*. New York: Cornell University Press.

Kersenboom, S. S. C. 1987. *Nithiyasumankali: Devadasi Tradition in South India*. Delhi: Motilal Banarsidass.

Khaled, L. 1973. 'My People Shall Live: The Autobiography of a Revolutionary', in G. Hajjar (ed.), London: Hodder and Stoughton.

Kirk, J. 2006. *Women in Context of Crisis: Gender and Conflict*. In <htpp://portal.unesco.org/education/es> as accessed on 18 April 2007.

Kitzinger, C. and S. Wilkinson. 1996. 'Theorising Representing the Other', in C. Klitzinger and S. Wilkinson (eds), *Representing Other: Feminism and Psychology Reader*. London: SAGE Publications.

Kleinman, S. and M. A. Copp. 1993. *Emotions and Field Work*. London: SAGE Publications.

Klein, U. 1998. 'War and Gender: What Do We Learn from Israel?', in L. A. Lorentzen and J. Turpin (eds), *The Women and War Reader*, pp. 148–154. New York: New York University Press.

Kline, C. and M. Franchetti. 2002. 'The Woman behind the Mask', *The Sunday Times* (Sunday edition), London.

Knauss, P. R. 1987. *The Persistence of Patriarchy: Class, Gender and Ideology in Twentieth Century Algeria*. New York: Praeger Publishers.

Knight, W. A. 2005. 'Female Face of Terror Increasingly Common'. In <http://www.uofaweb.ualberta.ca> as accessed on 28 January 2006. University of Alberta.

Kondo, D. 1986. 'Dissolution and Reconstitution of Self: Implications for Anthropological Epistemology', *Cultural Anthropology*, 1(1): 74–88.

Korac, M. 2004. 'War, Flight, and Exile: Gendered Violence among Refugee Women from Post Yugoslav State', in W. Giles and J. Hyndman (eds), *Sites of Violence: Gender and Conflict Zones*. Berkley: University of California Press.

Kulick, D. and M. Wilson. 1996. *Taboo*. London: Routledge.

Laslett, B. and R. Rapoport. 1975. 'Collaborative Interviewing and Interactive Research'. *Journal of Marriage and Family*, 37: 968–977.

Lee, R. M. 1995. *Dangerous Field Work*. London: SAGE Publications.

———.1999. *Doing Research on Sensitive Topics*. London: SAGE Publications.

Lee, R. M. and C. M. Ranzetti. 1990. 'The Problems of Researching Sensitive Topics: An Overview and Introduction', *American Behavioural Scientist*, 33(5) (May–June): 510–528.

Lee-Treweek, G. and S. Linkogle. 2000. *Danger in the Field: Risks and Ethics in Social Research*. London: Routledge.

Leon, J. P. 2001. *Our World is our Weapon: Selected Writings of Subcomandante Marcos*. London: Serpents Tail.

Lobao, L.M. 1998. 'Women in Revolutionary Movements: Changing Patterns of Latin American Guerrilla Struggles', in M. J. Diamond (ed.), *Women and Revolution: Global Expressions*, pp. 225–290. Boston: Kluwer Academic Publishers.

Machel, G. 2001. *The Impact of War on Children*. London: Hurst and Company.

Mackie, M. 1987. *Constructing Women and Men: Gender Socialization*. Canada, Holt: Reinhart and Winston of Canada.

Manchanda, R. 2001. 'Where are the Women in South Asian Conflicts?', in R. Manchanda (ed.), *Women, War and Peace in South Asia: Beyond Victimhood to Agency*, pp. 9–41. India: SAGE Publications.

Manogaran, C. 1987. *Ethnic Conflict and Reconciliation in Sri Lanka*. Honolulu: University of Hawaii Press.

Maps of Sri Lanka. 2007. Sri Lanka. In <www.tamilnation.org>, as accessed on 12 July 2007.

Massey, D. 1994. 'Double Articulation: A Place in the World', in A. Bammer (ed.), *Displacements: Cultural Identities in Question*, pp. 110–124. Bloomington: Indiana University Press.

Maunaguru, S. 1995. 'Gendering Tamil Nationalism: The Construction of Woman in Projects of Protest and Control', in P. Jeganathan and Q. Ismail (eds), *Unmaking the Nation: Politics of Identity and History in Modern Sri Lanka*, pp. 158–175. Colombo: Social Scientist Association.

———. n.d. 'Tamil Women's Movement in Sri Lanka', (unpublished manuscript), in Jayawardena, K. and M.de Alwis The Contingent Politics of the Women's Movement in Sri Lanka after Independence', in Jayaweera, S. (ed.) *Women in Post-independence Sri Lanka*. London: SAGE Publications, p. 265.

Maynard, M. and J. Purvis. 1995. *Researching Women's Lives From a Feminist Perspective*. London: Taylor Francis Ltd.

Mc Gowan, W. 1992. *Only Man is Vile: The Tragedy of Sri Lanka*. London: Cambridge University Press.

Mendis, G. C. 1932 (reprinted 2003). *The Early History of Ceylon*. New Delhi: Asian Educational Services.

———. 1943. 'The Cause of Communal Conflict in Ceylon', *Ceylon Historical Journal*, Issue no. 1 (April), pp. 41–44.

Minault, G. 1989. *The Extended Family: Women and Political Participation in India and Pakistan*. Delhi: Chanakya.

Morano, E. 1996. 'Rape in the Field: Reflection from a Survivor', in D. Kulick and M. Wilson (eds), *Taboo: Sex, Identity and Erotic Subjectivity in Anthropological Fieldwork*, pp. 166–189. London: Routledge.

Moser, C. and F. Clerk. 2001. *Victims, Perpetrators or Actors? Gender, Armed Conflict and Political Violence*. London: Zed Books.

Muller, T. R. 2006. 'Education for Social Change: Girl's Secondary Schooling in Eritrea'. *Development and Change*, 37(2): 353–373.

Narayan, U. 1997. *Dislocating Cultures: Identities, Traditions, and Third World Feminism*. New York: Routledge.

Narayan-Swamy, M. R. 2002. *Tigers of Lanka: From Boys to Guerrillas*. Colombo: Vijitha Yapa Publications.

———. 2006. *Inside an Elusive Mind: Prabhakaran*. Sri Lanka: Vijith Yapa Publications.

Navaratnam, C. S. 1959. *Tamils and Ceylon: From the Earliest Period up to the End of the Jaffna Dynasty with a Chart of Important Events up to 1900*. Jaffna: Saiva Prakasa Press.

Nordstrom, C. and A. C. G. M. Robben. 1995. *Fieldwork under Fire: Contemporary Studies of Violence and Survival*. Berkeley: University of California Press.

O'ballance, E. 1989. *The Cyanide War: Tamil Insurrection in Sri Lanka, 1973–88*. Oxford: Brassey's.

O'Conner, P. 1992. *Friendships between Women: A Critical Review*. Great Britain: Harvester Wheatsheaf.

Oakley, A. (ed.) 1981. 'Interviewing Women: A Contradiction in Terms', in R. Helen, (ed.), *Doing Feminist Research*, pp. 30–61. London: Routledge and Keegan Paul.

Oxford Dictionary. 2009. *English Language the Concise Oxford Dictionary of Current English*. London: Oxford University Press.

Page, N and C. E. Czuba. 1999. 'Empowerment: What Is It?', *Journal of Extension*, 37(5). In <www.joe.ord/archive.html> as accessed on 10 February 2008.

Pape, R. 2005. *Dying to Win: The Strategic Logic of Suicide Terrorism*. New York: Random House.

Peace in Srilanka. 2003. 'Inaugural meeting of Sub-committee on Gender Issues. *The official website of Sri Lankan Governments Secretariat for Co-ordinating the Peace Process (SCOPP)*, <http://www.peaceinsrilanka.org> as accessed on 20 October 2010.

———. 2006. Ceasefire Talks Session 1: February 22–23, 2006—Geneva, Statement Sri Lanka Talks. *The Official Website of Sri Lankan Governments Secretariat for Co-ordinating the Peace Process (SCOPP)*. <http://www.peaceinsrilanka.org> accessed on 10 September 2007.

Peritore, N. P. 1990. 'Reflections on Dangerous Fieldwork', *American Psychologist*, 21: 359–372.

Pfaffenberger, B. 1982. Caste in Tamil Culture: The Religious Foundations of Sudra Domination in Tamil Sri Lanka. *Foreign and Comparative studies/South Asian Series*, 7. Maxwell School of Citizenship and Public Affairs, Syracuse University.

Phoenix, A. 1995. *Practising Female Research: The Intersection of Gender and Race in the Research Process*. London: Taylor Francis Ltd.

Porteus, J. D. 1976. 'Home: The Territorial Core'. *Geographical Review*, 66(4): 383–390.

Porter, E., G. Robinson, M. Smyth, A. Schnabel, and E. Osaghae. 2005. *Researching Conflict in Africa: Insights and Experiences*. New York: United Nations University Press.

Pratap, A. 2001. *Island of Blood: Frontline Reports from Sri Lanka, Afghanistan and Other South Asian Flashpoints*. Colombo: Wijitha Yapa Publications.

Pujangga, P. 1997. *A Requiem for Jaffna (A Personal History about Sri Lanka)*. London: Anantham Books.

Puri, J. 1999. *Woman, Body, Desire in Post-Colonial India: Narratives of Gender and Sexuality*. New York: Routledge.

Rajasingham-Senanayake, D. 2004. 'Between Reality and Repression', *Cultural Dynamics*, 16(2/3): 141–168.

———. 2001. 'Ambivalent Empowerment: The Tragedy of Tamil Women in Conflict', in R. Manchanda (ed.), *Women, War and Peace in South Asia: Beyond Victimhood to Agency*, pp. 102–130. New Delhi: SAGE Publications.

Ram, M. 1989. *Sri Lanka the Fractured Island*. India: Penguin Books.

Ramachandran, S. 2005. 'Dying to be Equal: Women Militants and Organisational Decision-making', in F. Faizal and S. Rajagopalan (eds), *Women, Security, South Asia: A Clearing in the Thicket*. New Delhi: SAGE Publications.

Rapport, J. 1984. 'Studies in Empowerment: Introduction to the Issue', *Prevention in Human Services*, 3: 1–7.

Rasanayagam, M. C. 1926. *Ancient Jaffna: Being a Research into the History of Jaffna from Very Early Times to the Portuguese Period*. Madras: Everyman Publishers.

Reed-Danahay, D. 1999. 'Friendship, Kinship and the Life Course in Rural Auvergne', in S. Bell and S. Coleman (eds), *The Anthropology of Friendship*. New York: Berg Oxford International Publishers Ltd.

Refugees International. 2005. 'Sri Lanka: LTTE Must Halt Recruitment of Child Soldiers', 21 March. In <http://www.refugeesinterational.org/content/article/details/5474> as accessed on 12 June 2007.

Reinharz, S. 1979. *On Becoming a Social Scientist*. San Francisco: Jossey-Bass.

Reuter, C. 2004. *My Life is a Weapon: A Modern History of Suicide Bombing*. USA: Princeton University Press.

Reynolds, H. B. 1978. *To Keep the Tali strong: Women's Rituals in Tamil Nadu*. Religious Department, University of Wisconsin, USA.

———. 1980. 'The Auspicious Married Woman', in S. Wadley (ed.), *The Powers of Tamil Women*, pp. 35–60. USA: Syracuse University.

Rezende, C. B. 1999. 'Building Affinity through Friendship', in S. Bell and S. Coleman (eds), *The Anthropology of Friendship*. New York: Berg Oxford International Publishers Ltd.

Richter, D. C. 1997. *Lionel Sotheby's Great War; Diaries and Letters from the Western Front*. Ohio: Ohio University Press.

Roberts, M. 1994. *Exploring Confrontation: Sri Lanka—Politics, Culture and History*. Switzerland: Harwood Academic Publishers.

———. 1994a. 'LTTE Suicides and the Cankam World of Devotion, *Lanka Guardian Newspaper*, 15 July.

———. 1996. 'Filial Devotions in Tamil Culture and the Tiger Cult of Martyrdom', *Indian Sociology*, 30(2) (November): 245–272.

———. 2004. 'Narrating Tamil Nationalism: Subjectivities and Issues', *South Asia: Journal of South Asian Studies*, XXVII(1) (April): 87–108.

———. 2001. *Sinhala-ness and Sinhala Nationalism, a History of Ethnic Conflict in Sri Lanka: Recollection, Reinterpretation and Reconciliation*, Marga Monograph Series on Ethnic Reconciliation, No. 4, Marga Institute, Sri Lanka.

Rose, J. 2004. 'Deadly Embrace: Book Reviews', *London Review of Books*, 26(21), (4 November): 21–24.

Rovira, G. 2000. *Women of Maize: Indigenous Women and the Zapatista Rebellion*. London: Latin American Bureau.

Rowland, J. 1998. 'A Word of the Times', in H. Afshar (ed.), *Women and Empowerment: Illustrations from the Third World*, pp. 11–34. London: Macmillan.

Russell, D. E. H. 1996. 'Between a Rock and a Hard Place: The Politics of White Feminists Conducting Research on Black Women in South Africa', in S. Wilkinson and C. Kitzinger (eds), *Representing Other: Feminism and Psychology Reader*, pp. 89–93. London/New York: SAGE Publications.

Ryan-Flood, R. 2009. *Lesbian Motherhood: Gender, Families and Sexual Citizenship*. UK: Palgrave Macmillan.

Ryang, S. 2004. 'A Note on Transnational Consanguinity, or, Kinship in the Age of Terrorism, Social Thought and Commentary', *Anthropological Quarterly*, 77(4) (Fall): 747–770.

Sabaratnam, L. 2001. *Ethnic Attachments in Sri Lanka: Social Change and Cultural Continuity*. New York: Palgrave.

Salazar, C. 1991. 'A Third World Woman's Text: Between the Politics of Criticism and Cultural Politics', in S. Berger Gluck and D. Patai (eds), *Women's Words: The Feminist Practice of Oral History*. London: Routledge.

Samarasinghe, S.W. R. de A. 1984. 'Ethnic Representation in Central Government Employment and Sinhala–Tamil Relations in Sri Lanka: 1948–1981', in R. B. Goldman and A. J. Wilson (eds), *From Independence to Statehood: Managing Ethnic Conflict in Five African and Asian States*. New York: St. Martin's Press.

Samuel, K. 2000. 'Gender Difference in Conflict Resolution: The Case of Sri Lanka', in I. Skjelsbaek and D. Smith (eds), *Gender, Peace and Conflict*. London: SAGE Publications.

Sanders, C. R. 1980. 'Rope Burns: Impediments to the Achievement of Basic Comfort Early in the Field Research Experience', in W. Shaffir, R. Stebbins and A. Turowetz (eds), *Field Work Experience: Qualitative Approaches to Social Research*. New York: St. Martins Press.

Sangarasivam, Y. 2003. 'Militarising the Feminine Body: Women's Participation in the Tamil Nationalist Struggle', in A. J. Aldama (ed.), *Violence and the Body: Race, Gender and the State*. USA: Indiana University Press.

Schalk, P. 1992. *Bird of Independence: On the Participation of Tamil Women in Armed Struggle*. Sri Lanka: Lanka Publication.

———. 1994. 'Women Fighters of the Liberation Tigers in Tamil Ilam: The Martial Feminism of Atel Palacinkam', *South Asia Research*, 14(2) (Autumn).

———. 1997a. 'Resistance and Martyrdom in the Process of State Formation of Tamil Eelam', in <www.tamilantion.org/ideology/schalkthyiyagam.htm>, as accessed on 23 June 2007.

———. 1997b. 'The Revival of Martyr Cults among Ilvar'. In <www.tamilantion.org/ideology/schalkthyiyagam.htm> as accessed on 23 June 2007.

Schegloff, E. A. 1997. 'Whose Text? Whose Context?', *Discourse and Society*, 8: 165–187.

Schnabel, A. 2005. 'Preventing and Managing Violent Conflict: The Role of the Researcher', in E. Porter, G. Robinson, M. Smyth and E. Osaghae (eds), *Researching Conflict in*

Africa: Insights and Experiences, pp. 24–44. New York: United Nations University Press.

Schneider, D. M. 1984. *A Critique of the Study of Kinship*. United States: Michigan University Press.

Schrijvers, J. 1999. 'Fighters, Victims and Survivors: Constructions of Ethnicity, Gender and Refugeeness amongst Tamils in Sri Lanka', *Journal of Refugee Studies*, 12(3): 307–333.

SCOPP (Secretariat for Coordinating the Peace Process). 2005. *Peace Talks*. In <http://www.peaceinsrilanka.org/peace2005/Insidepage/PeaceTalks/PeaceTalksMain.asp.> as accessed on 10 September 2007.

Seiber, J. E. and B. Stanley. 1998. 'Ethical and Professional Dimensions of Socially Sensitive Research', *American Psychologist*, 43: 49–55.

Shaffir, W. B. and R. A. Stebbins (eds). 1991. *Experiencing Fieldwork: An Inside View of Qualitative Research*. California, London: SAGE Publications.

Shanmugaratnam, N. 2001. *Forced Migration and Changing Local Political Economies*. Colombo: Social Scientist Association.

Sibernews. 2007. Sri Lanka: Situation of Civilian Population in Jaffna Continues to Deteriorate: NPC, 8 September. In <www.Sibernews.com> as accessed on 16 September 2007.

Simons, A. 1995. 'The Beginning of the End', in Nordstrom, C. and A. C. G. M. Robben (eds), *Fieldwork under Fire: Contemporary Studies of Violence and Survival*. Berkeley: University of California Press, pp. 42–61.

Slinger, P. W. 2005. *Children at War*. New York: Pantheon Books.

Sivanayagam, S. 2001. *The Pen and the Gun; Selected Writings 1977–2001*. UK: Tamil Information Centre.

Sivathamby, K. 2006. 'What Do the Terms "Eelam" and "Ilankai" Mean? *Getting to Know the Sri Lankan Tamils—Part 2*', Ilankai Tamil Sangam, Association of Tamils of Sri Lanka in the USA, *Sunday Observer*, 2 April. In <http://www.sangam.org> as accessed on 20 August 2007.

Skaine, R. 2006. *Female Suicide Bombers*. North Carolina: Mc Farland and Company.

Skjonsberg, E. 1982. *A Special Caste? Tamil Women of Sri Lanka*. London: Zed Press.

SLMM. 2004. 'Ceasefire Agreement between the LTTE and the Government of Sri Lanka'. In <http://www.slmm.lk.> as accessed on 24 January 2004.

SLMM. 2007. Weekly Report 27 August-02 September 2007. In <http://www.slmm.lk/> as accessed on 10 September 2007.

Sluka, J. A. 1989. *Hearts and Minds, Water and Fish: Support for the IRA and INLA in a Northern Irish Ghetto*. England: Jai Press.

———. 1990. 'Participant Observation in Violent Social Contexts', *Human Organisation*, 49(2) (Summer) : 114–126.

Smith, A. D. 1986. *Religion and Legitimating of Power in Sri Lanka*. Chamsbersburg: PA: Anima Books.

Smith, C. October 2003. 'In the Shadow of a Cease-fire: The Impact of Small Arms Availability and Misused in Sri Lanka', *Small Arms Survey Occasional*, Graduate Institute of International Studies, Switzerland. In <www.smallarmssurvey.org> as accessed on 4 April 2007.

Smyth, M. 2005. 'Insider–Outsider Issues in Researching Violent and Divided Societies', in E. Porter, G. Robinson, M. Smyth and E. Osaghae (eds), *Researching Conflict in Africa: Insights and Experiences*, pp. 9–23. New York: United Nations University Press.

Somasundaram, D. 2002. 'Child Soldiers: Understanding the Context', *British Medical Journal*, in A. Jayantha (ed.), *Impact of War on children in Sri Lanka*. In <www.sangam.org/ANALYSIS/Children> as accessed on 28 May 2007.

———. 1998. *Scarred Minds: The Psychological Impacts of War on Sri Lankan Tamils*. London: SAGE Publications.

SPUR (Society for Peace, Unity and Human Rights in Sri Lanka. 2001a. *Child Soldiers, of LTTE in Sri Lanka*. In <www.spur.asn.au> as accessed on 20 September 2001.

———. 2001b. *War Games in Paradise: Child Soldiers of LTTE in Sri Lanka*. In <www.spur.asn.au> as accessed on 20 September 2001.

Sri Kantha, S. 2004. *Vignettes on Three Black Tiger Heroes in the Battlefield: Selected Writings by Sachi Sri Kantha*. In <www.tamilantion.org/forum/sachisrikanth/blacktigers> as accessed on 23 June 2007.

———. 2006. *On Suicide Bombers and Education Professor Robert Pape of University of Chicago*. In <www.tamilantion.org/forum/sachisrikanth/blacktigers> as accessed on 23 June 2007.

Sri-Jayantha, A. 2002 (revised in 2003). *Impact of War on Children in Sri Lanka*. In <www.sangam.org/ANALYSIS/Children> as accessed on 28 May 2007.

Stack-O'Connor, A. 2007. 'Lions, Tigers and Freedom Birds: How and Why the Liberation Tigers of Tamil Eelam Employs Women', *Terrorism and Political Violence*, 19: 43–63.

Stedman, S. J. and F. Tanner. 2003. *Refugee Manipulation: War, Politics and the Abuse of Human Suffering*. Washington: Brookings Institution.

Subrahmanian, N. 1996. 'Conditions of Women in Tamil Society', in A. Mukherjee (ed.), *Women in Indian Life and Society*. Calcutta: Punthi Pustak and Institute of Historical Studies.

Szczepanikova, A. 2005. 'Gender Relations in Refugee Camp: A Case of Chechens Seeking Asylum in the Czech Republic', *Journal of Refugee Studies*, 18(3): 281–298.

Taillon, R. 1999. *When History Was Made: The Women of 1916*. Belfast: Beyond the Pale Publications.

Tambiah, H. W. 1954. *The Laws and Customs of the Tamils of Ceylon*. Ceylon: Tamil Cultural Society of Ceylon.

Tambiah, S. J. 1986. *Sri Lanka Ethnic Fratricide and the Dismantling of Democracy*. London: B.Tauris and Co Ltd.

Tambiah, Y. 2002. *Women and Governance in South Asia: Re-imagining the State*. Colombo: International Centre for Ethnic Studies.

Tambiah, Y. 2005. 'Turncoat Bodies: Sexuality and Sex Work under Militarisation in Sri Lanka', *Gender and Society*, 19(2) (April): 243–261.

Tamil Canadian Services- Action Group of Tamils in the United States of America. 1995. *Failed Peace Process of 1994–95*, 15 November. In <www.tamilcanadian.com> as accessed on 25 January 2004.

Tamil Dictionary. 2003. *Tamil Language Dictionary (The Great Lifco)*. Chennai, India: The Little Flower Co.

Tamilnet.org. 2006. *Maa Veerar Lt.Col.Thileepan*. In <www.tamilnet.org/tamileelam/maveerar/thileepan> as accessed on 15 January 2006.

BBC History Channel. 2004. *Inside Story*. Aired on 17 July.

Channel 4. 2006. *The Cult of the Suicide Bomber*. Aired on 11 September.

Temple, B. 1997. 'Watch Your Tongue: Issues in Translation and Cross-Cultural Research', *Sociology*, 13(3): 607–618.

Temple, B. and R., Edwards. 2002. 'Interpreters /Translators and Cross Cultural Research: Reflexivity and Border Crossings', *International Journal of Qualitative Methods*, 1(2), Article 1. In <www.ualberta.ca> as accessed 25 January 2008.

The Asian Human Rights Commission (AHRC). 2000. 'Sri Lankan Press Council Commits Outrage in Incitement to Rape Case', Media Release, 7 June. In <www.ilga.info/Information/Legal_survey/Asia_Pacific/sri_lanka.htm> as accessed on 13 June 2007.

The Asian Tribune. 2007. 'Tamil Tigers to Fight Final War against Sri Lanka: In Canada Tamil Cinema Stars Billed to Participate in a Fund Raising Event'. In <www.asiantribune.com> as accessed on 21 March 2007.

The Hindu International. 2007. 'LTTE Planning Major Operation to Take Control of Jaffna', *Online edition of India's National Newspaper*. In <http://www.hinduonline.com>, as accessed on 22 January 2004.

The Hindu (online edition). 2002. 'How Enabled…?', 10 March. In <http://www.hinduonline.com> as accessed on 22 January 2004.

———. 2002a. 'Dispelling Notions', 10 March. In <http://www.hinduonline.com> as accessed on 22 January 2004.

———. 2002b. 'Show of Strength by Women Tigers', 13 October. In <http://www.hinduonline.com> as accessed on 22 January 2004.

The Ministry of Defence Sri Lanka. 2007. *Funding the Final War: UK-based LTTE Extortions—Al Jazeera*. In <www.defence.lk/new> as accessed on 15 March 2007.

The Refugee Council. 2003. *Sri Lanka: Internally Displaced Persons and Safe Returns*. Compilation of the information available in the Global IDP database of the Norwegian Refugee Council, Global IDP project, 7 March 2005. Sri Lanka: UNHCR, Profile of Internal Displacement. In <http://www.unhcr.org/home> as accessed on 14 June 2007.

The Terrorist. 2001. Film directed by S. Sivan. In Tamil with English subtitles. Distributed by Mertro Tartan, India.

Thiranagama, R., R. Hoole, D. Somasundaram and K. Sritharan. 1990. *The Broken Palmyra: The Tamil crisis in Sri Lanka—An Inside Account*. California: Sri Lankan Studies Institute.

Thiruchandran, S. 1993. *Ideological Factors in Subordination of Women: A Comparative Analysis of Tamil Women of Madras across Caste and Class*. Amsterdam: Amsterdam Publishers.

———. 1994. 'The Social Implication of Tecawalamai and Their Relevance to the Status of Women in Jaffna', *Nivedini: A Sri Lankan Feminist Journal*, 2(1) (July).

———. 1997. *The Politics of Gender and Women's Agency in Post-colonial Sri Lanka*. Colombo: Women's Education and Research Centre.

———. 1997a. 'The Construction of Gender in the Social Formation of Jaffna: Some Thematic Observations', *Nivedini: A Sri Lankan Feminist Journal*, 5(2) (December). Colombo: Women's Research and Education Centre.

———. 1997b. *Ideology, Caste, Class and Gender*. New Delhi: Vikas Publishing House Pvt Ltd.

———. 1998. *The Spectrum of Femininity: A Process of Deconstruction*. New Delhi: Vikas Publishing House.

———. 1999. *The Other Victims of War; Emergence of Female-headed Households in Eastern Sri Lanka*. New Delhi: Vikas Publishing House Pvt. Ltd.

Tickner, J. A. 1992. *Gender in International Relations: Feminist Perspectives in Achieving Global Security*. New York: Columbia University Press.

Turner, K. G. and P. T. Hao. 1998. *Even the Women Must Fight: Memories of War from North Vietnam*. USA: John Wiley and Sons.

UK History Channel (BBC UK Programme). 1992. *Inside Story* Series: *Suicide Killers*. Directed by D. Elliott. Aired on 17 July 2004.

UNICEF. 26 August 1996. *Promotion and Protection of the Right of Children: The Impact of Armed Conflict on Children*. In <www.unicef.org/graca/a51-306-en.pdf> as accessed on 27 July 2005.

———. 1996a. *Children as Soldiers*. In <www.unicef.org/sowc96/2csoldrs.htm> as accessed on 18 May 2005.

———. 1996b. *Fact Sheet: Child Soldiers*. In <www.unicef.org/protection/files/childsoldiers.pdf> as accessed on 18 May 2005.

UNIDP-Working Group. 2005. 'Profile of Internal Displacement: Sri Lanka', 7 March. Compilation of the Information Available in the Global IDP Database of the Norwegian Refugee Council. *UNHCR, Global IDP Project*. In <http://www.unhcr.org/home> as accessed on 14 June 2007.

United Nations Key Documents. 1996. 'The Impact of Armed Conflict on Children. *Children and Armed Conflict*', 6 September. In <www.un.org/special-rep/children-armed-conflcit> as accessed on 28 August 2005.

University Teachers for Human Rights (Jaffna). 2002. 'In the Shadow of Sattahip: The Many Faces of Peace Section 4:3 Child Soldiers: The Number Game and Public Relations', Special Report No.15, 4 October. In <www.uthr.org/SpeicalReports/spreport15.htm> as accessed on 20 January 2003.

———. 2002. 'Towards A Totalitarian Peace: The Human Rights Dilemma', 10 May, Special Report No. 13. In <www.uthr.org> as accessed on 3 March 2003.

University Teachers for Human Rights (Jaffna). 1994. *Someone Else's War*. Borelasgamuwa: CRC Press.

Updegraff, K. A., S. M. Mchale and A.C. Crouter. 2002. 'Adolescents' Sibling Relationship and Friendship Experiences: Developmental Patterns and Relationship Linkages', *Social Development*, 11: 182–204.

Usher, G. 1991. 'Children of Palestine', *Race and Class*, 4(23): 1–18.

Uyangoda, J. 2003. 'Tamil Question Is Not a Minority Issue', *Reporting to the World on Tamil Affairs*. In www.tamilnet.com, as accessed on 9 August 2003.

Uzzell, L. 2005. Profile of a Female Suicide Bomber, 396(2908), Article No. 23533. In <www.jamestown.org/publications> as accessed on 27 March 2005.

Van Maanen, J. 1991. 'Playing Back the Tape: Early Days in the Field', in W. B. Shaffir and R. A. Stebbins (eds), *Experiencing Fieldwork: An Inside View of Qualitative Research*. California/London: SAGE Publications.

Victor, B. 2004. *Army of Roses: Inside the World of Palestinian Women Suicide Bombers*. London: Constable and Robinson Ltd.

Vinogradova, L. 2003. 'Deadly Secret of the Black Widows', Cover Story, *The Times* (London edition), 22 October .

Vittachi, T. 1958. *Emergency '58: The Story of the Ceylon Race Riots*. London: Andre Deutsch Ltd.

Wadley, S. S. 1980. 'The Paradoxical Powers of Tamil Women', in S. S. Wadley (ed.), *The Powers of Tamil Women*. USA: Syracuse University.

Ward, M. 1983. *Unmanageable Revolutionaries: Women and Irish Nationalism*. London: Pluto Press.

———. 2001. *In Their Own Voice: Women and Irish Nationalism*. Ireland: Attic Press.

Warren, C. 1980. *Gender Issues in Field Research*. Newbury Park: SAGE Publications.

Weerasooriya, N. E. 1970. *Ceylon and Her People*. Colombo: Lake House Investments Limited Publishers.

Westley, W. 1970. *Violence and the Police*. Cambridge: IT Press.

Weston, K. 1991. *Families We Choose: Lesbians, Gays, Kinship*. New York: Columbia University Press.

White, J. B. 2004. *Money Makes Us Relatives: Women's Labour in Urban Turkey*. London: Routledge.

Whyte, W. F. 1984. *Learning from the Field: A Guide from Experience*. London: SAGE Publications.

Wilkinson, S. and C. Kitzinger. 1996. 'Theorizing Representing the Other', in S. Wilkinson and C. Kitzinger (eds), *Representing the Other: A Feminism and Psychology Reader*, pp. 1–32. London: SAGE Publications.

Wilson, A. 1991. *The Challenge Road: Women and the Eritrean Revolution*. London: Earthscan Publications.

Wilson, A. J. 1974. *Politics in Sri Lanka 1947–1979*. London: The Macmillan Press Ltd.

Wilson, A. J. 2000. 'Sri Lankan Tamil Nationalism: Its Origins and Developing in the Nineteenth and Twentieth Centuries'. In <www.international-alert.org/our_work/regional/asia/sri_lanka.php> as accessed on 17 April 2004.

Wray, S. 2004. 'What Constitutes Agency and Empowerment for Women in Later Life?', *The Sociological Review*, 52(1): 22–38.

Wriggins, W. H. 1960. *Ceylon: Dilemmas of a New Nation*. USA: Princeton University Press.

WSG-Women's Support Group. 2002. 'Lesbian Activism in Sri Lanka By the Women's Support Group (WSG)', *LINES*. In <www.lines-magazine.org/Art_May02/WSG.htm> as accessed on 13 June 2007.

Yancey, W. L. and L. Rainwater. 1970. 'Problems in Ethnography of the Urban Underclass's, in R. W. Habenstien (ed.), *Pathways to Data*, pp. 245–269. Chicago: Aldine.

Young, H. P. 2001. *Choosing Revolution: Chinese Women Soldiers on the Long March*. Chicago: University of Illinois Press.

Young, M. B. 1998. 'Reflections on Women in the Chinese Revolutions', in M. J. Diamond (ed.), *Women and Revolutions: Global Expressions*. Netherlands: Kulwer Academic Publishers.

Yuval-Davis, N. 2000. *Gender and Nation*. London: SAGE Publications.

Yuval-Davis, N. and F. Anthias. 1989. *Woman-Nation-State*. London: Macmillan.

Zackariya, F. and N. Shanmugaratnam. 2002. *Stepping Out: Women Surviving Amidst Displacement and Deprivation*. Colombo: Muslim Women's Research and Action Forum.

Zedalis, D. 2004. 'Female Suicide Bombers', *Strategic Studies Institute*. In <http://www.strategicstudiesinstitute.army.mil/pdffiles/PUB408.pdf> as accessed on 22 October 2006.

Zimmerman, M. A. 1984. 'Taking Aim on Empowerment Research: On the Distinction Between Individual and Psychological Conceptions', *American Journal of Community Psychology*, 18(1): 169–177.

Index

About the Author

Tamara Herath is a Criminal Justice Manager for a Policing organisation in Central London, UK. She has had a long career in criminal justice with many years of working in the Crown Prosecution Service. She was awarded the prestigious Bramshill Fellowship to facilitate the research that forms the basis of the book.

Dr Herath obtained a doctorate from the London School of Economics and Political Science (LSE), London. Her current publications include articles titled, *In My Honour: Contextualising Rape in Suicide Bombing* (2006), and *Black Widows, Army of Roses, and Armed Virgins: An Overview of Women's Involvement in Suicide Bombings* (2006).

She is in the process of writing a co-edited book with Dr Sabine Grenz from Humboldt Universität, Berlin, with a working title of *Gender, Security and War*.